acc. no. 3742

WESTERN EUROPE: ECONOMIC AND SOCIAL STUDIES

series edited by Eleonore Kofman and Allan Williams

Western Europe : Economic and Social Studies is a series of introductory texts dealing with the major countries of Western Europe. It provides a concise overview of the economic and social geography of individual countries or areas, using contemporary social science theories to interpret the evolution of geographical patterns. Each book covers the political and economic context; post-war economic and social development; rural transformation; urbanization; regionalization; future development, and includes a detailed bibliography. Each is suitable for use on a range of courses, including geography, language, economics and social science.

The United Kingdom   Ray Hudson and Allan Williams
France   Eleonore Kofman and Chris Flockton
West Germany   David Burtenshaw
Spain   John Naylon
Scandinavia   Viggo Plum
Ireland   Barry Brunt

Dr Russell King is Reader in Geography at the University of Leicester. He has been a frequent visitor to Italy for research purposes since 1966. His other publications include *The Industrial Geography of Italy* (1985, Croom Helm) and *Land Reform: The Italian Experience* (1973, Butterworth).

ITALY

ITALY

RUSSELL KING

Reader in Geography,
University of Leicester

WESTERN EUROPE:
ECONOMIC AND SOCIAL STUDIES

Harper & Row, Publishers
London

Cambridge
Mexico City
New York
Philadelphia

San Francisco
São Paulo
Singapore
Sydney

Copyright © 1987 Russell King

First published 1987

Harper & Row Ltd
28 Tavistock Street
London WC2E 7PN

British Library Cataloguing in Publication Data
King, Russell
    Italy. —— (Western Europe : economic and
    social studies)
    1. Italy —— Economic conditions —— 1945–
    I. Title   II. Series
    330.945′092   HC305

    ISBN 0-06-318364-1

Typeset by Inforum Ltd, Portsmouth
Printed by St Edmundsbury Press, Bury St Edmunds

CONTENTS

PREFACE

I wish to record my grateful thanks to the following who helped in various ways in the production of this book: to Kate Moore and Ruth Rowell for their cartography; to Rosemary Barber and Audrey Bingham for fast and accurate typing; to Zoë King for indexing; and to Allan Williams, Eleonore Kofman and Marianne Lagrange for editorial advice and forbearance. My visits to Italy for research and conference purposes over the years have been aided by various bodies, and in this respect I should like to acknowledge the financial help of the University of London, the University of Leicester, the Royal Geographical Society, the *Geographical Magazine*, the Nuffield Foundation and the Economic and Social Research Council. On the literature front my debts will be apparent from the bibliography at the end of the book. The economic, social, political, geographical and historical literature on Italy is truly vast. At the request of the series editors and in the interests of student readers, I have confined the bibliography very largely to the more accessible English-language items. Fortunately much of the key reference material is available in English for, unlike some of their continental colleagues, Italian scholars have not been slow to publish their findings in English. For economic issues the two English-language bank reviews published by the Banco di Roma and the Banca Nazionale del Lavoro are indispensable, while social issues have been given a critical airing in a series of contributions by Italian authors to journals such as the *International Journal of Urban and Regional Research*. For students wishing to assemble data themselves, the Italian government statistical agency ISTAT puts out a wealth of information, and its key annual publication, the *Annuario Statistico Italiano*, is to be found in many university libraries.

Russell King
University of Leicester

ONE

Historical and Political Context

1.1. Introduction

A book on the economic and social geography of modern Italy might logically be expected to start in the seventh decade of the nineteenth century when Italy finally emerged as a coherent nation. Prior to that decade political fragmentation had been the rule ever since the collapse of the Roman Empire. But in a country where history is so important, in the landscape and in the hearts and minds of the people, such a recent start would be to ignore the older characteristics and events which are still embedded in the Italian psyche. Who can study Italian transport without reference to Roman roads, or urban life without reference to Renaissance cities, or the problem of the South without reference to the colonial history of that most tormented of regions?

Italy's contribution of ideas and works to Western civilization has been incalculable. The Roman Empire, the Renaissance and the Catholic Church represent outstanding examples of administrative or cultural imperialism originating in the peninsula. In Ancient times the peninsula was the vehicle for the transfer of Greek culture to Western Europe as well as the central stage of great Roman achievements of engineering, architecture and public administration. During the early Middle Ages Italy alone of Western European regions had contacts with both Byzantium and the Arab realm, which allowed it to bring to the West much of the learning of the Middle East. Then from the tenth to the sixteenth centuries, it led the cultural revival of the Old World. In the Middle Ages and the Renaissance Italians developed new methods of agricultural and industrial production, built up a commerce with distant markets and created an intricate system of bank credit and money exchange. They produced many of the masterpieces of the Renaissance in painting, sculpture, literature and music. Men like Leonardo da Vinci, Galileo Galilei, Christopher Columbus and Amerigo Vespucci put Italy at the forefront of science and exploration. Luigi Barzini (1964) was not being excessively jingoistic when he wrote that his country's 'past is glorious, her achievements are dazzling, her traditions noble, her fame awe-inspiring, and her charm irresistible'.

1.2 Some geography and early history

But if contemporary social and economic patterns are to be interpreted at least partly in historical terms, it is also important to be aware of still wider-scale influences — the geographical pivot of Italian history. Despite the external uniformity of Italy's boot-shaped peninsula cut off from the rest of Europe by the Alpine watershed, the country's internal geographical contrasts are marked. Mountain chains, hill massifs, plains and islands provide a wealth of different regions with different historical personalities (Figure 1.1). Italy has found it difficult to establish cultural and political unity over such physical heterogeneity. At the same time, the central position of Italy within the European–Mediterranean realm helps to explain such centrifugal forces as the dominance of the Greeks in the southern part of the peninsula, the rise of Rome as a sea power, the Byzantine influence in the east of Italy, and the subsequent international character of its mediaeval history.

In his masterly survey of the geography of the western Mediterranean basin, Houston (1964) writes that few areas of the world have been so humanized as has Italy, and points out that this has largely been achieved through an urban mode of life. The cities of Italy are so venerable that they seem always to have been there. It is true that some of them, such as Ostia Antica, Tuscolo and Selinunte, have been abandoned because of shifting military strengths, changing commercial needs or declining sea levels, but the majority of Italian cities of today were well established at the time of the Romans, if not before. The Romans greatly developed the urban character of Italy, founding 36 new urban colonies in northern Italy, including many along the Via Emilia at the northern foot of the Apennines, as well as 25 in central Italy and 9 in the South. A much larger number of native centres was upgraded into Roman colonies. Agriculture too was developed in a rational manner. The Tuscan Maremma, the Roman Campagna and the Pontine Marshes were made rich by irrigation and almost the whole of the North Italian Plain laid out under the checkerboard pattern of centuriated estates whose square outlines may still be seen in the present-day field and road patterns of this region.

Under the Roman Empire, then, Italy was unified, with a single central government, a common language and a widespread sense of shared identity based on Roman citizenship, law and social institutions. Given this heritage of Roman unity, why did Italy fail to attain early national unification? Zariski (1972) suggests the following reasons. First, it should be pointed out that the Romans regarded Italy as simply a region of the Empire rather than as a potentially sovereign nation. Second, there were important pre-Roman ethnic contrasts. The Greeks only colonized Sicily and the southern third of

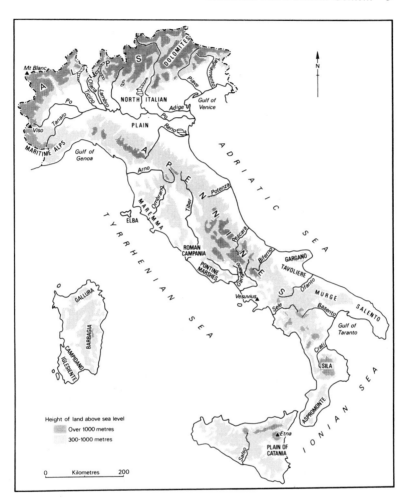

Figure 1.1 Physical geography of Italy.

the peninsula. Long before that, the Palaeolithic migrations from Africa had taken two major routes, one crossing to Spain and following the arc along the Riviera to Italy and the second making use of the then still apparent chain of islands and reefs to Sicily. The first never extended its influence below Tuscany, the second never much above Naples.

Third, for several centuries after the fall of the western Roman Empire, northern Italy was under Germanic political domination, while Moorish and Byzantine rulers controlled most of the South. Thus different attitudes and traditions were passed on by the various overlords, further accentuating already existing contrasts between the regions. Northern Italy came under the dominion of the Holy Roman Empire in the ninth century. The existence of this shadow empire was a constant temptation for its German rulers to intervene militarily south of the Alps to try to consolidate control over the North Italian Plain. On the other hand the Papal States in central Italy, controlled directly by the Pope, regarded any attempt to unite Italy as a threat to their own sovereignty, and so foiled all efforts by the Holy Roman Emperor to gain hegemony over Italy. Violent conflict between the Guelphs (supporters of the Pope's interests) and the Ghibellines (supporters of the Emperor) eventually resulted in the frustration of the Emperor's designs and perpetuated the political fragmentation of the peninsula.

Another reason for tardy unification was the distinctive pattern of development — or underdevelopment — followed by the South. After the Normans ousted the Moors from Sicily and Byzantine forces from the southern mainland in the eleventh century, the Kingdom of the Two Sicilies was established. Thus, at the very time the northern city-states were asserting themselves in terms of wealth and independence, the South was languishing under a centralized but mostly inefficient foreign autocracy which stunted urban and commercial growth.

Finally, the prosperous mediaeval cities of northern and central Italy played their own direct role in frustrating the nation-building process. Enjoying *de facto* sovereignty such city-states as Milan, Venice and Florence emerged as the principal commercial powers of Western Europe. Their very success served to heighten centrifugal forces that prevented the formation of a united Italy at a time when less-advanced countries such as Spain and France were establishing themselves as unified nation-states.

1.3 Italian unification

The French Revolution of 1789 and Napoleon's subsequent invasion and occupation of Italy paved the way for the rise of the nationalist movement or Risorgimento. The 'Napoleonic wind' blowing across Italy cleared away the traditional state boundaries, bringing a new efficiency in administration and financial matters and, even more pragmatically, creating many new roads, bridges, schools and other public edifices. Above all it imposed a new legal system, the *Code Napoléon*, which established equality of rights and destroyed the privileges of the nobility and the clergy, with revolutionary effects in the Papal States and Naples. The sense of unlimited horizons which many middle-class Italians suddenly experienced during the 20 years of French rule continued to influence Italian attitudes until long after the

Napoleonic tide had receded, and the Congress of Vienna (1815) had restored to power the traditional authorities, dominated by Austria firmly rooted in Lombardy and Venetia. Chafing under renewed confinement, the 'proto-nationalists' founded a series of secret societies, the most important of which was the *Carbonari* or 'charcoal-burners'. The societies' early attempts to foment nationalistic fervour were somewhat faltering. Uprisings in 1831 in the duchies of Parma and Modena and in the Romagna province of the Papal States brought down the wrath of Austria and were firmly suppressed. Esoteric and confused in their aims, the societies collapsed as a political force, to be replaced by a new movement, *Giovine Italia*, headed by Giuseppe Mazzini, one of the key figures of the Risorgimento. From his bases in exile, first in Marseille and later in London, Mazzini propounded a clear programme easily understandable to all: Italian nationhood via popular insurrection.

Mazzini's revolutionary programme also acted as a spur to more moderate opinion. Between 1815 and 1848 a number of Lombard journals published hundreds of articles on practical measures for the social and economic rehabilitation of Italy; usually it was implicit that such rehabilitation could best be achieved by promoting political and economic unification. Also important were books published in the 1840s by Piedmontese writers like Vincenzo Gioberti, Cesare Balbo and Massimo d'Azeglio. Together the Lombard journals and the Piedmontese school sum up the moderate approach to freedom, independence and unity — an approach which espoused monarchical government tempered by a liberal constitution, which accepted a federated rather than a centralized Italian state, which was founded on a policy of diplomacy and the military might of princes rather than a popular insurrection, and which walked the difficult tightrope between Mazzinian revolutionary republicanism and monarchical reaction (Clough and Saladino, 1968).

The 1840s also brought fresh political and military developments. In 1846 a new liberal pope, Pius IX, granted three important concessions: freedom of the press, a civil guard and a consultative council of state with lay as well as ecclesiastical representatives. These Roman reforms aroused ambitions for similar changes elsewhere. By early 1848 Sicily, Tuscany, Piedmont and the Papal States — half of Italy — were under constitutional government — a success for the moderate liberals. In fact the new constitution did not go very far towards meeting more advanced ideals. The statute of Piedmont, for instance, provided for a parliament consisting of two chambers, only one of which was elective, the other being chosen by the king; and the electoral law enfranchised only a restricted number of voters according to their income. Yet this subsequently became the constitutional charter for the whole of Italy after unification and lasted until the Fascist era.

1848 was also the year of European upheaval. Revolution spread from Paris to Berlin and Vienna, where Metternich was ejected after 30 years in control of Austrian policy. This encouraged revolt in Lombardy and Venetia, especially in their capitals Milan and Venice. The moment had come for open war against Austria and for the Piedmontese King Charles Albert to lead it. Initially his army was joined by forces from Naples, Tuscany, Parma and Modena. However, the subsequent withdrawal of papal support for this anti-Austrian crusade left the Piedmontese isolated and they were defeated at Custoza in 1848 and again at Novara in 1849. Charles Albert abdicated in favour of his son Victor Emmanuel II.

These defeats shattered the credibility of the liberals and encouraged the democrats to move more audaciously. In Rome a ministerial stabbing caused the Pope to flee and Mazzini, already back in Italy, proclaimed the Roman Republic. During its few months of existence, Mazzini tried to put into practice his cherished ideals: church lands were confiscated, the tax on grain lifted and urban poverty confronted. But the Republic was not to survive long. The Pope appealed to the Catholic powers of Europe to restore him and subdue the democratic government. France sent in an army and after heroic resistance on the Janiculum Hill by Garibaldi, the democratic forces were defeated. Other short-lived republican administrations in Venice and Florence collapsed at about the same time.

For the next decade the Italian patriotic movement had to endure bitter repression. The Austrians in Lombardy–Venetia and the Bourbons in the South reacted fiercely against the slightest attempt at insurrection. Only in Piedmont was the reforming zeal not put into reverse and this region became the focus of hopes for the revolutionary movement. Victor Emmanuel II maintained his father's promise of a statute, set in motion reforms abolishing ecclesiastical privileges and confiscating church property, and gave shelter to refugees from Austrian oppression. Piedmont's role in the unification process was also immeasurably boosted by its two outstanding prime ministers: Massimo d'Azeglio, Prime Minister between 1849 and 1852, and the even more gifted Count Camillo Cavour, who succeeded d'Azeglio.

Cavour came to the Piedmontese premiership with two major objectives (Grindrod, 1968). The first was to make Piedmont a thoroughly efficient and modern state with a sound administrative and financial organization, an egalitarian social system, an improved agricultural economy and a growing network of roads, railways and industries. The second aim was to cultivate Piedmont's position in the international sphere so that it could manoeuvre France into helping it to oust the Austrians from northern Italy, thus enabling Piedmont to spearhead the final drive for unification. In 1859 Austria was provoked into invading Piedmont; the French forces arrived

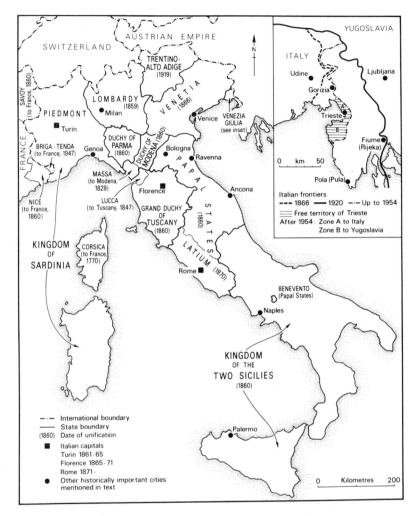

Figure 1.2 Unification of Italy and subsequent boundary changes.

quickly and within two months the Austrians were defeated. However, under the terms of the armistice concluded between France and Austria, only Lombardy was ceded to Piedmont; Venetia remained under the Austrians. In subsequent negotiations between Cavour and Napoleon III the former was allowed to annex Tuscany, Emilia and Romagna following local plebiscites in these provinces in favour of joining Piedmont. The other part of the bargain was that Piedmont would yield Savoy and Nice to France. This horse-trading of territory left Piedmont the strongest state in Italy; the Papal States, shorn of Emilia–Romagna, were reduced to a narrow belt between Rome and Ancona; and Venetia was the only northern Italian state still under Austrian rule (Figure 1.2).

Even more dramatic developments then took place in the South as Garibaldi launched his amazing expedition to liberate Sicily from Bourbon rule. In May 1860, accompanied by just 1000 volunteers, he landed on the Sicilian west coast; three months later he had captured Palermo and driven the Bourbon troops from the island. He then crossed the Straits of Messina and, amid escalating popular clamour, advanced on Naples, whereupon the Bourbon king fled the city. Piqued at Cavour's gift of his birthplace Nice to France, Garibaldi's ambition was to march on Rome and avenge his defeat there by the French in 1849. Events were thus running ahead of Cavour who saw that if Italy was to be united under the Piedmontese crown, it was essential for Piedmontese soldiers to be involved in some way in liberating the Centre and South as well as the North. So Cavour hastily despatched his troops southwards and defeated the papal army in September 1860. One month later the Garibaldian volunteers met the Piedmontese troops, headed by the King, at Montecassino between Rome and Naples. Garibaldi saluted Victor Emmanuel as King of Italy, laid down his arms and, spurning all rewards, retired to his tiny Sardinian island of Caprera to tend his beans and his bees.

Plebiscites followed in Naples, Sicily, Umbria and Marche in favour of annexation to Victor Emmanuel's kingdom. In February 1861 the first Italian parliament met in Turin; one month later the Kingdom of Italy was proclaimed. The only regions outside the Kingdom were Venetia, still Austrian, and Rome and its environs, still the domain of the Pope (Figure 1.2).

At this point tragedy struck the unification process. Cavour died unexpectedly in the summer of 1861, aged 50. Grindrod (1968) speculates that had he lived to guide the final phase of unification and then the early years of united Italy's existence, he might have profoundly influenced the course of public life through educating Italians in the true meaning of democracy and parliamentary practice. Instead events proceeded more haphazardly. Napoleon III's promise to Cavour to withdraw French troops from Turin lapsed and they remained until 1864, their eventual departure made conditional on the transfer of the capital to Florence, which duly took place in 1865. However, Rome had been declared the putative capital of Italy as early as 1861. In 1870, during the Franco-Prussian War, the French garrison was withdrawn from Rome and, as soon as the French were defeated and Napoleon III taken prisoner at Sedan, the soldiers of the Royal Italian Army

entered the 'Eternal City' and it was confirmed as capital in 1871. Eleven
centuries of papal temporal power came to an end.

The Venetian situation ended less conclusively. Bismarck had promised
Italy Venetia in return for help in the Prussian war against Austria. Italy
paid dearly for this, suffering heavy military defeats and then merely getting
the province of Veneto, not the Trentino or Venezia Giulia (Figure 1.2)
which were only acquired after the First World War.

1.4 Modern Italy: the first 50 years

Although unification is unquestionably the key event of Italian history, its
problems were manifold. Little consensus existed as to what kind of unified
Italy should be created. Cavour, Garibaldi and Mazzini each had different
ideas, and there were others too. It should be emphasized that the Risorgimento was largely the work of an urban minority and that the movement
lacked widespread peasant support. Even the ruling classes were intrinsically provincial in outlook, with little vision of a national culture. Cavour, like
most upper-class Piedmontese, was francophone; his Italian was apparently
so execrable that people winced when he spoke (Mack Smith, 1959). This
inherited provincialism was a very powerful obstacle to the formation of a
truly united Italy; indeed in some respects the process of 'making Italians'
out of Piedmontese, Lombards, Tuscans, Sicilians, etc. is still far from
complete today.

1.4.1 Emerging regional contrasts

In addition to the problem of language and dialects, unification brought
into the Italian fold a panoply of regions with different social and historical
characteristics. The Northwest, birthplace of Mazzini (Genoa), Cavour
(Turin) and Garibaldi (Nice), was close to France both geographically and
culturally. It brought into the new state an established tradition of political
skill, the Albertine constitution of 1848 and the major part of Genoa. The
Northeast, long under Austrian rule, exhibited old and new commercial
vitality in the cities of Venice and Milan plus a growing tradition of
manufacturing spread among a range of cities. Tuscany continued to enjoy
prestige as the birthplace of the Renaissance and of banking and credit. The
Centre contained the spiritual capital of Italy and the still powerful status of
the Catholic Church. The South, under foreign domination for over seven
centuries, contained in Naples the country's most populous city, but also
vast areas of rural backwardness and poverty. Sicily, removed from the rest
of the country by the Straits of Messina and the rugged terrain of Calabria,
had been governed by sundry chiefs and landowners who had done little but
drain the island of its produce and vitality. Sardinia had been politically tied

with Piedmont and the House of Savoy since 1720 but economically and socially this island was a world apart, sparsely populated by semi-nomadic shepherds.

Further contrasts existed between the coastal area and the interior. Centuries of history seemed to separate Genoa from the subsistence farming hamlets of the Apennines, Rome from the communities of the Ciociaria, Naples from the townships of Molise, Catania from Enna. With few exceptions, such as the Po Plain and the Tuscan valleys, the isolation of the interior was virtually complete, with the hilly hinterlands only reached by mule track in the face of many dangers and discomforts.

But the main regional contrast was between North and South, a divide which, if anything, sharpened during the post-unity period. The 50 years between the establishment of unity and the First World War saw, simultaneously, substantial economic growth in the North and stagnation in the South. The fledgeling southern industries nurtured behind the protective tariff wall of the Kingdom of Naples could not compete with more advanced businesses of the North, with the result that economically the South fell further and further behind. Although Eckaus (1961) has questioned the commonly held assertion that post-unification tariffs and taxes discriminatingly damaged a region that was already poorer than the North, the fact remains that the governments of the day did little that was positive to help development in the remoter parts of the Kingdom. The constitution allowed the northern capitalist bourgeoisie to impose its own structure, policies and types of institution on the South. The South accepted this damaging imposition because its ruling class benefited from these arrangements; landowners and local politicians were assured of state support for the protection of their privileges as a *quid pro quo* for northern economic freedom of manoeuvre.

Some indication of the differential development of northern and southern Italy after unification can be gained from Table 1.1, which reports census

Table 1.1   Occupational distribution of the working population by region, 1871 and 1911

% working population engaged in:	1871			1911		
	North	Centre	South	North	Centre	South
Agriculture	60.3	60.2	54.0	51.8	55.0	60.6
Industry	22.0	18.5	24.0	30.7	26.6	21.9
Other activities	17.7	21.3	22.0	17.5	18.4	17.5

Source: SVIMEZ: *Statistiche sul Mezzogiorno, 1861–1953.*

employment data for 1871 and 1911. Although it would be a mistake to assume a simple direct relationship between economic development and the percentage of the labour force employed in industry, the figures are quite striking; they imply that the North developed much more rapidly over the 40-year period and suggest furthermore the 'deindustrialization' of the South. The central region, roughly corresponding to Tuscany and the Papal States, behaved in similar fashion to the North.

Although the Italian natural resource pattern could not by any stretch of the imagination be described as rich, there is no doubt that nature gave the North an advantage over the South. The South had no stretch of fertile flat land comparable to that found in the Po Valley, which allowed regional-scale planning in the use of water, the key to productivity in Italian agriculture. By 1905 12 per cent of the North's agricultural area was irrigated compared to less than 2 per cent in the more drought-prone South. Reclamation of marshland also improved the agricultural potential of the northern plains. These improvements in the infrastructure of farming in the North allowed savings to be made from agriculture for investments in other economic activities. Moreover, whereas the South had few natural resources of minerals or power, the North had several steadily flowing rivers which could be tapped for power, and considerable iron deposits in the Alps and on the island of Elba. The North had at least one big navigable river — the Po — which could be used for carrying goods; more significantly, the flat land of the Po Plain facilitated the construction of roads, canals and railways. The South, on the other hand, had no navigable rivers and an awkward topography for transport and communications.

With these factors in mind it was not surprising that, apart from the brief industrial flourish around Naples in the mid-nineteenth century, it was the North which attracted united Italy's first manufacturing concerns. This was of tremendous importance for subsequent growth, for the well-known tendency of industries to draw satellite trades to them worked in favour of whichever area had the head start. Thus, the machine industry became located in the North, especially around Milan and Turin, because of the availability of iron and steel and because the chief users of machines, the textile industries, were nearby; the railway equipment industry became established in Turin, Milan and Genoa because of the supply of metals, proximity to the early market and local supplies of capital; and the rubber industry was founded by Pirelli in Milan because this was the largest centre of demand for rubber goods.

Another advantage which the North had over the South was that it had closer ties with the earlier industrialized regions of Europe north of the Alps. Cavour had studied in Geneva, Paris and London. Englishmen and Frenchmen who undertook the 'grand tour' to Italy seldom ventured beyond Rome; if they did reach Naples they found it 'heathen and primitive' (Clough and Livi, 1956). Backwardness in the North did exist — remote Alpine valleys, meagre hilltop villages in the northern Apennines, lowland areas of rural depression in Veneto — but what was the exception in the North was the rule in the South.

1.4.2 Political evolution

The manner in which national unification was achieved has strongly coloured the subsequent course and character of Italian politics (Allum, 1973a). First, the fact that unification was the heroic work of a minority, and not of a mass movement, has meant that Italian political life has continued to be dominated by a tiny oligarchy. Second, it ensured the establishment of a strongly centralized state as the only means by which the victors of 1860–70 believed that they could forge the 'geographical expression' of Italy into a modern nation state. And third, unification provoked a compromise between the ruling classes of the North and South which was responsible for the dualistic development of the country that has persisted to this day.

With the death of the great figures of the Risorgimento — Cavour in 1861, Mazzini in 1872 and Garibaldi, long since retired, in 1882 — the early political life of the new nation lacked charismatic leaders. Moreover, the transition to proper democratic rule was slow to come. Under the Piedmontese constitution of 1848 power was exercised jointly by the King and the two Chambers, only the lower of which was elected. The right to vote was restricted to literate males over 25 years of age paying a certain minimum amount of tax; this meant that only about 500 000 out of a total population of 27 million were enfranchised. Even after 1871, when Rome became capital, Pope Pius IX refused to recognize the united nation of Italy and the Holy See forbade Catholics to participate in Italian elections or hold political office. Only after 1890 was this attitude softened.

Meanwhile the Italian parliament degenerated into an amorphous mass of deputies, dependent on the skilful orchestration of a kind of official majority-monger. Depretis, Prime Minister for much of the period between 1876 and 1887, developed the system of *trasformismo* or 'transformism' whereby the voters of opposing factions in Parliament were bought by incorporating their leaders in the government. He also perfected the tactic, well-used by Italian political figures ever since, of 'timely resignation', and successively in 1883, 1884, 1885 and 1887 resigned so as to leave himself free to change direction and reshape his coalition (Mack Smith, 1959).

In spite of their coalitionary character, the Depretis administrations did effect some improvements. The franchise was widened, compulsory education was initiated, taxation became less punitive, and the first laws for the protection of workers were introduced. The death of Depretis in 1887 brought in Francesco Crispi, an energetic and capable Sicilian who had moved considerably to the Right since his days as a Garibaldian revolutionary. Now a fervent monarchist and antisocialist, Crispi's main impact was in foreign policy where he was keen to promote Italian interests in the Horn of Africa. In 1890, following a treaty with the Abyssinian King Menelik, Crispi made Abyssinia and Somaliland into Italian protectorates. Three years later, however, the Abyssinians revolted, eventually wiping out 8000 Italian troops in the massacre of Adowa in 1896. This disastrous episode, which reduced Italian colonial territory to Somaliland and Eritrea, led to Crispi's downfall, although his career had already been blighted in a series of banking scandals during 1889–93.

There then followed a period of undistinguished government accompanied by rising discontent and strikes among workers in various parts of the country. The climax was reached in 1898 in Milan where, in a series of violent disorders, soldiers turned cannons on the crowds, killing 80 and wounding 450. Martial law was proclaimed in many cities. Indignation at such harsh military repression prompted an anarchist to assassinate King Umberto I in 1900, so that the twentieth century opened in an atmosphere of shock and bitter disillusionment.

Umberto was succeeded by his son Victor Emmanuel III, whose long reign was only terminated in 1946 with the ending of the monarchy itself. His prime minister during most of the period up to Italy's entry into the First World War was Giovanni Giolitti, an astute Piedmontese politician of the Centre, judged by Procacci (1970) to be the only modern Italian political leader to stand comparison with Cavour. Giolitti proved to be a master of the art of *trasformismo* pioneered by Depretis. Of course, this tactic did little to improve the standard of parliamentary life, but in other respects Giolitti's liberalism brought a period of stability and economic progress such as united Italy had yet to experience. He introduced some progressive social legislation, thereby neutralizing the power of the socialists, and with a balanced budget was able to undertake important and long overdue public works such as the building of the Apulian Aqueduct which brought Apennine water to the arid southeast of the country. He also reformed the electoral law in 1911, giving votes to all adult males, including illiterates over the age of 30 years; this meant that the electorate rose to 8.5 million. At the same time Giolitti embarked on the second of Italy's colonial wars, this time to conquer Libya from the waning Ottoman Empire. This was duly achieved, although it soon appeared obvious that Italy's new colonial territories of Cyrenaica and Tripolitania had limited possibilities for the settlement of Italians and would become a heavy financial burden.

In the 1913 general election Giolitti's transformism finally overreached itself. He rashly extended government support to any candidate who nominally adhered to his programme. The result was a majority containing so many different and often antagonistic shades of opinion that not even Giolitti's consummate political skill could weld them all together. In 1914 he resigned and for the next seven years held no office, although he still controlled a majority of deputies in Parliament.

1.4.3 Social conditions

Faltering political evolution was paralleled by the abortive social character of national unification. The cliché 'Having created Italy, we must now create the Italians' reflected this problem. Cavour was not alone in his inability to speak proper Italian: in 1871 only about 1 per cent of the population outside Rome and Tuscany had learned the national language. Regional dialects reigned supreme.

Furthermore, united Italy started life as a nation of illiterates. Three-quarters of the population could not read or write, a proportion which varied from 54 per cent in Piedmont to nearly 90 per cent in Sicily and Sardinia. Fifty years later a programme of basic education had halved the national illiteracy figure to 37 per cent in 1911, but it was clear that the standard of education improved much more rapidly in the North than in the South. Piedmont's illiteracy figure was down to 13 per cent but in the South and islands nearly 60 per cent could not read or write.

From various sources such as the parliamentary inquiries carried out in the late nineteenth and early twentieth centuries by people such as Jacini, Vittorio Elena and Franchetti and Sonnino, we know that life in both town and country was a perpetual struggle for survival for the majority of people. In many rural areas less than 1 in 10 farmers possessed their own land or were holders of stable tenancy contracts; the majority of rural dwellers were simple landless labourers, with luck employed for half the year, whose standard of living was barely above subsistence level. Most peasants rarely if ever ate meat, their food generally consisting of pasta, bread and beans. This was true even in Piedmont where peasants survived the winter on a diet of roots and chestnuts (Saunders, 1980). Urban and industrial conditions were no better. Cholera epidemics killed 55 000 in slum areas between 1884 and 1887. In industries like silk and cotton a working day of 12 or even 14 hours was common, and this was combined with low wages, insanitary working conditions and housing in hovels. The fact that millions of Italians 'voted with their feet' and emigrated to relieve themselves of drudgery and a seemingly hopeless situation is vivid testimony of their miserable condition.

In fact emigration became a fundamental characteristic of the Italian population almost immediately after unification. As can be imagined, pressure on employment opportunities and therefore for emigration was greatest where the natural increase in population was higher, where economic growth was lowest, and where agriculture, which was particularly depressed during 1874–96, was poorest. The regions most heavily affected by emigration were Veneto and, later, the South. Between 1880 and 1914 7 million people emigrated, mostly to the United States. In 1913 the high point was reached when 872 600 people, 1 person in every 40, left the country in a single year.

Improvements in social conditions came rather slowly. Until 1889 trade unions were virtually forbidden and strikes were illegal unless the workers could demonstrate 'just cause', which was difficult in practice. After 1889 labour organization progressed more quickly. Many socialist unions were founded – the ideas of Marx were widely diffused in Italian in the late nineteenth century — and two national federations, for printing workers and railwaymen, were established before 1900. By 1902 24 such workers' federations had come into existence. During 1900–03 there were general strikes in Genoa, Turin, Florence and Rome. Agricultural strikes were common in the South, especially in Apulia and Sicily, regions where big estates run with landless labourers survived in their most feudal form. In the North Mazzini's adaptation of the teachings of Robert Owen had spawned a thriving cooperative movement which was particularly strong in and around the cities of Bologna, Reggio Emilia and Ravenna. However, by the turn of the century the idealism of Mazzini and the anarchism of Bakunin, who had left Russia to settle in Italy in 1864, had split the Italian labour movement. A big labour congress in Milan in 1906 then created the unified Confederazione Generale del Lavoro. Collective wage and work contracts were soon made for whole industries, and a major object of improvement was the length of the working day and the conditions of employment of women and children who up till then had received wages of only one-third to one-half of those of adult men. In 1902 a new law prohibited the employment of children under 12 years of age (under 14 in mining) and restricted the working day for those under 15 to 11 hours and for women to 12 hours (Clough, 1964).

1.5 War, Fascism and war again

The Giolittian programme of social reform and political stability was abruptly reversed by the outbreak of the First World War. Giolitti himself, with most members of the government, the Catholic Church and the majority of the Italian population, opposed Italy's participation in war because he was convinced that the country could not withstand the shock of a major conflict without suffering irreparable damage both to its economy and to its political institutions. For a year or so Italy remained neutral, but then events led towards a more bellicose posture. Italy was technically still a member of the Triple Alliance with Germany and Austria, signed in 1882 and confirmed as recently as 1912, but in 1915 Foreign Minister Sonnino secretly signed the Treaty of London with the Entente powers (France, Britain and Russia), promising to aid them in war in return for Trento, Trieste, Istria, Dalmatia, Rhodes and the Dodecanese Islands. These were prizes evidently worth fighting for, and nationalist military fervour was fanned by inflammatory speeches by the poet Gabriele D'Annunzio and the young renegade socialist Benito Mussolini.

1.5.1 Italy at war, 1915–18

Italy declared war on Austria in 1915 and on Germany a year later. Initially, the Italian army made steady progress, occupying the Trentino and capturing Gorizia. But in 1917 the collapse of Russia released Austrian resources for the campaign against Italy and the tide turned. Thousands of Italians fell in the futile push for Trieste and further reverses followed. Then in 1918 British and French help enabled the Italians to redeem themselves by routing the Austrians at Vittoria Veneto; Italian troops once more occupied Trento and the navy entered Trieste.

Under the Treaty of St Germain (1919) Italy achieved most of her irredentist objectives. Trento, Trieste, Venezia Giulia, Istria, Rhodes and the Dodecanese were annexed as a result of the Allied victory. In fact the northern frontier was pushed forward to the Brenner Pass, thereby placing 229 000 German-speaking Tyrolese under Italian domination, while the acquisition of the Istrian peninsula involved incorporation of 77 000 ethnic Slavs. Thus were implanted seeds of ethnic and linguistic tension which were to last beyond the Second World War. Italy was disappointed at not gaining Dalmatia, which she had claimed on account of its former participation in the Venetian Republic, and especially Italian-speaking Fiume, whose inhabitants had voted in a plebiscite to join Italy. Subsequently D'Annunzio and a band of commandos occupied Fiume for 15 months during 1919–20 in defiance of the Treaty and against the wishes of the Italian government, but the flamboyant soldier-poet was eventually evicted and the port passed to the new state of Yugoslavia under the Treaty of Rapallo in November 1920.

These territorial disappointments helped to give rise to the 'myth of the mutilated victory' and the sense of profound disillusionment which followed the conflict (Procacci, 1970). Far more important was the loss of 600 000 Italian lives during the three years of war. It rapidly transpired that the pyrrhic victory had solved none of the perennial problems and imbalances of Italian society; indeed, in many respects it had made them worse.

Few years in the history of modern Italy were so troubled as 1919. It was a year of revolutionary restlessness and of deep social crisis. In the cities violent demonstrations against the cost of living took place. The labour force was greatly agitated, the frequency and magnitude of strikes exceeding anything experienced in the troubled years at the turn of the century. Factory workers managed to win substantial wage increases and an eight-hour day. Strikes broke out among public servants — railwaymen, post office workers, even the normally contrite government clerks. Rural workers in the Po Valley also struck. In the South peasants took more direct action; organized by ex-combatants' associations, they forcibly occupied some of the big estates and achieved government recognition of their *faits accomplis*.

The days of the liberal state appeared numbered. The November 1919 elections — the first in Italian history to be held on the basis of proportional representation — were contested by two main parties: the Socialists and the recently formed Popular Party, the latter a Catholic party founded by the Sicilian priest Luigi Don Sturzo to mark the return of the Vatican to political life. The Socialists were victorious, their majority based on re-sounding electoral triumphs in the industrial cities and fertile countrysides of the Po Plain, the country's economic nerve-centre. But, internally divided between the reformists and those of more revolutionary bent, they lacked a coherent policy platform. Their Prime Minister, F. S. Nitti, was a politician of deep democratic conviction and considerable knowledge, especially on economic matters — qualities rare in Italian political leaders both before him and since — but he lacked vigour when quick decisions had to be made, as they did when D'Annunzio's legionaries were in Fiume. Nitti soon resigned, unable to cope with the threat of insurrection and a worsening economic situation caused by a bad harvest in 1920 and a banking collapse the year after.

Giolitti was recalled but he too was unable to stabilize the deteriorating social and economic position; moreover, he failed to come to terms with the new scheme of proportional representation, a system which prevented him from operating the old-style transformism. Meanwhile the Socialist Party had been seriously weakened by the secession first of the left wing to form the Italian Communist Party in 1921, and then of the reformists in 1922. Out of this political confusion a new, more sinister, force emerged.

1.5.2 Mussolini and the rise of Fascism

The Fascist Party that now appeared on the political scene was the creation of one man — Benito Mussolini, ex-Socialist and a former soldier, teacher, journalist and vagabond. Mussolini had been a great admirer of D'Annunzio's swashbuckling occupation of Fiume; although little more than comic-opera, this short-lived republic provided a dress rehearsal for Fascist demagogy. The poet's theatricality and balcony oratory and his legionnaires' black shirts, outstretched arm salute and battle-cry were all to be incorporated into the Fascist code of behaviour. The social and economic origins of Fascism lie in the confrontation of a problematic parliamentarianism with economic problems and an increasingly organized revolutionary working class.

Mussolini entered Parliament in 1921 as a member for Milan and as part of a bloc of 35 Fascists foolishly admitted by Giolitti as a bulwark against the Socialists and the Church-based Populists. In fact Giolitti was not alone in being slow to perceive how profoundly antiliberal and dangerous Fascism was. People believed that revolution could come only from the Left, and looked to Fascism to protect industry, farming and the interests of law and order at a most troubled time. The repressive way in which the Fascist *squadri* were meting out rough justice on behalf of the landowners of Emilia–Romagna (Mussolini's region of origin), beating back the socialist and cooperative movements of the peasants, was not appreciated as a model of things to come.

Having gained a foothold in Parliament, the Fascists lost no time in consolidating their power. Later in 1921 Mussolini called a meeting of his followers to formally establish the Partito Nazionale Fascista and to set out the party's programme. Its main points were calculated to have a wide appeal: social reform, an end to strikes, financial stabilization and the restoration of prestige abroad. Some of these goals were, however, highly nebulous. In reality Mussolini sacrificed ideology for opportunism and his followers were drawn from an extraordinarily wide range of political backgrounds — nationalists, ex-liberals, industrialists, landowners, *petite bourgeoisie*, former soldiers and rootless students. Many of Fascism's provincial organizations retained an individual character. In Trieste they were anti-Slav, in Sicily they were against land occupations by landless peasants, in Apulia they were allied to cliques of local political bosses. Local Fascist leaders could be republican or monarchist, socialist or conservative, Catholic or secular. Mussolini was adaptable enough to ally himself with all of these diverse elements, which is why he remained party leader (Mack Smith, 1959).

As fresh outbreaks of strikes and disorders propelled the country along the path towards civil war, Mussolini waited in the wings to make his grand entry. In August 1922 the Fascists were instrumental in breaking a general strike by running the essential services themselves. Soon Fascist groups occupied many key points in the country's economic organization, including the town councils at Milan, Ferrara, Cremona, Parma, Ravenna and

Leghorn and the lines of communication between Rome and the North. At the end of the year came the King's invitation to Mussolini to form a government and he set off for his 'march on Rome' by train. He thus came to power not as a dictator but with all the necessary façade of constitutionalism, arriving on the overnight sleeper from Milan.

Mussolini began his rule as prime minister of a broad coalition government in which Fascists were very much a minority. But gradually his opponents both within and outside the coalition were eliminated; some, as in the case of the Socialist deputy Matteotti, murdered in the woods outside Rome, in highly suspicious circumstances. As the surviving vestiges of a liberal state disappeared between 1923 and 1928, new authoritarian organs were created. The Grand Council of Fascism was set up in 1923 as a kind of parallel Cabinet, while the *squadri* blackshirts were formed into a Fascist militia, separate from the regular army. Electoral reform assured Mussolini and the Fascists a big majority in the 1924 elections which were conducted in an atmosphere of intimidation and violence towards adversaries of the government. After the elections Fascism continued to transform itself from a government into a totalitarian regime in which the 'Duce', the leader, was all powerful and always right. The activity of other parties was checked by a law on associations; the liberty of the press was crushed, to be replaced by daily broadcasts over the state-controlled radio of the regime's achievements; dissidents were expelled from the Chamber; the bureaucracy was purged of suspected anti-Fascists; the autonomy of local administrations was severely restricted; and the General Confederation of Labour, the last stronghold of trade unionism, was dissolved and replaced by Fascist corporatism as expressed by the Charter of Labour. Active persecution of Fascism's critics began. Many were imprisoned or sent into exile in remote parts of the South. The artist and doctor Carlo Levi, a Piedmontese Jew, wrote his classic *Christ Stopped at Eboli* while confined to a remote Basilicatan hill-village by the Fascists in the mid-1930s. Other political activists emigrated. The socialists Treves, Turati, Nenni and Saragat holed up in Paris, Don Sturzo went to London and then America, while Togliatti, leader of the Communist Party, went to Moscow. Saddest case of all was the Sardinian Communist Antonio Gramsci, who died in 1937 after 11 years of Fascist imprisonment.

Economically the early years of the Fascist regime were successful. The favourable state of the Western economy between 1922 and 1929 meant that the Fascist government had to do little more than assist the general trend for expanding production and trade and falling unemployment. In 1929 industrial production was 50 per cent up on 1922. Spectacular progress was made by the chemical and rayon industries, dominated by the state-supported firms of Montecatini and Snia Viscosa respectively. Mechanical engineering, headed by Fiat, also enjoyed buoyant growth. Agricultural production too showed a general increase although partly this was due to the regime's special campaign, launched in 1925, for the country to grow more wheat in order to eliminate food imports. This policy had significant ecological consequences, for it caused the ploughing-up of much unstable hill land.

Mussolini's aims during the early years of his regime were mainly domestic. One particular objective was to boost the Italian population. Emigration was discouraged as demeaning the ability of Italy to look after its own people, and tight controls were also imposed on internal movement, partly to avoid a build-up of what were seen as politically threatening urban problems by keeping people on the land. Various measures were introduced to discourage celibacy and encourage the raising of large families; these included a 'bachelor tax', birth premiums and income tax commutation for parents of 'very large families' (usually defined as more than seven dependent children). Mussolini believed that 'to count for something in the world, Italy must have a population of at least 60 million by 1950' (Glass, 1967). Not only was this objective not reached (in fact the 60 million mark still has not been passed today), but the population growth policies had no noticeable effect. This was probably just as well since Italy was clearly overpopulated given its level of economic development. Much more appropriate, therefore, was Mussolini's programme of extensive public works to provide employment. Some of these projects, although over-vaunted at the time, were of lasting service to the country, notably the vast Pontine Marshes land reclamation scheme, the establishment of farm settlements for ex-servicemen and the beginnings of the motorway system. The regime was also active in constructing low-income housing, schools and grandiose public buildings. Other praiseworthy Fascist achievements — apart from the hyperbolic running of the trains on time and the removal of beggars from the streets — were the granting of social security and free medical care to the lowest income groups, and the institution of a Christmas bonus to workers.

The prestige of the Fascist government reached its zenith with the signing of the Lateran Treaty with the Catholic Church in 1929. Although raised in an anticlerical family (his father was a prominent atheist) in an anticlerical region, Mussolini's attitude to the Catholic Church had always been ambiguous. His own behaviour was often overtly antireligious but he was too hard-headed a politician not to realize the prestige that the regime would receive both at home and abroad if it could achieve a rapprochement with the Church. Under the Lateran agreement, the Italian government recognized papal sovereignty over the territory named the Vatican City and revived the 1848 statute that declared Catholicism to be the national faith. The Holy See, for its part, declared that the 'Roman question' was closed, and agreed to regulate its relations with the Italian state with a concordat. This 'conciliation' was one of Fascism's most historic and lasting achievements.

1.5.3 The corporate state and Fascist foreign policy

The economic boom came to an abrupt end with the stock market crash of 1929, the effects of which in Italy lasted through to 1933. Foreign trade fell by two-thirds during this period, and the price of securities slumped by an equal amount. Over the same four-year period automobile production was halved, steel output dropped by one-third and unemployment jumped from 300 000 to over 1 million. Per capita income declined by 7 per cent, and consumption and food intake were also reduced. Frustration and hunger became widespread once more.

Fascism's reaction to the economic crisis was to increase its central direction of the life of the country: hence the evolution of the 'corporate state'. An early and ambitious statement of corporatism was contained in the Labour Charter of 1927. This 'magna carta of Fascist economic dogma' (Clough, 1964) subordinated the interests of the individual to those of the nation, which controlled both capital and labour. Such central control was extended to intervene ever more deeply in the country's economic and constitutional affairs. The organization of 'corporations' — Fascist labour unions — was perfected and made operational in 1934. The state thus declared itself sole moderator between the interests and conflicts of employers and workers and the harmonizer of private and public sectors. In practice Fascism's control over the capitalist and managerial groups was less complete than its dominance of labour. Although several semi-public institutions such as the Istituto Mobiliare Italiano (IMI) and the Istituto per la Ricostruzione Industriale (IRI) were founded to salvage and support industries in difficulty in the recession, private groups like Fiat, Snia Viscosa and Montecatini managed to strengthen their monopolistic hold over certain sectors of the industrial economy and to silence any remnants of working-class protest. In 1939 came the last nail in the coffin of Italian democracy: the abolition of the Chamber of Deputies and its replacement by the Fascist Chamber of Fasci and Corporations.

Meanwhile, in the field of foreign policy, Mussolini embarked on a policy of colonialism and war which was to prove even more disastrous. In spite of the fact that previous colonial adventures initiated by the Liberal governments of Crispi and Giolitti had been far from economically rewarding, the Duce believed that Italy's economic ills could be relieved by the acquisition of new colonial territories. In 1935 he launched a military campaign to conquer Abyssinia, the last independent African state, without having any real idea of the region's economic potential and without acknowledging that elsewhere the tide of European colonialism was already receding. In 1939 Albania, an Italian protectorate for the previous decade, was also invaded and occupied.

The war in Abyssinia led to economic sanctions, which naturally worsened Italy's economic predicament. Mussolini's reaction was typically bone-headed; he launched the country on a self-sufficiency drive and allied Italy with Germany in a mutual preparation for war. Both policies were foolhardy. With its limited natural resources, a country like Italy could only prosper through a high level of international trade. And how could Italy have benefited economically or politically from helping Hitler establish a German-dominated Europe?

Although the successful conquest of Abyssinia in 1935–36 strengthened the prestige of the regime, the nation's economic strength was sapped by the effort, and by Italy's participation in the Spanish Civil War in support of Franco. Between 1934 and 1939 the nation's public debt rose by 43 per cent, largely because of military spending. All the indications were that Italy was ill-prepared for any large-scale conflict, a fact which Mussolini's advisors frequently warned him of but which the dictator eventually chose to ignore.

Mussolini's alliance with Hitler, a bond fuelled by envy and jealousy as much as by admiration, sealed the regime's eventual downfall. The alliance was initiated by the two countries' common participation on the same side in the Spanish Civil War in 1936. In 1937 came the Anti-Comintern Pact between Germany, Italy and Japan, and in 1938 the transplanting of German racist legislation against Jews — one of the most unjustifiable and monstrous acts of the regime. Italo-German fraternity was then consolidated in the 1939 'Pact of Steel' by which Italy promised to support Germany in the coming war.

1.5.4 The Second World War and the collapse of Fascism

Italy was totally unprepared for war. Mussolini's public statements that 8 million bayonets could be immediately mobilized and that Italy's aeroplanes 'were so numerous they could blot out the sun' were hopelessly exaggerated claims; quite apart from the fact that modern war was no longer fought with bayonets, only 2 million soldiers could be mobilized, and Italy's air fleet numbered only 1400 antiquated planes.

With German victory seemingly imminent, Mussolini launched a 'shadow war' to try to achieve quick military success and so arrive at the peace negotiations in a good bargaining position. A pointless assault was launched on France in the Western Alps, while Germany's occupation of Rumania irritated Mussolini into a disastrous 'parallel invasion' of Greece in which thousands of ill-equipped Italian soldiers froze to death in the Greek mountains. Italian defeats also occurred in North Africa, resulting in the loss of the Italian African Empire by 1941; in the Bay of Taranto, where the Italian fleet, attacked by the English navy, incurred grave losses; and on the Russian front, where, during the winter of 1942–43 over half of the Italian expeditionary army of 110 000 died under enemy fire or from the cold. The screw was further tightened when the United States entered the war at the end of 1941; subsequent Allied bombing did considerable damage to many Italian cities and greatly sapped civilian as well as military morale. By the time the British and the Americans landed in Sicily in the summer of 1943, the Italians were heartily sick of war. Mussolini's promises of quick gains had proved false, and he had lost the confidence of both his people and his party and military leaders.

It was at this point that the Fascist Grand Council passed a vote of no confidence on Mussolini, who was then forced to resign by the King. Sixty years of age and racked by pain from stomach ulcers, Mussolini was bundled off into protective custody, first on the island of Ponza (where he had banished many of his own opponents), and then to a skiing hotel on the top of the Gran Sasso, the highest mountain in the Apennines.

While there was widespread popular rejoicing at Mussolini's downfall, the Badoglio government which replaced Fascism was not able to bring about a swift end to Italy's participation in the war. With the Germans in the North and the Allies, having conquered Sicily, making laborious progress in the South, the country was divided in two. Eventually, in September 1943, Badoglio signed an armistice of 'unconditional surrender' with Churchill and Eisenhower, and one month later Italy declared war on Germany. At the same time, German paratroopers dramatically rescued Mussolini from his mountain top and carried him off to Munich. A few days later he returned to Italy under German protection and set up his new 'Fascist Republican Government' on the shores of Lake Garda. The ill-fated 'Republic of Salò' made little impact, however. Although it staged a spectacular trial in Verona of the 'traitors' of the Grand Council who had brought about the Duce's earlier downfall (Mussolini's own son-in-law was executed after this trial), the resurgence of anti-Fascist movements, both liberal and left-wing, meant that the Fascists' days were numbered. Anti-Fascist Committees of National Liberation (CNLs) were set up in the main towns, functioning publicly in the Allied-controlled South but secretly in the North which was still under German and neo-Fascist control. The Communists worked actively for revolution, spearheaded by their leader Togliatti, who returned from Moscow in 1944. Also active were the Christian Democrats, the heirs of Don Surzo's Popular Party of the early 1920s. As the fighting moved northwards the CNLs progressively took over local administration. The King's government, which had earlier abandoned Rome for Brindisi, also shifted northwards in the wake of Allied progress, first to Salerno, then returning to Rome in June 1944. In Milan, Turin, Genoa and some other northern towns, the partisans themselves were successful in driving out the Germans before the arrival of the Allies. Mussolini was captured by Communist partisans while fleeing with his mistress at Dongo on Lake Como. They were put up against a wall and shot.

1.5.5 The aftermath of war

The war revealed all the inherent weaknesses of Fascism — its carelessness, corruption, insincerity, internal inconsistencies and total lack of realism (Blinkhorn, 1984). Yet politically and structurally, Italy at the end of the war seemed surprisingly unchanged by two decades of Fascism. The corporations vanished overnight. Trade unions reappeared with renewed force in the factories, having already established at a meeting in Bari in 1944 the united Confederazione Generale Italiana del Lavoro (CGIL) which embraced all workers' organizations. In the person of Ivanoe Bonomi, appointed prime minister when the Germans were expelled from Rome, a leader of the pre-Fascist era returned to office after an interval of 23 years.

The greatest problem was welding the two halves of the country back together after its division since 1943. A new Risorgimento was called for, since the North and South had endured very different experiences during the last years of the war (Ellwood, 1985). The South had largely been spared heavy fighting and the Allies had been responsible for the people's material needs: here the CNLs had operated openly under the watchful eye of both the Allied commanders and the Royal government. In the North, the realities of war had been much more severe, with food shortages, heavy bombing and destructive fighting. Politically the North had been much more active with the CNLs in hiding and a strong groundswell of partisan resistance against both the Fascist regime and the Germans.

When the various left-wing, liberal and Catholic parties met to select a candidate for the premiership their choice fell on CNL leader Ferruccio Parri, a dashing partisan activist and ardent republican. Parri's Cabinet included the Socialist leader Pietro Nenni as Vice-Premier, the Communist leader Palmiro Togliatti as Minister of Justice and the Christian Democrat leader Alcide De Gasperi as Minister of Foreign Affairs. All these statesmen were to play important roles in Italy's formative postwar years. Although some progress was made in lacing the country together again and in purging the remnants of Fascism, the Parri government was shortlived, torpedoed by disputes between the progressives and the traditionalists and by other domestic problems such as the flare-up of Sicilian demands for separatism.

Parri was succeeded by De Gasperi who was to dominate Italian political life for the next eight years.

Another end-of-war issue to be resolved was the future of the monarchy. Left-wing opinion found it impossible to forgive Victor Emmanuel's 20-year tolerance of Fascism. Sensing this mounting opposition Victor Emmanuel abdicated in favour of his son Umberto II, but this tactic failed to save the monarchy for the referendum of June 1946 voted by 12.7 to 10.7 million votes for a republic. The North, seat of the most courageous resistance to Fascism and now dominated by left-wing parties, voted solidly for republican government; the South, still influenced by royalist traditions dating back to pre-unification days, voted mainly for the monarchy. Umberto, having agreed to abide by the decision of the people, left for exile in Portugal.

Finally, there were the territorial issues. In contrast to the 'mutilated victory' of 1919, in 1947, when the Italian treaty was signed, it could be said that although Italy had lost the war, she won the peace (Procacci, 1970). The territorial concessions made to France (Briga and Tenda) and to Greece (the Dodecanese Islands) were relatively insignificant, while the Alto Adige, German-speaking and claimed by Austria, surprisingly stayed Italian. Only on the eastern border had Italy to cede to Yugoslavia those territories whose inhabitants were predominantly Slav, but she kept the city of Trieste which, after having been made a free territory under Allied control, finally returned to Italy in 1954 (see Figure 1.2). The African colonies of Libya and Eritrea were lost, but in an age of accelerating decolonization worldwide, not many Italians lamented this fact. Somaliland remained under Italian mandate until it achieved independence in 1961.

1.6 Postwar politics

The early postwar period saw the launching of Italy's remarkable economic development whose general character and social effects are considered in Chapter 2. In the remainder of this chapter we examine Italy's political evolution in the 40 years of postwar life — a political context dominated by the nebulous but all-pervading clientelistic power of the Christian Democrat (DC) Party, and commencing with the formation of the new republican constitution.

1.6.1 The Constitution

The 1948 Constitution, which replaced the Albertine statute of exactly 100 years before, represents a courageous attempt to combine into a single document all the aspirations which were burgeoning after 20 years of

Figure 1.3   Regions of Italy.

repression. It consists of 139 articles divided into three sections on 'Fundamental principles', 'The rights and duties of citizens' and 'Organization of the Republic'.

Article 1 opens the Constitution with the statement that Italy is a democratic republic founded on work. Sovereignty belongs to the people, and citizens have the 'inviolable right' to equality before the law irrespective of race, religion, language or political persuasion. All religions are equally free before the law, with Article 7 affirming the independence and sovereignty of the state and the Catholic Church and the regulation of their relations by the 1929 Lateran agreements. The sovereignty of the people is exercised through their parliamentary vote and, if need be, through referenda on key constitutional or moral issues. Parliament is bicameral, consisting of the Chamber of Deputies and the Senate, both elected for five-year terms. Executive power is vested in the Cabinet, under a Prime Minister designated by the President of the Republic and approved by Parliament. The President is elected by both Chambers in a joint session and serves a seven-year term. His political powers are limited; they include the appointment of the Prime Minister, the dissolution of Parliament and the right to veto parliamentary laws.

Apart from numerous legal structures which need not concern us here, the final key provision of the Constitution deals with the sphere of local government. In reaction to overcentralization, the 'region' is confirmed as an autonomous administrative unit. Initially regional autonomy was only put into practice in four 'special statute' regions with specific linguistic or cultural characteristics (Figure 1.3). These were Val d'Aosta (French speaking), Trentino–Alto Adige (partly German speaking) and the islands of Sicily and Sardinia where separatist tendencies needed to be neutralized. Creation of the fifth autonomous region, Friuli-Venezia Giulia, was delayed until 1963 owing to the difficulties concerning Trieste. Extension of regional autonomy to the 14 other regions (15 after the splitting of Abruzzo and Molise in 1964) had to wait until 1970; this issue is dealt with in Chapter 6.

Vercellone (1972) demonstrates that in reality the Constitution was a complex and occasionally contradictory compromise between the various political and ideological currents operating in the early postwar period. For while it was not possible for the left-wing groups to achieve a socialist constitution, the social problems and economic plight of large sections of the population did not allow the more conservative elements merely to erect a constitution based purely on administrative criteria. The strongest of the moderate parties, the Christian Democrats, had a broad popular base and could not risk alienating a large section of its members who, although they rejected radical upheaval, demanded greater social justice. The result was a compromise of a very special type. To compensate left-wing parties for their failure to effect a revolution, the right-wing forces did not oppose the inclusion in the Constitution of clauses which could be interpreted as the promise of a revolution, doing this in the belief that the moderate majority in parliament would always prevent a socialist transformation from taking place.

This constitutional confusion is greatest when dealing with the basic concepts which identify a capitalist social system: private enterprise and property. Article 41 begins with a statement of a clearly liberal flavour: 'Freedom of private enterprise is guaranteed'. But this is immediately qualified: 'Private enterprise cannot be allowed to conflict with social utility'. This caveat is a wide and vague expression which could permit the prohibition of all private economic activity. In a similar manner, Article 42 recognizes and guarantees private property, but reserves the right to determine its limits 'so as to ensure its social function'. One Italian commentator (quoted in Vercellone, 1972) made a shrewd comparison between the Constitution and a middle-aged man with two mistresses, one young and one old: the former pulled all his grey hairs out to make him look younger, and the latter pulled all his black hairs out to make him look older, so that in the end he was left completely bald!

1.6.2 The era of De Gasperi, 1945–53

It was under the leadership of De Gasperi, this astute politician from the Alto Adige, that many of Italy's difficult early postwar problems were resolved, among them the peace treaty, the question of monarchy, the establishment of the new constitution, the strategy for economic reconstruction, the land reform and the beginnings of a policy to develop the South. De Gasperi's eight governments in seven years may not betoken great political stability but he reigned as prime minister uninterrupted. In fact an average of one government every 10–11 months has proved to be the long-term norm for Italy both before (67 governments in 61 years) and after (45 governments in 40 years) the Fascist interlude.

The 1946 general election was the first free election to be held in Italy since 1922, and the first in which women voted. The great majority of votes went to the three 'mass' parties: the Christian Democrats (35.1 per cent), the Socialists (20.7 per cent) and the Communists (18.9 per cent). This was the only postwar election in which the Socialists surpassed the Communists; subsequently the Socialist vote was split by the secession of the Social Democrats under Saragat in 1947. The DC drew support from all over the country and from all classes of voters but was especially strong among the middle classes and among peasants in Veneto and the South; they were also the party to benefit most from the extension of the franchise to women. The Socialists and the Communists found their main support in the northern industrial towns and among the agricultural workers of Emilia.

The 1948 elections, the first under the new Constitution, brought a sweeping victory for the DC, its vote now boosted to 48.5 per cent of the total, as against 31 per cent for the Democratic Popular Front, the name under which the Communists and Socialists fought this election on joint lists (Table 1.2). The DC now had an absolute majority in the Chamber, though not in the Senate. Although under pressure from the Vatican to form a single-party DC government, De Gasperi settled for a four-party coalition with the Social Democrats, Republicans and Liberals; this combination of Catholic and secular centrist parties, known as the *quadripartito*, represented the De Gasperi ideal.

Also in 1948 a new head of state was elected. This choice fell on Luigi Einaudi, former Professor of Economics at Turin University. His anti-Fascist views were well known and he had already been instrumental in bringing financial stability to the country in the years following the war, first as Governor of the Bank of Italy in 1945 and then as Finance and Treasury Minister in 1947.

Muriel Grindrod (1968) judges the five years between 1948 and 1953 to be the highlight of government in postwar Italy. In Einaudi and De Gasperi the country had a president and a prime minister of genuinely statesmanlike stature. The *quadripartito* formula fitted the times, although it was to collapse later on. On the economic side the foundations were laid for future economic prosperity, while in the realm of foreign affairs the fruitful partnership between De Gasperi and Foreign Minister Count Sforza saw Italy taking her place among the nations of the West and sharing the moves towards a united Europe. In 1948 Italy was among the 16 nations joining the Organization for European Economic Cooperation (OEEC) and in the following years Italy joined both the Council of Europe and the North Atlantic Treaty Organization (NATO). Her membership of the United Nations was delayed by persistent Russian veto until 1955.

On the domestic front the late 1940s and early 1950s were a volatile period. In Parliament politicians unaccustomed to the luxury of democratic debate found it hard to reach decisions. Factions developed in most parties. This was most marked in the DC itself, a vast heterogeneous party whose members ranged from peasants to progressive intellectuals, from trade unionists to businessmen and landowners, with little in common except their Catholicism. An attempt on Togliatti's life in 1948 sparked off strikes and road blocks and the threat of insurrection was only contained with the help of the Communist Party leaders. Meanwhile in the South these same leaders were encouraging landless peasants to occupy undercultivated semi-feudal estates. It was during a fracas in the desperately poor region of Calabria that the police killed some peasants and sparked off nationwide protests that led to the land reform, rushed through in 1950. The background to, and effects of, this important piece of postwar social policy are considered in detail in Chapter 5. Here it is sufficient to note the horrified reaction on the part of the southern landowners who deserted the DC for the right-wing parties which thereby enjoyed an upturn of popularity in the

Table 1.2   Results of postwar elections

	1946 Vote (%)	Seats	1948 Vote (%)	Seats	1953 Vote (%)	Seats	1958 Vote (%)	Seats	1963 Vote (%)	Seats
Communist PCI	19.0	104 ⎫	31.0 ⎫	183 ⎫	22.7	143	22.7	140	25.3	166
Socialists PSI	20.7	115 ⎭	⎭	⎭	12.7	75	14.2	84	13.8	87
Social Democrats PSDI	—	—	7.1	33	4.5	19	4.6	23	6.1	33
Republicans PRI	4.4	23	2.5	9	1.6	5	1.4	7	1.4	6
Christian Democrats DC	35.2	207	48.5	305	40.1	261	42.2	273	38.3	260
Liberals PLI	6.8	41	3.8	19	3.1	14	3.5	16	7.0	39
Monarchists PNM	2.8	16	2.8	14	6.9	40	4.8	23	1.7	8
Neo-Fascists MSI	—	—	—	—	5.8	29	4.7	25	5.1	27
Other parties	11.1	50	4.3	8	2.6	4	1.9	5	1.3	4
Totals	100.0	556	100.0	574	100.0	590	100.0	596	100.0	630

	1968 Vote (%)	1968 Seats	1972 Vote (%)	1972 Seats	1976 Vote (%)	1976 Seats	1979 Vote (%)	1979 Seats	1983 Vote (%)	1983 Seats
Communists PCI	26.9	177	27.2	179	34.4	227	30.4	201	29.9	198
Socialists PSI	14.5 ⎫	91 ⎫	9.6	61	9.6	57	9.8	62	11.4	73
Social Democrats PSDI	⎭	⎭	5.1	29	3.4	15	3.8	20	4.1	23
Republicans PRI	2.0	9	2.9	15	3.1	14	3.0	16	5.1	29
Christian Democrats DC	39.1	266	38.8	267	38.7	263	38.3	262	32.9	225
Liberals PLI	5.8	31	3.9	20	1.3	5	1.9	9	2.9	16
Monarchists PNM	1.3 ⎫	6 ⎫					0.6 ⎫	— ⎫		
Neo-Fascists MSI	4.5 ⎭	23 ⎭	8.7	56	6.1	35	5.3 ⎭	30 ⎭	6.8	42
Other parties	5.9	27	3.4	3	3.4	14	6.9	30	8.5	24
Totals	100.0	630	100.0	630	100.0	630	100.0	630	100.0	630

Source: Clark (1984).

1950s. The Monarchists, led by the nostalgic oratory of the Neapolitan shipowner Achille Lauro, increased their proportion of the vote by two and a half times between 1948 and 1953, while the neo-Fascists, with their new Movimento Sociale Italiano (MSI) party, captured a not insignificant 5.8 per cent share of the 1953 electorate (Table 1.2).

As the 1953 election approached, the *quadripartito* lost its stability. The Liberals left the government in 1950, the Social Democrats in 1951. In the politically capricious South the DC lost out both to the Right, through the land reform, and to the Left which had successfully 'politicized' large sections of the southern working class. The 1953 election, in spite of a disgraceful DC attempt to tamper with the electoral system, saw the centrist parties lose their overall majority. Henceforth they were to be more dependent on parliamentary support from what were regarded as more unpalatable extreme groups. Support from the Left was taboo as long as the Socialists remained in league with the Communists, while support from the Right, although eagerly proffered, was almost equally distasteful. The result was political paralysis and the end to most of the reforms initiated by De Gasperi. Nevertheless economic progress continued for the next 10 years, while in foreign affairs the most important event was Italy's participation in the Common Market.

1.6.3 Italy and the European Community

Integration within the European Community (EC) has been one of the key features of postwar Italy and undoubtedly conferred substantial benefits on the Italian economy, particularly in the field of industrial exports. The process started with the formation of the European Coal and Steel Community (ECSC) in 1952. Some Italians viewed this move with great trepidation, fearing that their nation's steel industry would be swamped by the longer-established industries of France, West Germany and Belgium. In fact, precisely the opposite happened. The competitive fillip caused the Italian steel industry to expand much faster than that of other ECSC countries with the result that by 1980 Italian steel capacity was the second largest in the whole of Western Europe after that of West Germany, accounting for 21.5 per cent of the total of the EC Nine. Further details on the steel industry are provided in Chapter 3.

Most Italian politicians were enthusiastic supporters of European economic and political integration. None worked harder to achieve it than Foreign Minister Martino, whose diplomacy and fluency in all major European languages made him a key figure in the formation of the European Economic Community. Italy gave unwavering support to the ideal of the Community, and the locations of the three key meetings, the first at Messina, Martino's home city, in 1955, the second at Venice in 1956, and the third when the Treaty was signed, at Rome in 1957, are testimony to this.

The first decade of the Community saw Italy's enthusiasm for European integration amply vindicated (Masera, 1967). With one-quarter of the Common Market's area and 29 per cent of its population, Italy was one of the three big members of a population mass of 180 million and of a bloc that became the single greatest trading entity in the world. Italy produced about one-third of the Community's wheat, two-thirds of its maize, half of its grapes and fruit, half of its natural gas output, one-fifth of electric power and automobiles, one-quarter of cotton textiles and one-third of woollen goods. The aggressive European marketing strategies of Italian companies led to remarkable successes in sectors like clothing, shoes, automobiles and electrical appliances. Italy was also able to benefit substantially from the Community's regional aid programmes — notably the European Investment Bank and the European Regional Development Fund — which have pumped large quantities of money into developing the South.

However, there have also been negative aspects of Italy's participation in the EC (Podbielski, 1974). Italy's hope for political union seems to be far from realization. The conflict between adherence to Community rules and the pursuit of domestic development objectives has been more acute in Italy than in other member states; indeed Italy holds the record for the number of infringements of the Treaty of Rome. At the same time, some of the benefits which should have accrued from EC membership have not materialized. The clearest illustration of this is found in agriculture. Substantial financial resources allocated to agricultural transformation have been only partially used, and large unspent reserves have accumulated at the Ministry of Agriculture. Structural change in Italian farming has thus been slow, failing to profit from Community aid theoretically available. Meanwhile the EC's agricultural price subsidies, geared largely to supporting northern European products like cereals, milk and meat, on which Italy is highly import-dependent, fail to boost the production of Italy's typically Mediterranean crops like olives, vines, tobacco and fruits to anything like the same degree. Thus Italy, with a numerically strong but economically weak agricultural sector, has consistently been a net contributor to the Common Agricultural Policy, helping to underwrite the production of substantial surpluses by the strong farm sectors of France, West Germany and the Netherlands. This problem is further discussed in Chapter 5.

Italy's relative position — geographical, economic and political — has changed considerably over the three decades of the Community's existence. Originally Italy was the poorest member economically and the most peripheral locationally. This peripherality became more exaggerated with the northward extension of the EC in 1973 to incorporate Great Britain, Eire and Denmark. The 1980s, on the other hand, have seen the EC's southward or Mediterranean enlargement, with the accession of Greece in 1981 and Spain and Portugal in 1986. In this new context Italy occupies a more central position within the Community, not only geographically but also as a possible spokesperson for the Mediterranean tier.

1.6.4 The 'opening to the Left'

De Gasperi's resignation in 1953, followed by his death the following year, precipitated a long period of governmental crisis dominated by the attempts of Amintore Fanfani, DC party secretary and several times prime minister, to weld a coalitionary power base around the Christian Democrats. For a time DC coalitions leaned to the Right. The 1959 Segni government and the 1960 Tambroni government depended on the votes of the Monarchists and neo-Fascists to stay in power — a far cry from De Gasperi's centrism. But violent clashes between neo-Fascists and anti-Fascists, first in Genoa and then in other northern cities, convinced the DC leadership that a move to the Right was a dangerous course to follow. The conviction took root that only a movement or 'opening to the Left' could provide a stable majority under DC control. Such an opening, championed by Fanfani and Moro, successive DC party secretaries, was conditional on the Socialists' leader, Pietro Nenni, formally breaking his alliance with the Communists. Also associated with such a break was the never-abandoned hope of reuniting the two socialist parties, the PSI under Nenni and the PSDI (Social Democrats) under Saragat.

In 1959 the Socialists succeeded in breaking with the Communists, in 1960 they collaborated with the DC in the formation of municipal administrations in Milan, Genoa and Florence, and in 1961 they supported the election of a DC president for the Sicilian regional government. In the national arena, PSI support for the DC was made conditional on certain reforms such as the nationalization of the electricity industry, duly completed by Fanfani's government in 1962, and the move towards regional devolution, which the Christian Democrats stalled on apart from the peripheral region of Friuli–Venezia Giulia which was granted regional autonomy in 1963. The Socialists, for their part, renounced their claims for Italy's withdrawal from NATO. It should also be pointed out that the Centre–Left ideology was actively supported by two of the country's biggest industrial concerns, Fiat and the semi-public oil company ENI, each of which controlled a mass circulation newspaper, respectively *La Stampa* of Turin and *Il Giorno* of Milan. Even Pope John XXIII showed sympathy for the merger, his 1963 encyclical *Pacem in Terris* supported the idea of collaboration between people of different persuasions in the pursuit of peace and social justice.

The Centre–Left union was finally consummated in the 1963 government of Aldo Moro, which had Nenni as Deputy Prime Minister and Saragat as Minister of Foreign Affairs. The coalition was further strengthened when Saragat was elected President in 1964. Moro's Cabinet ushered in a period of relatively stable government backed by a substantial parliamentary majority. The move of the Socialists to the Centre was cemented in their reunion in 1966 with the Social Democrats.

The 'opening to the Left' was, nevertheless, bitterly opposed by groups both outside and on the fringes of the coalition. Right-wing Christian Democrats and left-wing Socialists had profound misgivings while the Communists, earlier renounced by Nenni, accused the Socialists of seceding to the imperialists and betraying the workers to the class enemy. Within the coalition the Socialists were angry at the DC's refusal to make progress towards regional devolution, and in 1964 a third socialist party was formed as the left-wing socialists peeled off to form the Socialist Party of Proletarian Unity (PSIUP), taking up a position to the left of the Communists.

The 1963 election results reflected some of these tensions, but also contained other surprises (Table 1.2). The DC vote dropped considerably, while the PSI and PSDI made steady gains and the small Liberal Party doubled its share of the vote. But the most solid progress was made by the Communists (PCI) who gained one million new voters and whose support exceeded one-quarter of the electorate. Clearly, one of the objectives of the opening to the Left, that of disarming Communism, had failed.

Conservative opinion put the blame for the increased Communist vote on the Pope's naively friendly view of Communism. *Pacem in Terris*, published just two weeks before the election, probably encouraged many women, previously afraid of voting Communist, to follow their menfolk and vote for the PCI. The previous month the Pope had granted an audience to Khrushchev's son-in-law, the editor of *Izvestiya*. Prime Minister Moro pointed to more fundamental reasons for the Communist advance. These were to do with the dramatic transformation of a society in the midst of an industrial revolution. The vast migrations from countryside to industrial town, and from South to North, had brought formerly conservative peasants, who under the influence of the village priest had previously voted DC, or perhaps Monarchist in the South, into an urban-industrial working-class milieu dominated by Communist ideology. Moro alluded to specific causes of discontent such as rising prices, lack of housing and inadequate public services, and admitted that the PCI had been able to exploit these discontents (Kogan, 1981). Consolidation of Communist power in the 'red belt' of Emilia, Tuscany and Umbria was based on longer-established traditions of left-wing ideology, and on the simple fact that the local PCI administrations in cities like Bologna and Reggio Emilia were progressive and efficient.

The 'opening to the Left' was an unfortunate victim of its own timing, for it coincided with the end of the postwar economic boom in 1963. On the political side, opponents of the Centre–Left coalition blamed the recession on loss of confidence in the government, which they maintained was alienating investment by opening the door to socialism and state planning. Centre–Left supporters, on the other hand, accused industrialists of spreading panic and even of provoking the recession in order to bring down the government. Both sides' accusations were exaggerated, but they had their psychological effect, and Moro's government nearly foundered amid fears of economic collapse. As it happened the economists at the Bank of Italy had the situation under control and steady growth resumed until 1969.

The Centre–Left Moro remained prime minister for five years. Little tangible was achieved during this period, the commitment to planning being generally evaded. A Five-Year Plan was eventually put into operation but lack of precise definition and the muddle-headedness of the bureaucracy prevented its effective implementation. Meanwhile the mid-1960s saw many sad events. In 1964 two key postwar political leaders, Segni (DC) and Togliatti (PCI), were struck down by strokes. Further tragedy struck in 1966: there were disastrous floods in Venice and Florence, and a landslide at Agrigento which led to the collapse of many blocks of flats which had been built on unstable ground without proper planning permission. The Agrigento disaster revealed the corruption of the Sicilian building industry by the Mafia and implicated a number of DC officials. In 1967 an earthquake struck western Sicily, killing 300 in one of the most backward parts of the country. Official dilatoriness in responding to these various natural — and not so natural — disasters did much to discredit the DC.

1.6.5 The 'hot autumn' and the 'historic compromise'

By the end of the 1960s, the party strategies of the Centre–Left had gone badly wrong. Politics had come to seem something separate, out of touch with the more dynamic pace of life in the country as a whole. Parliament had become subordinate to the party political machines, and the government was overshadowed by parastatal organizations whose vested interests tended to obstruct change. Growing social unrest led to a wave of popular protest in which both students and workers participated. As students took to the streets in 1968, universities were closed down for long periods. Later in 1968 a series of wildcat strikes hit many industrial firms in the North. In April 1969 serious riots broke out at Battipaglia, near Salerno, when a tobacco factory closed down. Matters came to a head in the autumn of 1969 when the metal workers, striking for a new national wage contract, virtually brought the entire economy to a halt.

This period, known as the 'hot autumn', acted as a catalyst for great social and political change (Slater, 1984). The conflict contained two particularly radical and new features. First, the importance of the movement lay partly in the fact that it constituted a grass-roots or shopfloor protest against the prevailing system of industrial relations in Italy. It bypassed the traditional union structure, whose ideological divisions seemed so irrelevant to the problems of workers in the factory. This opened up the second new feature of the protest: the egalitarian nature of many of the grievances. Whether one was a Communist, a Socialist or a Catholic Christian Democrat made little difference to the problems one faced as a worker in a big factory or as a migrant weighed down by problems of housing, health care, transport or discrimination in the alien urban environment. In the end, government and employers yielded to workers' demands, a capitulation which added an estimated 28 per cent to the costs of Italian industry over the next three years (Giugni, 1971). Politically, the 'hot autumn' meant that a government policy based on the exclusion of the working class was no longer possible, at least for the foreseeable future.

The 1968 election was a bitter blow for the reunited Socialists, whose share of the vote dropped by 27 per cent. Although the DC vote held steady, the loss of Socialist support spelled the end of the Centre–Left alliance. The Communist vote continued its long-term trend upwards, reaching 26.9 per cent (Table 1.2), while the new ultra-Left socialist party, the PSIUP, polled 4.5 per cent and gained 23 seats. As the social protest boiled over, the Socialists and the Christian Democrats moved further to the Left, trying to leave as little space as possible for the Communists as the voice of dissent. This strategy failed in that it ignored the right-wing backlash which manifested itself in the 1972 elections when the Monarchists and neo-Fascists made spectacular gains, polling 8.7 per cent of the vote nationally and emerging as the dominant force in certain southern towns like Catania.

Partly as a result of the 1972 elections, the major parties, except the MSI, shifted their ideological positions. The change in ideological colour was most marked in the PCI whose leader, Enrico Berlinguer, proposed in 1973 a 'compromise' which amounted to a government of national unity, linking all the democratic parties in an onslaught against Italy's social, economic and civil crises. Growing terrorism, which had begun in 1969 with the bombing of a Milan bank in which 14 people were killed, gave rise to fears of a neo-Fascist revival. Berlinguer's demand for a compromise government was also an admission that Catholicism still existed in Italy as a potent political force among the working classes. Moreover, Berlinguer's overtures had some willing listeners on the left wing of the DC, most notably Aldo Moro who had sounded out the Communists with the aim of bringing them into the government five years earlier.

As a political strategy, the historic compromise was a big success, at least in the short term (Slater, 1985). The PCI made substantial electoral gains, and by the 1976 election came within touching distance of the DC: 34.4 per cent as against 38.7 per cent of the electorate (Table 1.2). The move to regional autonomy in the early 1970s meant that by 1975 the Communists ran six regions as well as most of the big cities. In spite of some electoral decline since 1976, the PCI remains the only Western Communist Party to retain the support of a large section of the electorate. It represents not just a party but a political culture.

The historic compromise has been described as a 'flirtation of convenience' between the two biggest parties in the country (Clark, 1984). Each had little choice but to court the support of the other. The DC regime was collapsing amid economic chaos, financial scandal, rampant secularization and incipient terrorism; and it had no alternative allies. Drastic economic and social reforms were necessary, and these presupposed agreements — between parties, between the major labour confederations and on the shopfloor. Berlinguer, too, was worried by the national crisis and what it might do to the long-term fortunes of the PCI. He believed that many key institutions — the police, the army, the judiciary — were under Fascist influence. Labour militancy and Communist success at the polls might frighten the middle classes into the Fascist fold. The PCI was not strong enough, or respectable enough, to go it alone in government; nor would Italy's allies have tolerated a Communist government (Allum, 1980). Power-sharing, with the outwardly respectable DC, was the only alternative for them too.

In 1978 a series of events occurred to scupper the compromise. Moro's kidnapping and death at the hands of the Red Brigades removed one of the most persuasive advocates of the DC–PCI understanding. In the Vatican, the election of Cardinal Wojtyla as Pope John Paul II strengthened Catholic opposition to Communism. International events too played a role: the Italian Communists lost credibility after the Soviet Union's invasion of Afghanistan (even though Berlinguer had distanced himself from Moscow and was, for instance, strongly in support of the 'Solidarity' movement in Poland). And there was, in reality, little love lost between most DC members and PCI voters.

In 1979 the PCI withdrew its support from the government, provoking new elections. Its share of the vote dropped sharply to 30.4 per cent — its first decline in more than 30 years — while the position of the DC and other Centre parties held steady (Table 1.2). The main beneficiary of the PCI's decline was probably the small anti-establishment Radical Party which increased its share of the vote from 1.1 per cent in 1976 to 3.4 per cent in 1979.

1.6.6 Italian politics in the 1980s: the crisis of governability

The present decade has seen new twists and turns in Italy's convoluted political path. 1980, like 1968, was an apocalyptic year. In August a bomb exploded by right-wing terrorists at Bologna station killed 84 people, injured 200 and horrified the nation as to the unbridled audacity of extremists and their capacity for mindless murder. In October came the famous 'right to work' march by 40 000 Fiat workers through the streets of Turin. This protest by a large segment of the vehicle company's workforce, acting in defiance of their union, signalled the collapse of the militant posture adopted by the unions since their victories in 1969. The significance of the event was noted all over Italy. Industrial tribunals began upholding the dismissals of employees who rarely turned up for work. The employers' federation challenged the system of automatic wage indexation in operation since 1975 and managed to get it modified. Italian industry began to look as if it was capable of getting to grips with some of its problems.

Calamity struck again in November 1980 when a severe earthquake centred inland of Naples killed 3000 in the highlands of Campania and Basilicata and made over 200 000 homeless. By an ironic tragedy the tremor struck at the heart of the country's most poverty-ridden district, the barren yet overpopulated Irpinia. The aftermath of the earthquake revealed once again the inability of the inert DC administration to cope with such emergencies (Allum, 1981). Five years later political recrimination in the earthquake zone is still rife, many of the displaced population are still in temporary accommodation and the local Neapolitan Mafia, the Camorra, is deeply involved in creaming off profits from the reconstruction process.

Politically, the withdrawal of the Communists from government in 1979 did not prove to be as destabilizing as might have been thought, for the Socialists, now under the dynamic leadership of Bettino Craxi, were once again ready to participate in a coalition government. Craxi benefited enormously from media exposure; his forthright, dominant manner, linked to a scarcely concealed ambition for power, had wide appeal.

One of the Socialists' strongest arguments was that the office of prime minister should not necessarily be filled by a Christian Democrat. After 1981, when the P2 Masonic corruption scandal (whose ramifications reached London when an Italian banker was found hanging under Black-friars Bridge) weakened the moral authority of the DC, the smaller lay parties of the Centre were finally successful in having the premiership assigned to one of their leaders. This was the first time the country had

had a non-DC premier since 1964. Initially the premiership went to the Republican leader Spadolini but his reign was short lived. Craxi's chance came when the 1983 elections brought further votes for the lay Centre parties. Now, with 23.1 per cent of the electoral vote overall, they could claim to represent a powerful 'third force' in Italian politics, running quite close behind the DC, whose vote collapsed from 38.3 to 32.9 per cent, and the PCI, whose share held steady at around 30 per cent (Table 1.2). With their house in disarray, the DC were prepared to accept Craxi's leadership on four conditions: (1) an acceptance of DC superiority in Cabinet numbers; (2) collaboration in forming DC–PSI local government administrations (previously the PSI had cooperated with the PCI on town councils); (3) modification of the PSI's economic programme to include public expenditure cuts and deceleration of wage increases; and (4) acceptance of Cruise missiles, to be stationed at Comiso in Sicily (Slater, 1985). Thus the Socialist Party's experience with the Centre–Left formula has come full circle. It had entered the first Centre–Left government with a strong commitment to change but was given little freedom to implement its reforms. Twenty years later the Socialists control the levers of power but are no longer committed to reform.

The future of the DC, which has dominated 40 years of postwar Italian politics, seems finally to be under threat. In the North it has lost power as part of the growing secularization of Italian society; in the South voters are deserting because they are disgusted at the party's record of corruption and clientelism. Leonardi (1984) suggests that the vote may soon be whittled down to the core of Catholic subculture which represents about one-quarter of the population: the way may then be open for either the Communists, still mourning the recent death of Berlinguer, or the Centre lay parties to take over.

As the latter half of the 1980s approaches the political and economic future of Italy is far from clear. Craxi's five-party coalition (DC/PSI/PSDI/PRI/PLI), which appeared relatively stable by Italian standards, wobbled in late 1985 following an event of relatively low domestic significance — the hijack of the cruise liner *Achille Lauro* by Arab extremists and Craxi's decision to allow the Palestinian activist Abul Abbas to escape to Yugoslavia without first consulting with the Republican leader Spadolini. Externally, the event of greatest long-term significance is the enlargement of the EC (Slater, 1984). The accession of Greece to the EC in 1981 has benefited Italian agricultural and industrial exports, but that of Spain will pose problems. Spain will offer competition in many agricultural products, including vegetables, fruit (especially citrus), wine and olive oil, and in some areas of industrial production, such as footwear, steel, shipbuilding and cars. The EC's Mediterranean enlargement will also probably weaken Italy's share of the regional and social funds, to the obvious detriment of the Mezzogiorno.

TWO

Economic and Social Development in the Postwar Period

2.1 Introduction

The political euphoria accompanying the collapse of Fascism during the Second World War was tempered by the existence of a plethora of economic problems requiring immediate action and policy decisions at the end of the war. Allen and Stevenson (1974) provide the following catalogue of war damage. In the rural field one-quarter of livestock was lost and agricultural production was cut by 40 per cent. Industrial output in 1945 was only one-quarter of the 1938 level, and just about equal to that of 1884. Communications were also badly hit: one-quarter of railway track destroyed, one-third of bridges broken, 60 per cent of railway wagons lost, 35 per cent of roads damaged, 90 per cent of lorries destroyed or damaged, merchant shipping capacity reduced to one-sixth of its wartime peak, port facilities almost wiped out. In 1945 real income per head was less than half the 1938 level and below that at unification. Mean daily calorie intake was 1737 per head, compared to 2652 during 1936–40; large numbers of people were close to starvation.

In addition, basic decisions were needed on the future structure of the economic system and on the mechanism of economic development. A long period of protectionism followed by war had produced an autarkic economic structure strongly regulated by government controls; agriculture was too dependent on cereals production, while industry was dominated by traditional and technologically backward sectors such as textiles and food processing. Raw materials such as coal, as well as vital inputs like iron and steel, were in desperately short supply; shortages of foreign currency curtailed resort to imports. The wartime inflation continued, becoming particularly acute in 1947; by the time it was brought under control in 1948 the retail price index (1938 = 100) stood at 4844. Mass unemployment was a further disturbing problem: 2.4 million persons, 12 per cent of the active population, were out of work (Podbielski, 1974).

2.2 Postwar reconstruction

In spite of such a formidable array of problems, the economy regained its prewar strength within five years. Manufacturing industry had recovered 1938 levels of production by 1948, agriculture by 1950, per capita income by 1951. How did this dramatic recovery come about?

First, it should be pointed out that the picture painted above was not as catastrophic as it might appear. With the major exception of steel capacity, war damage to industrial plant turned out to be less serious than was at first anticipated, especially when compared to that of other countries. The Bank of Italy eventually estimated war damage suffered by Italian industry at only 8 per cent (but that by metallurgy at 25 per cent).

Second, reconstruction and recovery benefited from the availability of an ample, cheap and high-quality labour supply, as well as from a high degree of labour mobility which followed on naturally from demobilization. Wartime upheavals and the collapse of Fascism helped to break down traditional patterns of outlook and to orient people's thoughts to new ways of shaping the future. Italy was fortunate at this time to be served by an exceptional group of talented leaders such as Alcide De Gasperi, Amintore Fanfani and Luigi Einaudi, who worked tirelessly for their country's regeneration.

A third key factor was the large quantity of international aid, much of which originated from the United States. Between 1943 and 1948 Italy received outside aid valued at $2230 million, 70 per cent in the form of non-repayable grants. The greater part of this aid was spent on imported fuel and food: the former was an important component of industrial recovery, the latter was vital to feed a near-starving population until agriculture could find its feet again. US aid continued after 1948 under the Marshall Plan which channelled $1310 million to Italy during 1948–51, mostly in the form of grants. Few would dispute that, without US Marshall Aid, the Italian postwar recovery would have been much more protracted (Allen and Stevenson, 1974).

2.2.1 Italy in 1950

Although Italy had largely recovered from the war by 1950, it was neverthe-less still a poor and backward nation. Some 44 per cent of the working population were employed in agriculture, much of which consisted of small-scale uneconomic peasant farming; agriculture's contribution to GDP was only 23 per cent. Underemployment was endemic to many rural areas, both those operating under conditions of peasant self-sufficiency and those worked by large estates employing wage labour (Dickinson, 1955a). In many respects, farming functioned as a 'refuge sector' for those unable to find other kinds of employment.

Much industry was also backward and small scale. The average manufacturing enterprise employed less than six people, and 90 per cent of industrial establishments had a workforce of fewer than five. The steel industry was technologically backward while industries such as vehicles and chemicals lagged behind their counterparts in the more advanced European countries.

The deficient economic structure was matched by poor performance on many social indicators. Infant mortality in 1950 was 63.8 per 1000 live births (cf. 31.4 in the UK and 29.2 in the USA), and illiteracy was 12.9 per cent of the population aged six years and over. Housing conditions were also very poor. Of the 11.4 million dwellings recorded in the 1951 census, only 10.4 per cent had a bath, only 35 per cent had piped drinking water within the dwelling, and only 43.5 per cent had an inside toilet.

Italy in 1950 was also a spatially dualistic society. The North–South differential was wider than it had ever been — a consequence not just of the war but of decades of neglect and non-existent or ineffectual regional planning. The southern economy was more agricultural than that of the North, yet southern farms were smaller and the land intrinsically poorer. Agriculture employed 57 per cent of the labour force in the South and 38 per cent in the North; comparable figures for manufacturing industry were 13 per cent and 27 per cent respectively (Allen and Stevenson, 1974).

These striking regional contrasts were further authenticated by the publication of detailed parliamentary inquiries into poverty and unemployment in the early 1950s. On the combined criteria of diet, clothing and housing, 11.8 per cent of the Italian population were found to be destitute, enduring a standard of living far below any acceptable average. This national percentage was, however, made up of widely differing regional averages: 1.5 per cent in the North, 5.9 per cent in the Centre, 24.8 per cent in the islands of Sicily and Sardinia and 28.8 per cent in the mainland South. Peak figures were found in Basilicata (33.2 per cent) and Calabria (37.7 per cent). Of the 11.8 per cent, or 1.37 million people, condemned to destitution, two-thirds lived in shacks, caves or basements with two, three or four persons to a room, half never consumed meat, sugar or wine and half were wretchedly dressed (Montini, 1955). Urban poverty was particularly acute in Naples where, according to the inquiry, '80 000 persons in the city do not know when they get up in the morning, what they will eat that day or whether they will eat at all'.

2.2.2 Strategy for recovery

The year 1950 marked the commencement of a range of policies to deal with the country's most pressing social and economic problems. The land reform attempted to redress inequalities in the agricultural sector, transferring land from inefficient and socially oppressive landowners to landless peasants. This policy was reinforced by the establishment, also in 1950, of the Cassa per il Mezzogiorno, a special government agency for developing the South. The land reform is described in more detail in Chapter 5, the work of the Cassa in Chapter 6.

More important in the long term than these institutional measures was the kind of economic strategy chosen to guide postwar recovery and subsequent economic development. Although there were many advocates of a strongly controlled economy, the dominant economic philosophy was the liberal one of restoring the free market economy and opening up international trade. These views were shared by many powerful figures in industry who saw export expansion, and readily available imports, as essential to the enlargement of their operations. The liberal philosophy provided a strong stimulus to the export-orientated industrial development of the ensuing decade, but it was also responsible for laying the foundations of a series of structural problems which continue to afflict the Italian economy to this day.

2.3 The long boom

In 1950, the task of economic reconstruction completed, Italy turned towards the future. During the next dozen or so years the country enjoyed a period of unprecedented economic growth remarkable for both its speed and sustained momentum. This golden period is often referred to as Italy's economic miracle; sometimes this term is applied to the entire growth period but more often the 'miracle' is confined to the last five years, i.e. 1958–63. More apt, therefore, is Hildebrand's (1965) description of the entire period as the 'long boom'; this forms the basis for a division into two phases, one of domestic-led growth (1950–58) and one of the export-led 'miracle' (1958–63).

A few facts and figures will illustrate the profundity of the economic transformation achieved during the long boom. Gross domestic product more than doubled, growing at 5.9 per cent per annum between 1950 and 1963, 6.9 per cent during 1958–63 and 8.3 per cent in 1961. Industrial output rose by an annual average of 8.1 per cent, exceeding 10 per cent in some of the 'miracle' years, faster than anywhere else in the world except Japan and possibly also West Germany. Whole new industries — motor-scooters, washing machines, refrigerators — emerged from virtually work-shop backgrounds and dominated world markets within just a few years. More established mechanical industries strengthened their position. Thus by the early 1960s Fiat was outselling all other car firms, even Volkswagen, in Europe, while Olivetti's annual production of typewriters approached 1 million and Necchi turned out 500 000 sewing machines (Clark, 1984). The fastest growing industry of all was chemicals, producing not only fertilizers, its traditional product, but also oil-based plastics and fibres on a huge scale.

2.3.1 The 'pre-miracle' years, 1950–58

The years before 1958 saw growth spurred largely by internal forces, especially by the increase in fixed investment achieved by both the public sector and private entrepreneurs. Gross capital formation rose by 10 per cent per annum between 1951 and 1958, with the investment share of GDP increasing from 18 to 24 per cent. The most dynamic component of investment was residential construction, a reflection largely of postwar reconstruction and urbanization needs. Conversely, private consumption remained subdued in line with only moderate growth in the level of real wages. The latter reflected the situation of excess labour and the acceptance by the then weak trade unions of relatively low wages. Total employment rose very little and the rate of unemployment fell only slightly between 1950 and 1958, despite a net emigration flow estimated by Rey (1982) as equivalent to 5 per cent of the labour force.

Agriculture's role in the early stages of the boom is frequently overlooked in the literature on this period. Between 1951 and 1958 1.75 million people left the land, supplying much of the labour required by the manufacturing and construction sectors. Moreover the volume of agricultural investment almost doubled over this period. The combination of growing investment and a declining farm labour force resulted in agricultural productivity rising by 6.3 per cent per annum. However, the rewards of this productivity leap were not, for the most part, reaped by the farmers themselves but by middlemen and those responsible for the technical inputs in agriculture, such as fertilizer and tractor manufacturers (Barberis, 1971). Another developmental boost provided by agriculture was the healthy surplus in the balance of trade for foodstuffs.

2.3.2 The miracle years, 1958–63

The outpouring of labour from agriculture continued and intensified during the five years of the 'miracle'. Between 1958 and 1963 GDP growth was extremely rapid at nearly 7 per cent per annum; investment rose at 10 per cent per year and in 1963 reached a share of GDP of 27 per cent — one of the highest levels recorded by any European country in the postwar period (Rey, 1982). By the early 1960s Italy enjoyed near full employment. As the boom gathered strength, a scarcity of skilled workers created bottlenecks in certain northern industries. Advertisements were placed in Swiss newspapers encouraging Italian emigrant workers to return home to work in Italy!

Several differences distinguish the character of growth during the miracle period from the pattern during the years prior to 1958 (Rey, 1982). As before, investment rose extremely rapidly, but instead of residential construction industrial equipment became the main destination for investment. A second distinguishing feature was the phenomenal rate of growth of merchandise exports, a fact closely connected to Italy's accession to the Common Market. Manufactures rose to 78 per cent of total exports, while the share of foodstuffs declined. On the imports side, foodstuffs increased sharply, and the trade balance in agricultural products lurched into deficit in 1960, and has remained negative ever since. A third, and very important, change from the 1950–58 period was the growth of private consumption, especially of durable goods, whose level of purchase doubled during the five miracle years. Symbolic of all three characteristics just mentioned — intensifying industrial investment, rising exports and increasing consumer demand — was the production of Italian cars, leaping from 319 000 in 1957 to 1.1 million in 1963.

Rising consumer demand proved to be one of the needles which pricked the bubble. Between 1951 and 1961 consumer price inflation had been less than 2 per cent per annum. In 1962, however, consumer prices rose by 4.7 per cent and in 1963 the rate increased to 7.5 per cent; these were twice the rates pertaining in other Common Market countries. Inflation quickly spread to the labour market. The achievement of virtual full employment, with labour shortages in some job sectors, led inevitably to upward pressure on wage levels. Wages increased by 14 per cent in 1962 and by 20 per cent in 1963 (Fazio, 1981). Domestic inflation led to a sharp loss in competitiveness and, combined with excess demand, to a deterioration in the balance of payments. By 1963 the trade deficit was equivalent to 3.6 per cent of GDP. The economic situation was further aggravated by an increase in illegal capital exports, this flight of capital being partly attributable to lack of confidence in the Centre–Left experiment begun under Fanfani's premiership in 1962.

2.4 The continuing transformation of the economy

The year 1963 was an important dividing line for Italian postwar economic development. Up to then, rapid growth had been sustained primarily by a process of capital accumulation favoured by large productivity gains, restrained wage rises and rapid international integration. Few of these forces remained in operation for the rest of the 1960s. Exports no longer so consistently 'led' growth; the problem of inflation was never absent; unemployment rose in spite of continued massive emigration and a fall in the working population of around 4 per cent between 1963 and 1969; the balance of payments was placed in constant jeopardy by a volatile capital account; and in 1964 Dr Guido Carli, Governor of the Bank of Italy, had to petition for loans of $1225 million from the United States and the International Monetary Fund. In short, the whole economic environment in Italy changed, and consequently the nature of the growth process after 1963 was fundamentally different from the years of the long boom.

2.4.1 The late 1960s: faltering growth

The statistics of economic growth during the period between the 1963–65 recession and the 'hot autumn' of 1969 reveal a see-saw pattern. As against an annual average of 5.9 per cent during 1950–63, annual GDP growth slumped to 2.9 per cent in 1964 and 3.5 per cent in 1965. In 1966 and 1967 there were signs of recovery as the economy grew at 5.8 and 6.8 per cent respectively. However, from then onwards the growth rate fell steadily to reach a low of 1.6 per cent in 1971.

The reduced rate of growth during the latter half of the 1960s can be attributed to a number of causes. Of prime importance was the failure of industrial investment to recover from the 1963–65 recession. Over the period 1964–70 industrial fixed investment increased at an annual rate of only 1 per cent, compared to more than 9 per cent during 1952–63 (Allen and Stevenson, 1974). The relatively buoyant economic growth which did occur during 1966–68 was in many ways a 'false growth' insofar as it was not accompanied by investment increases but based on a more intensive use of existing plant and increased working hours. While these changes succeeded in raising output in the short run, the process was inevitably temporary and reaped its final reward in 1969 when labour disputes were marred by increased bitterness owing to the deterioration of working conditions suffered since 1963.

Another critical mechanism in the economic slowdown was the outweighing of modest productivity gains by soaring labour costs. Over the period 1964–71 industrial wages rose by 77 per cent, although for the workers much of this increase was swallowed up by price inflation. Because of the dramatic rise in social security payments (these became higher in Italy than in any other Common Market country) labour costs as a whole rose by a massive 90 per cent. At the same time, industrial productivity grew by only 42 per cent. Labour costs, having accounted for an average of 56 per cent of industrial value-added during 1951–62, rose to account for 65 per cent during 1965–70 and 71 per cent in 1971. The rapid rise in wage rates was probably due less to a tightening of the labour market than to increasing trade-union pressures (Allen and Stevenson, 1974). The state industries employers' association Intersind had given an unfortunate lead by negotiating separately with the unions so that wages in the public sector became much higher than those in the private sector, up to twice as much for some equivalent jobs (Clark, 1984).

On the other hand exports continued to rise at rates comparable to those of the boom: an annual average rate of 13.5 per cent during 1964–73 compared to 13.8 per cent during 1950–63. This anomaly is not easy to explain. Self-evidently Italian products were able to retain their price competitiveness in export markets, and it must be concluded that the export industries were better able to minimize labour cost increases by productivity gains than the domestically oriented industries.

The other principal characteristic of the changing economic structure of the late 1960s was the increasing part played by the state in industrial and economic affairs (Wiskemann, 1971). Both the nationalized industries, such as ENEL (the electricity corporation), and the state holding sector, especially ENI and IRI, expanded in many directions. IRI took control of the food firms Alemagna, Motta and Cirio, partly to ward off the threat of American takeovers. ENI subsidiaries became active in the nuclear power programme, and ENEL undertook a massive development of power stations in the underprovided South.

2.4.2 Feeble planning

The involvement of the Socialists in the government after the 'opening to the Left' inevitably led to a firmer commitment to planning, and the 1966–70 Five-Year National Economic Plan, sometimes called the Pieraccini Plan,was the first of its kind in Italy. The Plan, which emerged after considerable delay, envisaged an annual growth rate of GDP of 5 per cent (7 per cent for industry, 4 per cent for services and just under 3 per cent for agriculture and construction) and aimed at full employment by the creation of 1.5 million jobs by 1970. A special effort was to be made to improve the efficiency and productivity of five industries — food processing, textiles, construction, electronics and machine tools. The Plan also aimed at much closer integration than had hitherto been achieved between the plans for specific areas or problems (such as the Cassa per il Mezzogiorno's work in the South or the Green Plans for agriculture) and the overall planning for the economy as a whole. Among the longer-term aims, extending beyond the Plan's own term, were the elimination of the North–South gap, improvement in farm incomes and better social services. In the context of this last objective social expenditure was to be raised from 23 to 27 per cent of national income, the main increases going to education, health and scientific research. This denoted a conscious effort to make up for the deficiencies of the 1950s when government investment had favoured industry over welfare services.

The Pieraccini Plan failed to have any significant impact on economic events. Partly this was because the Plan was a victim of its own delays: discussed in the early 1960s when growth could be taken for granted, but implemented only after rapidly increasing GDP had ceased to be a reality. However, there were also fundamental cultural reasons why effective planning could never be instituted in Italy, and to a large extent these still apply today. Planning demands cooperation from the state bureaucracy, but such cooperation has rarely been forthcoming, the personnel of the overmanned civil service being overwhelmingly concerned to preserve the status quo and their own jobs and status. Effective planning also demands quick, incisive decision-making, whereas the Byzantine nature of the official bureaucracy, with its multifarious layers and overlapping responsibilities, inevitably prevents this from happening. State administrative inactivity has allowed vast amounts of budgeted funds to accumulate unspent. Under the Pieraccini Plan this was especially true of funds earmarked for investment in housing and schools. Another cultural problem has been the failure to appreciate the interdependence between scientific research and economic development in a technological era. Italian politicians and civil servants tend to regard scientific research as a luxury and its financing as a fringe activity.

The Five-Year Plan was never widely supported by any of the major economic groups — small or large firms, the state holding sector or trade unions. The major private sector employers' body Confindustria (roughly equivalent to the Confederation of British Industry) opposed the Plan intransigently, denouncing it as an attempt to destroy private initiative and to collectivize the Italian economy — a clear case of overreaction. Planning was also anathema to most members of the Christian Democrat government. Even Fanfani, one of the architects of the Centre–Left coalition, dismissed planning as a 'book of dreams' (Pasquino and Pecchini, 1975). And finally the unions, wary of a possible incomes policy element, were sceptical, especially after their unification and victorious gains as a result of the 'hot autumn'.

After the collapse of the Centre–Left coalition in February 1972, the impetus to planning faded. Discussions on a second Five-Year Plan for 1971–75 petered out, although the *Progetto 80*, the Plan's guiding document, was widely used as a reference point after the document was stolen from a minister's desk and leaked to the press! In sum, Italy's political and economic evolution provides the classic planning dilemma: when planning is possible, it does not take place; when it is needed, it is impossible (Allum, 1973a).

2.4.3 *The role of labour*

The postwar transformation of the Italian economy has been closely linked to the fluctuating power of labour, especially organized labour. As we saw earlier in this chapter, the long boom was partly built on an excess supply of fairly cheap and unorganized labour. The sharp rise in the price of labour in 1962–63 coincided with the end of the long boom, and the sequence was repeated in 1969 when further wage increases secured through the strike action of the 'hot autumn' ended the shorter boom of the late 1960s. As a result the 1960s was the decade in which Italian wages and labour costs came into line with European levels (Cavallari and Faustini, 1978).

Despite these achievements, the Italian labour movement has been curiously fragmented. Since the end of the Second World War it has been divided into four main strands. The two ideological extremes are occupied by the Communist-dominated Confederazione Generale Italiana del Lavoro (CGIL), which is the largest union confederation and finds its strength particularly among the highly paid mechanical and engineering workers, and the neo-Fascist Confederazione Sindacati Nazionali Lavoratori (CIS-NAL), which has few members and is of little importance. Between these two is a second pair of unions. The larger, the Confederazione Italiana Sindacati Lavoratori (CISL), is allied to the Christian Democrat Party and the Church; the smaller is the Unione Italiana del Lavoro (UIL), which is allied to the Social Democrats.

There have been many reasons why Italian unions have been slow to assume an autonomous role in representing the interests of the working class. The long years of Fascist rule, during which unions and strikes were outlawed, heightened the anti-union bias of the middle classes. When unions were permitted, the severe unemployment of the early postwar era did a great deal to dilute labour's bargaining power. Different unions have frequently taken divergent points of view, especially with regard to strikes, and there have been marked regional contrasts in union activities, especially with the survival of more traditional labour relations in the South. Further problems have been the practice of operating on limited budgets because of the tradition against substantial dues, and the system of double contract negotiations — one for basic issues for each industrial sector nationally, and a second for supplementary local matters. Finally, the close ties between unions and political parties have led to the parties' exploitation of the unions for their own purposes and to the diversion of union energies into matters that have little direct connection with workers' interests (Neufeld, 1960). The complexity of the labour market is further increased by the fact that only about half the labour force is unionized and by contrasts in employer attitudes which range from enlightened benevolence to almost mediaeval autocracy.

The unions' close involvement with party politics is paralleled on the employers' side. Confindustria is reputed to finance the Liberal Party and has had close ties with the DC. Industrial groups like Fiat, Pirelli and Olivetti, which supported the 'opening to the Left' in the early 1960s, can be assumed to have contributed to the party funds of the DC, Social Democrats and Republicans, while others, like Edison (later Montedison) and Assolombarda (the Association of Lombard Industrialists), which opposed the 'opening', almost certainly contributed to the funds of right-wing parties, such as the Monarchists and the Liberals. The cement group Italcementi is reputed to have financed the neo-Fascists (Allum, 1973a; Martinelli, 1979).

During the 1960s the fragmented, impotent stance of the labour confederations was replaced by more positive action. Individual industrial unions within the confederations developed collective bargaining strategies from 1960 onwards and during the 1962–63 national negotiations, CISL union leaders agreed to develop joint strategies with CGIL and UIL unions. By the late 1960s worker militancy had increased sharply, not just in terms of the number of strikes but also judged by the evolution of more radical forms of struggle, especially from the grass-roots level of the factory floor, and by greater and broader demands including issues, like housing reform, which lay outside the workplace. At their 1969 congresses both CGIL and CISL accepted the need for breaking ties with their respective political parties, with the result that by the 'hot autumn' the labour movement spoke with a unified voice on many issues of national concern. The unity of the labour movement was formalized in the 1972 CGIL–CISL–UIL pact establishing a unitary federation.

The main result of the 'hot autumn' was, of course, improved wage rates and better working conditions. However, the 1970s saw a retreat from the aggressive posture of 1969. Starting in 1971 (later in some industries or firms), the unions tried to confine strike activity to limited periods when it was strictly necessary. Since 1972 the number of strike days lost as a result of industrial action has steadily declined, with the exception of those years fixed for the renewal of the most important national collective wage agreements (i.e. 1973, 1975, 1979, 1983). Especially after the *svolta sindacale* or 'union turnabout' of 1978, trade union emphasis shifted to one of cooperation with government to solve problems related to the economic crisis. Characteristic of this period was the practice of wage restraint and moderation of other demands as a trade-off for more control over the ways in which economic policy — especially with regard to the location of new investments to solve unemployment — was formed.

The 1980s have seen a further erosion in the bargaining power of labour. The key events here have been the 1980 'march of the 40 000' in Turin, when Fiat's middle management and some of its skilled workers took to the streets to demonstrate their right to work in defiance of the labour confederations, and the dissolution of the CGIL–CISL–UIL Unitary Federation in 1984. It is important to realize that although these were the two headline events, they were manifestations of more deep-seated and gradual structural and political changes stretching back over the past 12 years. These include the oil crisis of the mid- and late 1970s, continuing high inflation and unemployment, the rapid spread of new technologies involving computers, robotization, etc., the collapse of the governments of 'national unity' when the PCI withdrew their cooperation in 1979, and the incapability of union leaders of understanding the new needs arising out of these political, economic and social changes (Giugni, 1984). As a result the labour movement has refragmented, and the gulf has widened between union officials and rank-and-file workers and between unionized and non-unionized labour.

2.4.4 Recession and restructuring, 1970–85

The period since 1969 has seen recurrent crises: indeed the situation of crisis seems to be so permanent that the very meaning of the word needs to be questioned (Tarrow, 1979). The overall mean annual growth rate for the decade 1970–80 — a fairly respectable 3.1 per cent — hides a fluctuating pattern of periods of recovery punctuated by phases of decline. In the early years of the decade, the economy had to absorb the consequences of the 'hot autumn'. Then, in the mid-1970s, the increase in oil prices hit with particular force a country highly dependent on imported energy. In 1974 the economy declined by 3.6 per cent — the first decline since the end of the war. The scenario repeated itself in the late 1970s and early 1980s, with the difference that the intervening years had seen a painful adjustment process which had increased the fragility of the economy. The early 1980s have witnessed continuous economic decline — by 0.2 per cent in 1981, 0.3 per cent in 1982 and 0.8 per cent in 1983 (Slater, 1985).

Since 1974 annual inflation has constantly been in double figures, exceeding 20 per cent in some years. Within Europe only Spain, Portugal, Turkey and Iceland have had higher inflation rates. It is now appreciated that one of the major sources fuelling this inflation is the *scala mobile*, the sliding scale of wage indexation to the cost of living, which came into operation in 1975 as one of the main achievements of union–government cooperation. Reform of the *scala mobile* is one of the major preoccupations of the present government. However, recent modifications, indexing wages to a level 15 per cent below the rate of inflation, and then to the targeted rate of inflation not the actual rate, have achieved only modest reductions in wage increases.

Another critical issue, familiar to students of the British economy, is the expanding public-sector deficit. Some cuts have been made by the Craxi government in social security payments. Further public expenditure cuts may have to be made, particularly in the nationalized industries whose problems of overcapacity and inefficiency have yet to be vigorously tackled. However, such cuts will tend to increase unemployment and risk further alienation of the working class and of their supporting parties. In addition, all policy-makers are aware that in a system rife with political patronage, any spending cuts carry high political risk (Slater, 1985).

Some interesting explanations have been put forward for the economic and structural crises of the past 15 years, especially by Giorgio Fuà and his colleagues at the University of Ancona. Fuà (1978) characterizes Italy as a 'lagging' or 'late-developing' country (in contrast to the earlier developing countries like Britain, France and West Germany), and points out that in such countries, where an export-led growth strategy has opened up the economy to international market influences, the growth process is likely to be speeded up in the initial stage, when the incorporation of modern technology combined with low labour costs encourages fast productivity growth. Later on, however, as the abundant supply of labour becomes exhausted and as European wage levels are imitated, growth slows down and increasing inflationary tendencies appear. At the same time the imitation of welfare systems built up by richer neighbours inflates government expenditures and deficits, thus lowering national propensity to save and invest (Pettenati, 1982).

The economic crisis, especially the high cost of labour since 1969 and the high momentum of wage increases driven on by the *scala mobile*, has led directly to the segmentation of the labour market. The most dynamic element of the economy in the 1970s and 1980s has been the small-firm sector, often linked to big industries through chains of subcontracting. Fiat, Italy's foremost private industrial giant, has perfected the subcontracting strategy; unable to reconstruct the social peace of the 1950s inside the factory after 1969, the firm has opted for the fragmentation of labour power into a multitude of small supplying firms. Unlike large firms, small concerns are able to employ a largely non-union workforce. The very strength of this sector has threatened to negate the claim of the unions to represent the working class.

The now-celebrated 'submerged' or 'black' economy is only sketchily represented in official statistics, but its existence caused the government statistics agency ISTAT to revise upwards by 10 per cent its figures for total national output in 1978. Other, more recent, estimates put Italy's black economy at 20 or even 30 per cent of GDP, by far the highest proportion of any Western industrial country. Informed observers estimate that there are

Table 2.1   National employment changes by sector, 1951–81

| | % **working population employed in:** | | | % **of total population** |
	Agriculture	Industry	Services	**in employment**
1951	42.2	32.0	25.8	43.5
1961	29.3	40.7	30.0	38.7
1971	17.6	44.7	37.9	34.7
1981	11.2	39.8	49.0	39.8

Source: ISTAT: *Censimento Generale della Popolazione, 1951, 1961, 1971, 1981.*

at least 2.5 million 'unofficial' workers, mainly the young, the elderly and the female (Clark, 1984). They work at home (e.g. in the knitting trade) or in small workshops (e.g. producing shoes or carrying out mechanical repairs); they are not unionized; they pay no taxes; and they are outside the social security system or, rather, parasitic on it. Many of them also receive sick pay or disability pensions from other jobs, and 'moonlighting', multiple job-holding, is common.

2.4.5 Employment changes

The transformation and restructuring of the Italian economy over the postwar period can be summed up by a brief examination of sectoral employment figures for 1951–81 (Table 2.1).

Agriculture exhibits a continuing decline from 42.2 per cent of the employed population in 1951 to 11.2 per cent in 1981. Despite the substantial exodus from this sector since 1951, farming still accounts for a bigger proportion of the working population than in most other major European countries with more cultivable land and better water resources. Recently, there are signs that the exodus from agriculture is slowing down.

Industry increased its share of the working population during 1951–71 but this declined markedly during 1971–81 so that the 1981 proportion was similar to that in 1961, a dramatic testimony to the incipient deindustrialization of the country's economy. As described in more detail in Chapter 3, the loss of industrial employment has been especially marked in textiles, metallurgy, chemicals and pharmaceuticals. The industrial decline is, however, by no means regionally uniform. Industrial employment has continued to increase in many central and northeastern regions, but this is outweighed by the shrinkage of industrial employment in the traditional industrial heartland of the Northwest and in the South.

The service sector shows continuing, indeed accelerating, employment growth over the 1951–81 era. In Italy the dramatic increase in tertiary employment has been faster than in most other industrial countries. This is far from being a healthy sign, for the per capita contribution of tertiary sector workers in Italy is low by international standards, indicating ineffi-ciency in the management of tertiary establishments typified by the prolif-eration of small shops and petty traders and by overmanned offices using backward methods of clerical work. The tertiary sector also has the highest proportion of self-employed workers. Whereas one-fifth of the total Italian labour force is self-employed, this proportion rises to 47 per cent in the service sector, and this trend to self-employment is increasing (Predetti, 1982). More than any other major European country, Italy is a nation of small shopkeepers, barbers, artisans, traders and peasant farmers.

Finally, Table 2.1 shows the changing percentage of the economically active population compared to the total population. This percentage de-clined over the first three censuses but then increased in 1981. Annual data analysed by Di Comite and Imbriani (1982) show that the upturn in activity rates originated in the years 1971–73, though somewhat later in the South. The recent upturn in the economically active population is a reversal of a trend which was at least a century old, the activity rate having continuously declined from the first Italian census in 1861 (when it was 59.5 per cent) to the 1971 value of 34.7 per cent.

Postwar activity rates in Italy are well below those of most other European countries. Fuà (1977) has shown that the key to this inactivity was the declining participation rate (until 1971) for young (15–24 years) and old (over 45 years) males. Males in the 24–44 age bracket have retained a stable activity rate of around 95 per cent. Female employment, relatively low in Italy anyway, especially in the South where there are cultural sanctions against women working outside the home, has also declined.

It has to be stressed that Table 2.1 and the foregoing discussion are based on official census data on employment; a distinction has to be drawn between these official figures and what might be termed the 'real' or 'effective' supply and distribution of labour. Estimates of the 'unofficial' or 'hidden' labour force generally exceed 2 million and include a multitude of temporary, part-time, marginal workers whom the census probably records as unemployed or economically inactive.

Another problem with the national figures in Table 2.1 is that they mask very wide regional variations. Accordingly, Table 2.2 shows the regional pattern of activity rates, sectoral employment and unemployment for the country's administrative regions in 1981. The main residues of agricultural employment lie in the South where many regions still have 20–30 per cent of their employed population working in farming. Lombardy, on the other hand, has only 4 per cent. Industrial employment exhibits the reverse pattern, being appreciably higher in the North and accounting for about

Table 2.2 Regional pattern of employment and unemployment, 1981

	% working population employed in:			% of total population in employment	% unemployed
	Agriculture	Industry	Services		
Piedmont–Val d'Aosta	8.3	49.2	42.5	43.7	8.8
Lombardy	4.0	51.4	44.6	43.7	7.5
Trentino–Alto Adige	11.4	31.8	56.8	41.2	7.9
Veneto	8.8	45.3	45.9	41.3	9.0
Friuli–Venezia Giulia	5.2	39.7	55.1	40.2	7.5
Liguria	4.9	32.0	63.1	38.6	11.5
Emilia–Romagna	12.9	40.4	46.7	45.3	7.3
Tuscany	6.7	43.8	49.5	41.9	9.1
Umbria	11.2	42.4	46.4	40.5	10.6
Marche	11.7	44.9	43.4	42.4	9.2
Latium	6.7	28.3	65.0	38.9	17.7
Abruzzi	14.5	37.8	47.7	37.5	14.2
Molise	29.3	30.7	40.0	38.0	16.4
Campania	17.8	31.3	50.9	36.5	31.3
Apulia	25.5	28.9	45.6	36.5	23.8
Basilicata	27.6	32.0	40.4	37.8	23.4
Calabria	23.7	28.6	47.7	35.0	27.9
Sicily	19.8	29.6	50.8	32.9	25.8
Sardinia	13.4	32.1	54.5	35.4	23.2
Italy	11.2	39.8	49.0	39.8	14.8

Source: ISTAT: *Censimento Generale della Popolazione, 1981*.
Note: For the location of these regions see Figure 1.3.

half the working population of Piedmont and Lombardy. In the South many of the 'industrial' workers are actually artisans or construction labourers. The level of tertiary sector employment exhibits a narrower range of regional variation, most regions having values of 40–55 per cent. Only Liguria (63.1 per cent) and Latium (65 per cent) have appreciably higher levels, the former because of tourism, the latter because of the state bureaucracy in Rome. Moving on to activity rates, in most northern regions the proportion is above 40 per cent, while in southern regions it is 33–38 per cent. This regional divide reflects the wider availability of employment opportunities in the North and the higher rates of unemployment and underemployment in the South. Female activity rates are particularly low in the South. The decline in overall activity rates from North to South is matched by a rise in regional unemployment figures; rates in southern regions like Campania (31.3 per cent) and Calabria (27.9 per cent) are four times those of northern regions like Lombardy (7.5 per cent) and Emilia–Romagna (7.3 per cent).

2.5 Demographic evolution

The impact of economic factors on demographic development is generally hard to determine with precision, but economic trends have obvious repercussions on migration patterns, both internal and abroad, and there are clear parallels between regional economic and demographic contrasts. The differences between the 'Mediterranean' demographic regime of the South and the 'European' type of the North of Italy are both causes and consequences of the North–South economic gap (Del Panta, 1979). These differences are particularly significant in relation to fertility and infant mortality, both of which are much higher in the South where socioeconomic conditions are poorer. Rapid population growth in the South is in turn a major determinant of high unemployment and of overcrowded living conditions in the region.

The vital rate patterns of the Italian population generally replicate the declines postulated by the demographic transition model (Di Comite, 1980). Current birth and death rates, viewed for the nation as a whole, are roughly comparable to those of the advanced nations of Western Europe. But the national figures obscure regional contrasts which are quite marked. In the North, early industrialization and urbanization were associated with sharp declines in birth and death rates as early as the turn of the century so that the demographic evolution of Piedmont, for instance, has followed very closely the French pattern. In the South, on the other hand, birth and death rates continued at a much higher level for at least the first half of this century. During the postwar era, the southern birth rate, although sharply declining, remains substantially higher than that of the North, while the South's death rate, now slightly lower than that in the rest of Italy, reflects improved medical facilities and a relatively youthful age structure. The fact that some southern regions, notably Basilicata, Calabria and Sardinia, are still some way off completing the demographic transition process to low and equal birth and death rates implies that these regions are still in the throes of economic transition, with low levels of urbanization and limited or unbalanced industrial development. Regional contrasts are only part of the story, however, for lower birth rates have also been characteristic of most urban as opposed to rural areas, and of higher as opposed to lower socioeconomic status groups.

2.5.1 Population change, 1951–81

The most recent population census, taken on 25 October 1981, recorded 56.2 million people. The growth in population since the 1971 census of 2.1 million people or 3.9 per cent is a smaller increase than previous intercensal changes of 6.9 per cent during 1961–71 and 6.6 per cent during 1951–61. This fall-off in the momentum of demographic growth is all the more remarkable considering the dramatic decline in Italian emigration which had been high during 1951–71, but tailed off sharply during the 1970s.

Again, however, it has to be stressed that the national picture is nothing but an amalgam of widely differing regional situations. These are set out in detail in Table 2.3, which also shows how temporal trends shift from one intercensal period to the next. The decade 1951–61 was a period of intense regional contrast in the pattern of population losses and gains. Lombardy, Piedmont, Liguria and Latium were all growing at 1–2 per cent per year, while population losses over the decade occurred in the Northeast (Veneto, Friuli–Venezia Giulia) and in central Italy (Umbria, Marche, Abruzzo and Molise). Much the same picture holds for 1961–71, except that the rhythm of population growth in the key northern industrial regions of Piedmont and Lombardy increased slightly, and the regions of population loss tended to extend further south to take in Basilicata, Calabria and Sicily. By contrast, the third intercensal decade — 1971–81 — shows radical departures from the previous two. First, the regional contrasts are much less intense. No region gained more than 1 per cent per year (or 10 per cent over the decade), and there was only one region of population loss, Liguria's ageing population failing to reproduce itself in spite of some inmigration. Second, the broad geographical pattern changes with the regions of strongest demographic increase now located in the South, in particular Campania, Apulia and Sardinia.

Table 2.3 Regional population changes, 1951–81

	1951	1961	1971	1981	% change 1951–61	% change 1961–71	% change 1971–81
Piedmont	3 518 177	3 914 250	4 432 313	4 447 362	+11.3	+13.2	+0.3
Val d'Aosta	94 140	100 959	109 150	112 662	+7.2	+8.1	+3.2
Lombardy	6 566 154	7 406 152	8 543 387	8 898 653	+12.8	+15.4	+4.2
Trentino–Alto Adige	728 604	785 967	841 886	870 475	+7.9	+7.1	+3.4
Veneto	3 918 059	3 846 562	4 123 532	4 309 607	−1.8	+7.2	+4.5
Friuli–Venezia Giulia	1 226 121	1 204 298	1 213 532	1 229 929	−1.8	+0.8	+1.4
Liguria	1 566 961	1 735 349	1 853 578	1 799 055	+10.7	+6.4	−2.9
Emilia–Romagna	3 544 340	3 666 680	3 846 755	3 939 488	+3.5	+4.9	+2.4
Tuscany	3 158 811	3 286 160	3 473 097	3 570 926	+4.0	+5.7	+2.8
Umbria	803 918	794 745	775 783	803 988	−1.1	−2.4	+3.6
Marche	1 364 030	1 347 489	1 359 907	1 409 326	−1.2	+0.9	+3.6
Latium	3 340 798	3 958 957	4 689 482	4 970 681	+18.5	+18.5	+6.0
Abruzzi	1 277 207	1 206 266	1 166 694	1 215 136	−5.6	−3.3	+4.2
Molise	406 823	358 052	319 807	324 741	−12.0	−10.7	+1.5
Campania	4 346 264	4 760 759	5 059 348	5 408 298	+9.5	+6.3	+6.9
Apulia	3 220 485	3 421 217	3 582 787	3 849 598	+6.2	+4.7	+7.4
Basilicata	627 586	644 297	603 064	603 959	+2.7	−6.4	+0.1
Calabria	2 044 287	2 045 047	1 988 051	2 030 505	+0.1	−2.8	+2.1
Sicily	4 486 749	4 721 001	4 680 715	4 863 587	+5.2	−0.9	+3.9
Sardinia	1 276 023	1 419 362	1 473 800	1 585 959	+11.2	+3.8	+7.6
Italy	47 515 537	50 623 569	54 136 547	56 243 935	+6.6	+6.9	+3.9

Source: ISTAT: *Censimento Generale della Popolazione 1951, 1961, 1971, 1981*.

2.5.2 *Internal migration*

The population changes detailed in Table 2.3 are the result of two components: natural change and migration. The former is a relatively stable variable; rates of natural increase have declined more or less uniformly over all parts of the country, although the southern natural increase is still significantly above that of the North where there are now five regions (Piedmont, Liguria, Friuli–Venezia Giulia, Emilia–Romagna and Tuscany) in which deaths outnumber births.

Migration bears the major responsibility for determining regional demographic development. Indeed, if the long boom was the most dominant feature of postwar economic life in Italy, massive internal migration has been the most important social phenomenon, uprooting millions of people from a rural lifestyle and placing them, but not necessarily integrating them, in an urban context. Figure 2.1 shows that 1951–61 and 1961–71 were the decades of most intense interregional mobility; since 1971 the rate of movement has noticeably slackened as the economic boom has collapsed and the market for jobs contracted.

Most of the flight has been from marginal upland areas such as the eastern Alps, the Apennines, Calabria and Sicily, and directed towards the major metropolitan centres of Rome (in Latium), Milan (in Lombardy), Turin (in Piedmont) and Genoa (in Liguria). Over time it is possible to observe the centre of gravity of outmigration shifting southwards so that by 1971–81 some northern and central regions (e.g. Veneto, Friuli–Venezia Giulia, Umbria) which had earlier been sources of outmigration were now attracting net inflows (Figure 2.1). While the rate of outflow in the South has now been ameliorated, so too has the power of attraction of traditional destination regions like Piedmont, Lombardy and Latium.

Rural poverty has been the main 'push' factor accounting for the outmovement, industrial employment the main 'pull' factor. But there are other influences too. The diffusion of television and modern consumption patterns are also elements which have unsettled the rural population, leading indirectly to migration through accelerated aspirations of social mobility. Statistical analyses of local-level commune data show that, at least in the South, it is the level and buoyancy of tertiary employment which are the main economic factors determining net migration rates (King and Strachan, 1980; Strachan and King, 1982). In coastal districts the presence or absence of a tourist sector in the local economy is a major controlling variable (White, 1985).

Rural outmigration is probably greater than official statistics indicate. This is so quantitatively because not all moves are notified to the authorities, especially those moves which are temporary or seasonal. It is also true

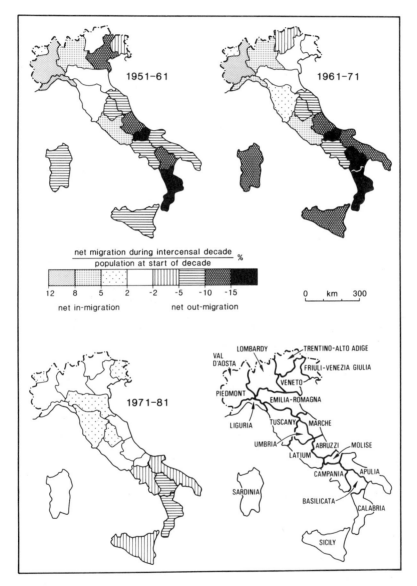

Figure 2.1 Regional migration rates, 1951–81.

qualitatively since the statistics do not indicate that it is often the most qualified and ambitious individuals who leave first. The demographic situation of the highland areas of the South has reached a highly critical juncture. On the one hand the depopulation of these upland areas has precipitated wholesale social disaggregation, but on the other hand any stoppage of outmigration or repopulation would lead to an unacceptably high rate of population increase, with serious economic consequences of unemployment. In some rural areas there are signs that this latter alternative is indeed prevailing. The excess of return migration over dwindling outflows is causing repopulation and, with farming largely abandoned at an earlier stage, existing employment levels are proving difficult to maintain.

2.5.3 Emigration

Of at least equal importance to internal movement has been emigration abroad. During its existence of more than 125 years, Italy is estimated to have 'exported' over 26 million people, while currently there are more than 5 million first- and second-generation Italians living abroad.

Since the end of the last war, Italian emigrants have moved to a variety of destinations (Table 2.4). Overseas emigration — to the USA, Canada, Argentina, Venezuela and Brazil — was important for a time, continuing trends traceable in some cases to the great migration waves of the late nineteenth and early twentieth centuries. By the late 1950s, however, these overseas currents had been largely replaced by movements to European countries. Switzerland's geographical proximity and expanding economy encouraged temporary and seasonal labour migration, and emigration during the 1950s and early 1960s was also strong to France, Great Britain and the Benelux countries. Access to the West German labour market was opened up in 1960, facilitated by the Common Market's free movement of labour charter which came into operation between 1961 and 1968 (King, 1976). By 1973, the eve of the recession, Italy had 858 000 workers residing elsewhere in the European Community. Italians had become the EC's own reserve of 'white labour', although numerically they were collectively outnumbered by non-Community migrants from countries like Spain, Portugal, Turkey and Algeria.

While most emigrants moved, willingly or reluctantly, to escape the 'poverty trap' of unemployment and low income in Italian rural areas, the structural relations of the international labour market dictated that they continued to suffer disadvantage and discrimination when abroad. They were welcomed only insofar as the receiving country required a source of relatively inexpensive, largely unskilled labour that could easily be dis-

Table 2.4 Italian emigration by major destination country, 1950–84 (annual averages by quinquennia)

	France	W. Germany	Benelux	Great Britain	Switzerland	USA	Canada	Argentina	Brazil	Venezuela	Total emigration
1950–54	34 397	276	15 299	6046	55 537	12 595	18 679	44 549	12 493	19 308	249 299
1955–59	75 991	11 733	16 793	9269	73 247	24 855	24 812	12 186	5821	19 596	301 462
1960–64	35 681	97 691	9346	7938	129 461	13 859	15 102	2054	1433	4671	334 547
1965–69	15 556	63 018	7090	5119	89 665	19 477	21 008	787	480	1480	241 263
1970–74	7709	43 150	4777	2218	49 135	12 825	5417	945	713	1226	139 450
1975–79	5333	28 869	3705	2037	25 921	5917	2834	690	1170	1236	90 414
1980–84	5185	30 457	3936	2238	22 626	4403	1944	858	641	1173	86 969

Source: ISTAT: *Annuario Statistico Italiano* and *Annuario di Statistiche Demografiche*, various years.

charged in the event of a downturn in the economy. Switzerland, in particular, discouraged permanent settlement by issuing one-year work permits: Italian migrants became *Gastarbeiter* — 'guestworkers' — rather than permanent settlers. Furthermore the migrants' living and working circumstances were far from favourable, especially in the early postwar years, and they were frequently the target for anti-Mediterranean racial discrimination.

In 1974 the tenuous position of the *Gastarbeiter* was underscored by the decision of Switzerland and Italy's Common Market partners to close their frontiers to new immigrants. In 1975 55 000 Italian workers were repatriated from Switzerland alone. While Italian residents in the Common Market countries are protected from forced repatriation, many are nevertheless choosing to return as the twin scourges of inflation and unemployment plague even the stronger economies of Western Europe. As a result return migration has outweighed a dwindling flow of emigrants for most years since the early 1970s, and Italy is now faced with the difficult prospect of reabsorbing hundreds of thousands of its migrant workers into an already faltering economy.

2.5.4 Immigration

As equally significant as return migration is the recent influx of foreign workers. Most of these are Third World migrants from countries as diverse as Ethiopia, the Philippines, Tunisia and Cape Verde. A rather different group comprises Yugoslav workers in Friuli–Venezia Giulia; this movement was already well established by the 1960s but received a boost from the reconstruction work following the 1976 Friuli earthquake (Neri, 1982).

The anomaly of immigration into a country with high unemployment and which has itself been a large-scale supplier of emigrants can be explained by wage levels and by variations in job status. Just as wage levels in Italy are generally below those in northern Europe, so too are they significantly above those of North Africa and the Third World. Hence workers from poor countries are willing to enter Italy and work for wages far lower than those demanded by Italians. They are also willing to work in those job sectors — domestic service, hospital orderlies, hotel cleaning, etc. — which are now largely shunned by Italian workers. Most of the foreign immigrants are concentrated in the major cities where such low-status marginal work is abundant, but there are also now large numbers of Tunisians working in agriculture and fishing in western Sicily.

This immigration is largely clandestine. Official Ministry of Foreign Affairs figures give 383 765 foreigners resident at the end of 1983, a threefold increase over 1970. However, the fact that nearly three-quarters of these 'officially' listed aliens were Europeans and North Americans reveals substantial failure to record Third World immigrants — only 6724 Ethiopians and 6722 Filipinos were enumerated by this source, and these were the largest Third World nationalities recorded. Unofficial surveys of Italy's Third World immigrant population often exceed the 500 000 estimate of the OECD migration agency SOPEMI in 1980. Difficulties of enumeration are heightened by the illegal status of most of the migrants and the fragmented, concealed nature of their employment in domestic households, hotels, restaurants, small workshops, fishing boats and scattered rural areas. Their illegal position also allows them to be shamefully exploited, with poor working conditions and low rates of remuneration.

2.6 Social structure and social issues

Italian society has yet to recover from the regional and class fratricidal bitterness of its past. Like Spain, Italy has traditionally had a rigidly stratified society, with serious conflict between social classes and a relatively low degree of social mobility. Centuries of fragmented colonial rule, the chronic persistence during most of Italy's modern history of a large mass of marginalized labour, and the employers' eagerness to exploit this last condition are some of the factors which have helped to deepen the cleavages separating Italy's social classes. In rural areas feudal aristocratic attitudes linger on despite the passage of land reform laws more than a generation ago. In industry the small number of large firms, many of which are still the property of a single entrepreneur, jealous of his prerogatives and dependent on low wage scales for his profits, tends to accentuate authoritarian relationships between management and labour. At the same time provincialism is still a very potent force and exists at a variety of scales from the *campanilismo* or local village allegiance of a suspicious rural population to the autonomist movements of regions like the Alto Adige and Sardinia. The South has its own distinct subculture based on a range of traits such as fierce loyalty to the family, suspicion of outsiders and a more rigid concept of female honour.

Regional particularism makes it difficult to outline a social structure at the national scale, but Acquaviva and Santuccio (1976) proffer the following schema. The *upper stratum* comprises: those who derive large incomes from ownership of agricultural land and urban property or from capital invested in industry, commerce or finance; those who exercise control over the means of production and receive high incomes as directors and managers of privately owned or state-controlled businesses; heads of government departments and other high-ranking and highly paid civil servants; and well-placed professionals such as lawyers, doctors, scientists, university professors and successful writers and artists. This upper stratum has widened considerably in recent decades. Until the early 1950s the upper crust of Italian society was a small, elite circle of landowners, bankers, industrialists and intellectuals with a culture that was, on the whole, Catholic or free-thinking or both. Over the past 30 years the content of the upper stratum has become much more fluid. The state bureaucracy has expanded enormously, with vast new organizations like the Cassa per il Mezzogiorno, and so has the welfare state. This creates a new elite of high-level administrators. Even more important has been the rise of the managerial class in both private and public industry. Industrialization has meant the arrival on the scene of huge complexes like Fiat, Pirelli and the international oil companies, each with its own close-knit bureaucracy and pyramid of power. Executives, directors and general managers of such firms have assumed a considerable importance in the life of the nation. Because members of this newer elite have often risen from quite humble backgrounds and because they have their own ways of exercising power, the upper stratum of yesterday is thrown into disarray. One final fact of critical importance about the upper classes is their locational concentration in the big cities, particularly Rome and the major industrial centres of the North.

In the course of the postwar industrial revolution there has also developed another distinct and regionally specific group which falls midway between the upper and middle strata of Italian society. This intermediate group comprises a large number of small industrialists who have sprung up from a working-class craftsman or even peasant background to become the owners and managers of a dense network of small factories in the North Italian Plain and, more recently, in some central regions. In spite of their humble origins, they display a great spirit of business initiative and are often highly export-oriented, selling clothes, shoes and mechanical goods all over Europe and beyond. These *padroncini* ('little bosses'), as they are called, tend to have a political outlook that is traditional and conservative; in Lombardy and Veneto they are the backbone of the Catholic Party. A broadly analogous group is to be found in coastal and tourist areas where hotel owners and restauranteurs have evolved into a similar independent middle bourgeois class.

The *middle stratum* divides into two groups, united by their general income levels but divided by the nature of their work and their social position. The *upper middle stratum* has at its core Italy's vast army of office workers who work for or under the control of members of the upper stratum. Their earnings may be no different from those of the skilled factory workers, but they are paid a monthly salary instead of a weekly wage. Also part of this stratum are the less affluent, small-scale *padroncini* who may also do some manual work themselves, the better-off owner-farmers (who are the small *padroncini*'s rural counterpart, and who are also numerous in the North Italian Plain), and other intermediate groupings such as teachers, police officers, priests, shopkeepers, army officers, etc.

Acquaviva and Santuccio (1976) are vehement in their criticism of the parasitic role played by the Italian office workers. Such people worry little about efficiency and productivity; their incomes are not related to their effectiveness or the number of hours worked; they enjoy the protection of their own organizations; they are jealous of their distinctions in social rank and of their ability to exploit their positions; they have no social concern for the nation's common good and their survival and proliferation are based on well-established techniques of corruption and clientelism. This system obviously has Rome as its hub but it flourishes particularly in the South where, because of the extension of welfarism and government development policy, the state bureaucracy has become the dominant class in the absence of an industrial bourgeoisie and in the wake of the decline of the landed aristocracy.

The *lower middle stratum* comprises a hard core of highly qualified skilled manual workers whose pay does not differ greatly from that of many clerical workers, and a satellite group of less qualified labour which receives somewhat lower wages but nevertheless enjoys regular employment, this fact distinguishing it from the lower stratum of Italian society which consists of marginalized labour and lumpenproletariat. The hard core of the lower middle stratum is found in the docks, metal workshops, engineering factories, car plants, oil refineries, chemical works and weaving sheds; pay is relatively high and working conditions quite good, for trade unions are firmly established in these industrial branches. The satellite group includes workers in small firms doing contract work for the big firms, in small and medium industries supplying local and regional markets, and in the building trades. Workers in these fields are generally not unionized.

The recent industrialization of Italy means that many factory workers have come from farming backgrounds bringing with them an inherited rural outlook; this is particularly so in the case of southerners, whether they work in new industries in the South or are migrants to the North. Nevertheless the culture of the present-day industrial working class is now thoroughly geared to the consumer society as the hypnotic influence of urban industrialism and the mass media cast their spell over the masses (Quartermaine, 1985). Again, Acquaviva and Santuccio (1976) are disdainful of this process: according to them the break-up and reshaping of culture along lines that reduce the individual to the status of an anonymous unit in an amorphous mass have proved to be the bane of the lower middle stratum, and are infecting the whole of society.

Though far from homogeneous in composition, the *lower stratum* has its own definite characteristics, chief among which is its estrangement from the technological and social structures of modern industrial society and its alienation from the mainstream working class. Although poor peasant farmers and underemployed rural labourers figure in the lower stratum, the bulk of the lumpenproletariat lives in the town, scratching a living on the fringes of the urban economy with intermittent work on building sites, in workshops, or functioning in low-grade self-employment as street-hawkers, rubbish recyclers, etc. Their work is insecure and spasmodic, they work inconvenient hours, they have unjust conditions of employment and are grossly underpaid. Domestic female outwork and even child labour are particular facets of this problem of marginalized and exploited labour; indeed since the recessions of the 1970s the degree of exploitation of such disadvantaged groups has almost certainly increased (Cesare, 1982; Colombino, 1984). Italy's growing stock of Third World immigrants form a further subgroup within this lowest stratum.

The schema of Acquaviva and Santuccio (1976) described above is not a static one and this survey of social structure can be concluded by a brief note on the main directions of change. Italian society is bulging at the centre with the expansion of the upper middle stratum and of the more affluent portion of the lower middle stratum. While in the past one could speak of a polarized society — businessmen and workers, landlords and peasants — now the *embourgeoisement* of the working class and the more militant and self-conscious behaviour of white-collar workers creates an increasingly uniform modal group which tends to set the tone for the whole of society (Low-Beer, 1978).

Social change has been particularly rapid since the protest movement of 1968–72. The social bombshell exploded first among university students and intellectuals; its shock waves spread to younger students and to workers, and then affected other groups including women who were finally, and especially in the North, embraced into the international feminist movement. The 1968–72 events had more social importance in Italy than almost anywhere else in Europe. Most institutions, it is true, remained unaffected: what changed was people's social and political self-awareness. For instance, changes in sexual behaviour and the social emancipation of women, which were already taken for granted in other countries, were unleashed on Italy virtually overnight. At the same time the Second Vatican Council speeded up the secularization process within Italian society, pointing it increasingly towards religious agnosticism. Workers were released from their religious bonds to follow their own consciences and political inclinations, and the Church became a more separate and distinct part of society, instead of its very backbone.

Changes of this kind obviously did not take place everywhere at the same time or affect each social group to the same degree. They tended first to affect northern cities and the educated groups, and then spread to smaller towns and villages and lower social classes. While the net result is an increased social fluidity and homogeneity, the major social strata nevertheless remain clearly identifiable.

2.6.1 Education

The education system has generally failed to pave the way for any change in social stratification. Its rigidly centralized structure does not allow it to cope with the changing needs of Italian society. Although theoretically available to the masses, with school compulsory between the ages of 6 and 14, the educational system and its curricula are still geared to a period when education was mainly for the elite. With the exception of the universities and, to some extent, the upper forms of secondary school, the teachers are women from the middle stratum who impart to their pupils their own brand of bourgeois culture. This way of teaching involves a rejection of children from the lower strata, from the South and from areas with a closed or distinct culture (Acquaviva and Santuccio, 1976).

One particular expression of pupils' regionally and culturally varied background is the problem of dialect. In 1951 more than 35 per cent of the population used dialect as their sole means of communication. Still today it frequently happens that pupils starting school have to learn Italian almost as a foreign language. Although the use of Italian is now standard in schools, offices and the workplace, a linguistic duality persists with dialect still used as the language of the home, the neighbourhood and the village. Many old people are unable to speak standard Italian.

Another index of cultural backwardness is illiteracy. While this parameter has fallen dramatically since unification when it was 75 per cent, there has consistently been a higher rate in the South — double the national average and five or six times the rate in the North (Table 2.5). Calabria has always been the region with the highest illiteracy rate: 26.3 per cent in 1961, 9.4 per cent in 1981, three times the respective national averages. In recent decades illiteracy in northern regions like Lombardy and Piedmont has been mainly confined to immigrants from the South.

At the other end of the educational spectrum, regional differences in the proportions of the population who are graduates are much less marked (Table 2.5). The higher figures for central Italy are accounted for by Latium which contains Rome, the main focus for the Italian civil service and intelligentsia. Saville (1968) points out that the proportion of young people attending university is higher in the South than in the North and is increasing more rapidly in the former. This can be explained by the greater prestige of university work in the South (where there is no industrial or

Table 2.5 Illiteracy and graduates, 1951–81

	% of population over 6 years who are illiterates				% of adult population who are graduates			
	1951	1961	1971	1981	1951	1961	1971	1981
North	4.5	2.8	1.6	0.9	1.6	2.0	2.4	2.6
Centre	11.5	7.3	4.3	2.8	2.2	2.7	3.5	3.6
South	24.4	16.0	10.7	6.3	1.5	1.8	2.3	2.5
Italy	12.9	8.3	5.2	3.0	1.7	2.1	2.6	2.7

Source: ISTAT: *Censimento Generale della Popolazione, 1951, 1961, 1971, 1981.*

commercial tradition) and by the fact that many young people go into higher education as a refuge against unemployment. This higher southern parti-cipation does not show up in Table 2.5 because after graduation many southerners move to Rome or to the North to obtain employment.

With 30 per cent of Italian school-leavers going on to university and more than 1 million students, Italy has one of the highest participation rates in higher education in the world. Numbers of students multiplied explosively after university entry restrictions were lifted in 1969. Now Rome University, the largest in Italy, has more than 100 000 students and several big city universities like Milan and Bologna have over 50 000 each. Yet these figures are slightly misleading in that many students follow university courses at home and visit the universities but rarely, sometimes only to take the examinations. Moreover only 15 per cent of students come from working-class or peasant backgrounds, while more than 50 per cent are children of professional, business or white-collar families (Acquaviva and Santuccio, 1976).

In spite of the international success of some Italian academics and scientists in fields as diverse as physics and economics, the traditional emphasis of the Italian higher education system on humanities and law leaves the Italian economy starved of expert technological help. Italy has been slow to develop its polytechnics. The bias against science subjects originates in schools, where science receives minimal coverage. Of course, arts subjects also lend themselves more easily to study at home by students who have enrolled at, but who do not attend, university because of the expense of travelling to, or lodging in, a distant city. The bloated bureau-cracy is the traditional outlet for many of these graduates, but competition for white-collar jobs is now so fierce that graduates now make up nearly half the total unemployed. And herein lie the roots of another Italian problem, the political extremism and terrorism which are born out of intellectual frustration and alienation.

2.6.2 Terrorism and protest, Mafia and banditry

The expansion of the universities led to many more students but worsening conditions for study. Clark (1984) wrote that the universities were turned from elite factories into intellectual parking lots, somewhere to put 'young age pensioners' for a few idle years. Autocratic absentee professors were as remote as ever, libraries overcrowded and laboratories ill-equipped. A little learning proved a dangerous thing, for a huge, disgruntled 'intellectual proletariat' appeared in the 1960s and 1970s. Student unrest started as early as 1962 when the Great Hall of Pisa University was seized during a visit by the Minister of Education. Sporadic student protest continued in the main university cities throughout the 1960s, culminating in the riots of 1968. In Rome, students battled with the police two months before the more famous outbreaks in Paris and Berkeley. Years of neglect had caught up with the academic establishment.

With the 1970s we enter the present period of social instability and recrimination which neither the government nor the traditional institution of the Church has been able to contain. This is what Fraser (1981) calls the 'crisis society'. By the late 1970s the student movement appeared to have blown itself out, but it had given birth to something more permanent and dangerous, for extra-parliamentary groups like Lotta Continua, Potere Operaio and Autonomia Operaia are run by former student leaders. Renato Curcio, former student at the notoriously left-wing Faculty of Sociology at the University of Trento, was one of the founders of the Red Brigades, established in Milan in 1970, while Toni Negri, former lecturer in political science at Padua University, is widely regarded as the intellectual theoretician behind ultra-left groups dedicated to violent protest. Nor is the revolutionary movement without its more bizarre characters, among them the guilt-ridden millionaire publisher Giacomo Feltrinelli, killed on an electricity pylon while supposedly planting explosives.

The wider causes of the terrorist movement are many and varied. Outside of the seething universities it had its roots in the overcrowded urban ghettoes and suburban slums of the industrial cities; these were the festering sores of an economic boom which had raised expectations but not satisfied many of the emerging social demands. What both students and workers had in common was a basic mistrust of the ruling class and of the prospect for peaceful change. The 'historic compromise' promoted by Berlinguer of the PCI and the DC's Aldo Moro from 1973 on merely increased the tensions on the far Left. Indeed the compromise was directly responsible for the Red Brigades' most outrageous act, the kidnapping and eventual murder of Moro in 1978. Negri was arrested under accusation of involvement in this act, and of being the 'moral leader' of terrorist groups. Imprisoned without trial until 1983, he later fled to France and taught at the Sorbonne. He was finally acquitted of the 'moral leadership' charge by a Padua court in February 1986.

No less extreme has been the terrorism of the far Right. The most important neo-Fascist terrorist groups are Avanguardia Nazionale, Ordine Nuovo and Nuova Destra. The last of these was founded as recently as 1977 but already has an estimated 4000 members evenly spread over the country (Quartermaine, 1985). The common ideology of such groups encompasses a nostalgia for past hierarchical systems of law and order, an antidemocratic view of the world, the acceptance of inequality, and the need for paramilitary cultural uniformity. Apart from beating up student leaders and Communists, one of their main strategies has been to provoke chaos in order to force the army to step in, impose martial law and overthrow parliamentary democracy. This so-called 'black terrorism' has links with the Mafia and with the official neo-Fascist party (the MSI), and is reputed to have infiltrated the police and the State Secret Service.

Between 1969, year of the Piazza Fontana massacre in Milan, and 1980, year of the Bologna station explosion, there were 12 690 instances of terrorist violence in Italy, killing 326 people and wounding 4254; in no other contemporary European society have so many people been killed and injured as victims of the tyranny of both left- and right-wing ideology (Drake, 1984). Italy leads the world in the 'art' of kidnapping — more than 300 *reported* cases annually. Of the 597 terrorist groups that have claimed credit for violent acts, 484 are of the Left and 113 of the Right. However, there are only about 15 major groups. Estimates of the actual number of full-time combatants vary, but 3000 is a commonly quoted figure, together with perhaps another 3000–8000 'part-timers' and maybe 200 000–300 000 'active sympathizers' (Ronchey, 1979).

The Mafia has its own statistics of violence and should not be confused with any of the above, except its tenuous relationship with neo-Fascist events. Unlike student protest and urban terrorism which are recent and have their roots in the North, the Mafia is a long-established Sicilian phenomenon. It originated among the feudal estates of the western part of the island where it functioned as a parallel system of law and organized power, an alternative to ineffective colonial rule from the North. Its classic activities were defence of the landed estates and the control of agricultural markets, livestock and irrigation (Blok, 1974). These activities are still common; farmers have to pay protection money, and theft or destruction of livestock or of valuable crops like oranges are the threats by which the control is exercised. Since the 1950s Mafia activities have expanded along with the development of the Sicilian economy. The centre of gravity of Mafia power has shifted from rural areas to Palermo and the other major towns of western Sicily. The Mafia now draws most of its vast profits from urban activities like property speculation, the construction industry, food markets and chain stores. Most significant in recent years has been its involvement in the international smuggling of drugs, especially heroin. Sicilian emigration to the USA, and the subsequent feedback of the more ruthless methods of the American Mafia into Sicily, has been instrumental in transforming the Mafia into a more overtly criminal organization. At the same time, Mafia links have developed at all levels of Sicilian, and Italian, society — to the police, the prisons, the banks, the planners and the politicians (Pantaleone, 1966). Threats have become more violent and murder almost second-nature — a chilling average of one a week since the end of the war. Some of the killings have been of natural enemies of the Mafia — policemen, journalists and other 'informants' — but much of the strife is internecine, between Mafia factions battling for control of a particular patch of territory or lucrative line of trade. Recently Mafia killings have become increasingly audacious. In 1980 Piersanti Mattarella, DC president of the regional government of Sicily, was assassinated. In 1982 Pio La Torre, head of the Sicilian Communist Party, was ambushed and murdered. Other victims have included two police chiefs and two judges. All had been involved in anti-Mafia campaigns. The final straw came with the murder in 1982 of General Della Chiesa, Prefect of Palermo, his newly wed young wife machine-gunned with him. Since then new laws have given the police unprecedented powers to act against the Mafia and a massive programme of arrests and trials is now under way. The 'confessions' of Tommaso Buscetta, a *mafioso* who decided to break the law of silence after his entire family was wiped out by clan killings in the Italian–American drugs war of the early 1980s, are a crucial part of the prosecution case in the massive trial of 474 suspected *mafiosi* which started in Palermo in February 1986. The trial is expected to last at least a year and fears have been expressed for the lives of the judge, the prosecuting witnesses and the jurors. Whether the Mafia will be eradicated remains to be seen. Palermo has become a bleak and frightened city, for so many of the population have been involved, willingly or otherwise, with the Mafia. A new wave of violence has erupted among the would-be Mafia bosses over the inherited empires of those arrested and in prison. The anti-Mafia war is a long way from being won.

Within Italy the Sicilian Mafia is not unique for parallel organizations or phenomena exist elsewhere in the South. Three of these may be mentioned. The Calabrian Mafia or *'ndrangheta* emerged on the plains and undulating hills of Italy's poorest region, where similar historical and agrarian patterns to those of Sicily are to be found (Arlacchi, 1983). Less prominent than their Sicilian counterparts, the Calabrian Mafia has engaged in a similar range of racketeering and protectionist activities, with a special emphasis on kidnapping. It too has had the wind taken from its sails by the recent wave of arrests. Of more specifically urban origin is the Neapolitan Mafia or Camorra, a secret society which dominates the underworld of Naples and its hinterland. The Camorra is also involved in an analogous range of activities to those of the Sicilian Mafia: marketing of agricultural produce from the rich Neapolitan hinterland, the construction industry, smuggling of cigarettes and drugs (Allum, 1973b).

The third parallel movement, banditry, is rather different. Originally banditry was endemic throughout the highland South and was especially virulent in Calabria and Campania. The Sicilian bandit Salvatore Giuliano achieved international fame for his daring exploits in the late 1940s. Francesco de Rosi made a magnificent film of his life and Gavin Maxwell (1957) wrote a sympathetic biography. Significantly, Giuliano was probably killed by the Mafia, although the police claimed responsibility.

Today banditry survives only among the mountain shepherds of Sardinia. Indeed this is the only locus of contemporary banditry in the whole of Europe. Sardinian banditry is an expression of the pastoral culture of highland Sardinia and originated as a spontaneous protest against high rents for pasture imposed by outside laws and absentee landowners. Before the law controlling pasture rents was passed in 1971, major outbreaks of banditry always coincided with the time of the year when the rents were due. Theft of livestock was, and still is, the classic bandit activity, and this is also the principal way in which interfamily vendettas and intervillage feuds are perpetuated (King, 1973a). Kidnap for ransom and murder have also been common occurrences, reaching epidemic proportions in some years in the 1960s. It was during this period that banditry shifted to a more outward-looking orientation, with the kidnapping of rich industrialists setting up businesses in the island and of occasional foreign tourists. Like the three Mafia organizations described earlier, the work of bandits is generally surrounded by a blank wall of 'honourable silence' which makes the work of the police (many of whom are not native to the island and therefore do not understand its dialects and ways) very difficult.

2.6.3 The family, women and the Church

To return to the mainstream of Italian society, we conclude this chapter with a discussion of the changing nature of family life. Traditional Italian society has always been regarded as familistic, an impression which owes a lot to the pioneering anthropological work of Edward Banfield in the rural South. Banfield (1958) developed the concept of 'amoral familism' to explain the social atomism and lack of a community spirit in his case-study village in Basilicata. Amoral familism is a situation in which the paramount loyalties of each individual are to his or her nuclear family, to the detriment of the wider society. It is expressed in Banfield's famous dictum: 'Maximise the material short range advantages of the nuclear family; assume that all others will do likewise'.

To what extent is Banfield's portrayal of inward-looking nuclear families typical of Italian society, especially rural society, today? Structural changes within the Italian space economy, notably industrialization, urbanization and rural depopulation, have had a critical impact on the male-dominated, family-centred traditional society. Over the past 30 years emigration has ripped apart the fabric of rural life, dispersing family members across the world and to other parts of Italy. In the South, villages are full of *vedove bianche*, or 'white widows', whose husbands labour elsewhere, returning home perhaps two or three times a year. In other cases rural households are composed of grandparents caring for young children whose parents work abroad. The rural family thus becomes a fragmented, contracted unit, temporarily reconstituted in the summer months or perhaps at Easter when the emigrants return, but otherwise only a partial social base. Different processes are at work in urban areas where the influence of industrial society is pervasive. Here families have become less authoritarian and more 'cooperative', less a grim, inflexible structure designed for economic and psychological survival, and more a voluntary association aimed at a more 'human' life in an increasingly impersonal society (Clark, 1984).

The crisis within the traditional family runs parallel with the increasing social emancipation of women, a process which has made great strides in the past 15 years. Symptomatic of the changed pattern of life, apparent especially in towns, are the different attitudes towards the woman who has committed adultery (until quite recently in the South the murder of an unfaithful wife was 'divorce Italian style' and considered an honourable act), the more widespread practice of birth control, and the less dogmatic insistence on female premarital virginity. Such changes have been far from painless, especially for males and the older generation. The male-dominant character of Italian society, part of a wider Mediterranean cultural field of *machismo*, is deeply rooted and resistant to change. Male 'superiority' is partly inculcated by the differential treatment of children — girls are trained to be demure and submissive, boys are spoilt and encouraged to be boisterous show-offs. So the transition to equality, if it is ever achieved, will take at least another generation yet. For most middle- and lower-status groups, and in some upper-income families, the dominant role-model for the woman is still that of full-time housewife and mother. Such a role-model is still applied considerably more rigidly in Italy than in most other European societies. Exceptions to this rule, whereby the woman has a full or part-time job outside the home, tend to mean that she becomes physically exhausted and suffers from nervous tension, while the rest of the family feel that their personal needs are being neglected (Balbo and May, 1975).

Another indication of the crisis of the traditional Italian family is the progressive decrease in average household size evident in the postwar censuses: 4.2 persons in 1951, 3.6 in 1961, 3.3 in 1971, 3.0 in 1981. The reasons for this are clear: the birth rate is falling; there is an increasing number of one-person households; and the cohabitation under one roof of extended families is becoming less common. Nevertheless ties of kinship — and also of godparenthood — remain extremely important. The extended family may have declined as a residential unit but it still functions as a network of primary social contact and of support in times of need.

The final correlate of the declining influence of the family as a social institution is the waning influence of religion. By the end of the 1970s only one-third of Italians attended mass weekly (mostly women); over half declared themselves indifferent to religion (Wertman, 1982). Church-run institutions — schools, cooperatives, trade unions — appealed to only a minority. Religious practice had ceased to be a social habit and had become a minority subculture.

The Church's ability to control and influence family life has been repeatedly dented since the divorce law was introduced in 1970. Catholics campaigning for a repeal of the divorce law, i.e. for a return to 'no divorce', forced a referendum in 1974, the first since the 1946 vote on the monarchy. But the campaign backfired; only 13 million voted against the law, and 19 million voted for its retention. Antidivorce sentiment prevailed only in the Catholic Northeast (Veneto, Trentino–Alto Adige) and in the mainland South, although in all regions the countryside was more traditional than the towns. The result was a crushing defeat for the Catholic Church and its DC allies; it was a victory for the 'lay Left' and for the up-and-coming Radical Party.

Divorce was perhaps the most spectacular aspect of the 'crisis of the family', but it was not the only one. In 1971 the law banning the sale of contraceptives was repealed. In 1975 dowries were abolished, wives were allowed to keep their maiden name, and it was stipulated that husbands and wives should jointly agree where and how to live. Civil marriages became more common, increasing from 1 per cent of total marriages in 1967 to over 12 per cent in 1980. In the big cities one-third of marriages are civil, and cohabitation has also become more accepted.

After the divorce battle had been won, the second great campaign of anticlerical and feminist opinion centred around abortion. In 1978 the 'lay' majority in Parliament passed an abortion law, in spite of the DC-dominated government. Again, committed Catholics petitioned for a referendum, and again the referendum, held in 1981, backfired. Indeed the decrease in the 'Catholic' vote from the 42.1 per cent against divorce in 1974 to only 32.1 per cent against abortion in 1981, is a significant reflection of the shrinking power of the Church in family and moral issues and a powerful reflection of how deep rooted secularization has become (Furlong, 1985).

THREE

The Development of the Industrial Economy

3.1 Introduction

Few major European countries are so handicapped by a lack of industrial raw materials as Italy, whose inhospitable Alps and geologically young peninsula, as well as being unfavourable to agriculture, yield grudgingly few minerals of economic value. The modern industrial era, which in Italy began towards the end of the nineteenth century, has seen the country struggle with, and eventually overcome, these natural handicaps. Initially the narrow, inhospitable peninsula, so thin in resources and poor in market potential, set an early pattern of imbalance, of foreign ties and enmities, that in some respects has persisted to the present day in the uneven sectoral and spatial distribution of industry and in the structural polarization between big enterprises funded partly by foreign capital and the small craft-style workshop industries that still proliferate in most parts of the country. Later, however, native inventiveness asserted itself and this, in combination with an eventually skilled and adaptable labour force, triumphed in the postwar export boom of Italian industry by which many European markets, notably for shoes, clothing, cars, typewriters, refrigerators and washing machines, were conquered by Italian products.

3.2 Early industry

Italy's somewhat tardy development of modern industry should not be allowed to obscure the fact that there have been earlier periods when the Italian peninsula was, considering the historical era, extremely advanced industrially. Accounts of Roman industry describe metal industries based on the lead, copper, tin and iron deposits of Elba and Etruria, while Milan was a major centre of Roman arms and textile manufacture. In mediaeval times many industries flourished in northern Italy. The political and economic revolution of the emergent city-republics provided the stimulus not only for the expansion of traditional economic activities but also for the development of new industries. The mediaeval textile industry provides a good illustration of this. Traditional productive processes associated with wool, linen and hemp underwent a transformation both of technique and of regional specialization. The proliferation of towns devoted to woollen manufacture created demands for foreign supplies of raw material, especially the wools of North Africa, Spain and England, and for international markets for a wider range of products. At the same time, new industrial specialisms such as silk and cotton arose, dependent from their inception on distant sources of raw materials and thus from the beginning susceptible to new forms of entrepreneurial control. The diffusion of cotton manufacture among northern cities from the twelfth century onwards meant the regulation, by powerful merchants' and industrialists' associations, of standards of production (Mazzaoui, 1972). Uniform standards backed by guild control of quality and individual firms' trade marks assured an easier penetration of foreign markets, a fact of great importance in an emergent mass production industry like cotton or wool or silk. Thus mediaeval industry had organizational characteristics of modern industry. Meanwhile Venice and Genoa grew as ports, serving the expanding industrial towns, and developed important shipbuilding industries. By 1400 the Venetian shipbuilding industry employed 16 000 workers and was the largest and most technologically advanced in the world — a far cry from its present situation. Venice also developed the industrial production of luxury items such as jewellery, glass, soap and, later, books. Apart from ships, Genoa concentrated on iron working, textiles and paper. Milan specialized in textiles, metal working and armaments.

The post-Renaissance decline of industries in northern Italy, which in simple terms was due to the collective failure of producers to confront competition from the expanding Atlantic community, lasted until the eve of the Risorgimento by which time Italy was an economic backwater industrially overtaken by England, The Netherlands and France.

During the first half of the nineteenth century new life appeared in the textile industry. Woollen manufacture took hold at Biella in Piedmont and Prato in Tuscany, locations that are still important today. The silk industry revived around Como, and cotton manufacturing expanded along the river valleys north of Milan, where some factories employed up to 500 workers (Clough, 1964). Arms manufacture spread from Milan to Turin and Genoa, and shipbuilding consolidated at Genoa (the Orlando yards) and, under Austrian control, at Trieste. In the South some embryonic industrial growth was fostered by the Bourbon kings at Naples, where Italy's first railway line was built in 1839, and the Sicilian sulphur mines were developed to the extent that they accounted for 90 per cent of world output.

Real industrial growth finally came in the 1880s and continued, fitfully, through to the First World War. Having missed the first round, Italy's industrial take-off thus took place in the European industrial revolution's 'second wind', the main technological features of which were the wide employment of new materials like steel and chemicals, the use of new sources of energy and the rapid development of the machine industries (Cafagna, 1971). Gerschenkron (1955) estimates an overall average annual rate of industrial growth of 3.8 per cent for the period between 1881 and 1913, and fixes Italy's industrial 'big push' within the years 1896–1908, although he stresses that it occurred in a more jerky fashion than in many other countries, indicating continuing structural weaknesses and entre-preneurial uncertainties.

One of these underlying weaknesses was the feeble development of iron and steel, the driving force behind nineteenth-century industrial develop-ment elsewhere. At the beginning of the industrial spurt Italy produced 10 000 tons of pig iron per year and 55 000 tons of steel; English figures were 9 million and 3.3 million tons respectively. The chief reasons for Italy's backwardness in ferrous metallurgy were the perennial problems of scarcity of iron ore and coal, and lack of investment capital and advanced technology. Italian annual coal production at this time was less than 300 000 tons, most of it low-grade lignite from peripheral locations in Sardinia; English output was 300 million tons and German 200 million tons. Never-theless by 1914 metallurgy and the vital machine trades, pulled along by the demands of the merchant marine and the railways, were more important than any other branch of Italian industry, measured by value-added. They helped Italy effect the transition from wood to steel — one of the great steps in the country's economic history (Clough, 1964).

The turn of the century thus saw particular expansion in heavy industry. The birth of the hydroelectric power industry was critical here. New iron and steel plants were founded at Piombino on the Tuscan coast in 1903 and at Bagnoli near Naples in 1905. In mechanical engineering vehicles were the leading sector; Fiat was founded in Turin in 1899, Alfa in Milan in 1910. Moreover the vehicles industry nurtured a whole series of ancillary indus-tries such as electrical products, rubber tyres and aluminium. Another important industrial empire was founded at this time: Samuel Olivetti started production of typewriters at Ivrea in Piedmont in 1911.

The First World War retarded the industrial growth that had been steady for 20 years and inflicted great long-term damage to Italian industry (Webster, 1975). Although there were short-term positive effects on some industrial sectors such as steel, shipbuilding, chemicals and armaments, the distortion of the industrial economy proved difficult to correct when peace came. Steel output, up by one-third during the war, dropped back by 45 per cent between 1917 and 1921. At the end of the war, industries dependent on the Ministry of Munitions employed 918 000 workers, many of whom subsequently lost their jobs. Unemployment was further massively boosted when demobilization reduced the armed forces from 3 million to 500 000.

Sarti (1971) has suggested that one of the most important roots of Fascism is to be found in the industrial disorder and imbalance that characterized the immediate post-conflict period. Fascism's rise to power created the authoritarian climate the industrial leaders needed to crush union opposition. Early Fascist policy was 'productivist' and, indeed, during the period to 1927 industrial output improved steadily, increasing by 41 per cent between 1920 and 1925. Foreign investment was buoyant and unemployment dropped dramatically. Key transport improvements were made and by the mid-1920s the railways were paying substantial profits into the Treasury.

The economic situation turned sour after 1928. Industrial output slumped to one-third during 1929–32, factory wages were slashed and industrial unemployment reached an estimated 20 per cent in 1931 (Hildebrand, 1965). Within industrial sectors a process of monopolistic concentration set in as a natural response to shrinking markets at home and abroad: Fiat increasingly dominated in vehicles, Edison in electrical engineering, Montecatini in chemicals.

In 1933 the Institute for Industrial Reconstruction (IRI) was founded to shore up the main banks suffering from the decline in the value of industrial securities. IRI eventually found itself taking over many businesses that it was supposed only to help via the banks. Thus began IRI's profound controlling influence on the character of the Italian industrial economy. The number of businesses it controlled became so large that it began to group them under subsidiaries: STET (for telephones) in 1933, Finmare (shipping) in 1936 and Finsider (steel) in 1939. By the late 1930s the Italian state controlled a larger share of national industry than any other West European country — a position that has been maintained to the present day. Within the framework of Mussolini's increasing autarkic ambitions, special efforts were made to expand branches of industry dominated by imports. The state-owned Azienda Generale Italiana Petroli (AGIP) built oil refineries and carried out intensive exploration for oil and gas in the North Italian Plain. Another state subsidiary, Azienda Nazionale Idrogenazione Combustibili (ANIC), was established for hydrocarbons. Coal production in the Sardinian Sulcis mines was pushed to its maximum extent.

These monopolistic and autarkic measures should be seen not only as instruments of industrial policy (however misguided) but also in relation to the political leadership's even more mistaken imperialist and military ambitions. In fact, had Italy remained neutral in the Second World War substantial industrial benefits would almost certainly have accrued in terms of supplying the combatants (Clough, 1964). Instead, the war proved militarily and economically catastrophic for Italy.

3.3 Regional and sectoral patterns of industry in the postwar period

Chapter 2 described in some detail the general economic, political and social conditions which favoured the rapid growth of Italian industry in the early postwar period, especially during the long boom of 1950–62. Although Italian governmental policies and international economic conditions were extremely favourable, especially for exports, it was to a large degree the innovation and improvisation of a host of small and medium-sized industrialists which enabled Italian products to succeed abroad.

Table 3.1 shows that the numbers of both factories and industrial workers have increased strongly throughout the postwar period, at least as recorded by the industrial censuses taken between 1951 and 1981. There has, however, been a tendency for these increases to slacken off. Thus the intercensal increase in industrial employment was 32.1 per cent during 1951–61, 16.3 per cent during 1961–71 and only 9.6 per cent during 1971–81. The changing regional distribution of employment shows some significant features: the relative share of the South, both of factories and of workers, has tended to decline, while that of the Centre has increased. The 1981 census, however, indicates an interruption of long-term regional trends, especially for the North and South.

3.3.1 Structure of industry

The 1981 industrial census reveals a remarkably large number of firms in relation to the numbers employed: 900 322 firms and 6 061 445 employees in manufacturing industries, an average of 6.7 workers per firm. To these must be added 7535 firms and 70 460 workers in extractive industries and 326 000 firms with nearly 1.2 million employees in the construction industry. The size distribution of industries is highly skewed: a few large private and state enterprises contrast with a multitude of small concerns many of which employ no labour outside the owner and his family. In the manufacturing sector less than 500 firms employ over 1000 workers, for a total workforce of 930 000 as against 1.6 million working in firms employing less than 10 workers and 2.6 million in firms with 10–100 workers.

Perhaps more surprising is the fact that the number of workers in small and medium-sized firms has expanded faster than the number of workers in big firms. From 1951 to 1981 the largest firms (those employing over 1000 workers) expanded their employment by about 400 000, but firms employing less than 100 workers experienced an increase of more than 1 million employees. Decline in size of industrial enterprises was especially characteristic of the more recent intercensal period, 1971–81. The average

Table 3.1 Factories and industrial workers by region, 1951–81

	1951		1961		1971		1981	
	Factories	Workers	Factories	Workers	Factories	Workers	Factories	Workers
Italy	691 426	4 241 901	692 084	5 602 795	806 902	6 514 125	958 576	7 140 326
North	347 285	2 854 622	361 052	3 857 740	440 406	4 416 695	571 395	4 630 130
Centre	119 860	653 570	129 290	881 390	163 102	1 123 545	197 646	1 320 820
South	224 281	733 709	201 742	863 665	203 394	973 885	189 535	1 189 376
% North	50.2	67.3	52.2	68.9	54.6	67.8	59.6	64.8
% Centre	17.3	15.4	18.7	15.7	20.2	17.3	20.6	18.5
% South	32.5	17.3	29.1	15.4	25.2	14.9	19.8	16.7

Source: ISTAT: *Censimento Generale dell' Industria, 1951, 1961, 1971, 1981.*

size of production unit declined in 23 out of the 32 branches into which Italian manufacturing is divided. In some cases, for instance in artificial fibres, the change can be attributed to the decline in the level of manufacturing activity with the closure of some very big factories. In other cases the change in size may indicate a reorganization of production with the setting up of many new small and medium-sized units specializing in particular products or aspects of the production process. This appears to be happening particularly in the motor industry, in textiles, in agricultural, industrial and office equipment, and in electrical goods (Zanetti, 1983). The dynamism of the small-firm sector thus contrasts with the stagnation and even decline of the big firms.

This fractioning of industrial production is a major structural change, reversing longer-term tendencies towards larger units and concentration of production. In Italy it is often accompanied by deverticalization (the splitting up of sequential industrial processes originally under one management into small firms concentrating on single phases) and by spatial decentralization of such industry into formerly rural areas which are peripheral to, but not completely detached from, the traditional industrial core area of Lombardy, Piedmont and Genoa. The overall phenomenon is known as *decentramento produttivo* – productive decentralization – and has been closely studied by Italian economists in very recent years. It is most characteristically found in regions of northeast and central Italy which are adjacent to the industrial triangle. Because it was first studied in Emilia where it seems to reach its most highly developed form, productive decentralization is often called the 'Emilian model' (Brusco, 1982). Further discussion of this model of regional development, which also includes significant non-industrial inputs, is made in Chapter 6.

3.3.2 *The role of the state holding sector*

The practice of state participation in industrial development started under Fascism and has evolved, somewhat haphazardly, into a major structural component of Italian economic life. Although primarily involved in the key industries of steel, heavy engineering, shipbuilding, telephone services, hydrocarbons, chemicals and banking, the state holding sector has also developed strongly in recent years in other areas — in vehicles, motorways, electronics, nuclear engineering, computer software and supermarkets. Many well-known Italian products and services are now within the system: examples are Alfa Romeo, Alitalia, AGIP petroleum, Cinecittà film studios and the Banco di Roma. There are approximately 350 firms in the state holding network; together they employ around 700 000 people and account for 45 per cent of the increase in manufacturing employment between 1951 and 1971, since when their rate of expansion has slowed (Allen and Stevenson, 1974).

The Italian state holding sector is a unique combination of public and private enterprise. Its organization is basically pyramidal. At the top is the Ministry of State Holdings, which issues general directives and is responsible to Parliament. Below the Ministry are the *enti*, the most important of which are IRI, ENI (oil) and EFIM (manufacturing industries in difficulty). From a financial viewpoint, the *enti* are wholly government controlled in the sense that all their equity capital is put up by the state. At the base of the pyramid are the various firms and enterprises in which the *enti* have a controlling interest but whose capital can also be partly privately subscribed. In fact, given the fragmented nature of private shareholding in many firms, a state controlling interest can be maintained with as little as 15 per cent of the equity capital. The state holding sector thus differs from the Italian nationalized industries which are wholly state financed.

The giant of the state holding system, accounting for three-quarters of its employment, is IRI, which can be considered the largest service and investment company in Europe. Bethemont and Pelletier (1983) question whether the state controls it or vice versa. Its activities are so vast that they are split into sectorally defined subholding companies, the most important of which are Finsider (steel), Finmeccanica (mechanical industries including Alfa Romeo), Fincantieri (shipbuilding), Finmare (shipping lines), STET (telecommunications) and Italstat (infrastructure construction — roads, airports, etc.). In towns specializing in these basic industries (especially steel and shipbuilding) IRI is thus responsible for the majority of industrial employment; cases in point are Genoa, Trieste, Naples, Piombino, Terni and Taranto. IRI has also played an important role in developing industry in the Mezzogiorno in the postwar period; this is described in more detail in Chapter 6.

ENI is responsible for 13.5 per cent of state holding sector employment but a greater proportion — 29 per cent — of its fixed capital investment (Keyser and Windle, 1978). ENI was set up in 1953 with the original objective of disposing of the assets of AGIP, founded in the Fascist period. Under the dynamic leadership of Enrico Mattei, who died in an air crash in 1962, it expanded rapidly into an organization which comprises oil exploration, drilling, importing and marketing, and which has pioneered the development of natural gas exploitation and the petrochemical industry. ENI now embraces both AGIP and ANIC and has minor interests in nuclear energy, textiles and engineering.

The way in which the state holding sector has been developed has made it more and more difficult for IRI, ENI and EFIM firms to remain profitable. Frequently they have been used as a 'sponge sector' for labour that under

86 *Italy*

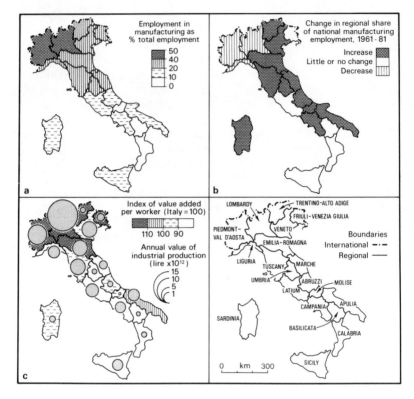

Figure 3.1 Regional structure of Italian industry. a, Employment in manufacturing, 1981. b, Trends in manufacturing employment, 1961–81. c, Value-added per industrial worker and regional industrial product, 1981.

private enterprise would have been laid off. In order to stabilize economic growth rates, the state sector has generally been expanded at times when private industrial growth is weak, and vice versa. The sector's operations in key areas like steel, oil and chemicals have made for lower costs in other industries dependent on these products, but world market crises in steel, shipbuilding, oil and petrochemicals have saddled IRI and ENI with huge losses over the past 10 years. Losses have also been made in fields where private firms have remained profitable. Thus the IRI food and confectionery firms of Alemagna and Motta have poor records in comparison to big private companies like Ferrero and Buitoni–Perugina, and Alfa Romeo's losses contrast with the continued profitability of Fiat (King, 1985).

3.3.3 Regional patterns

There is a clear decrease in the importance of industrial employment from North to South. Only two regions — Lombardy and Piedmont — have more than half their employed populations working in the secondary sector. The remaining northern and most central regions have 32–44 per cent in secondary employment, while Latium and all southern regions have below 29 per cent, the lowest being Molise, 22 per cent. If, however, we limit the discussion to manufacturing employment, the figures become even more contrasting: Lombardy 46 per cent and Piedmont 43.9 per cent down to Calabria 7.2 per cent and Molise 8.5 per cent (Figure 3.1a). This means that regions like Molise and Calabria have more people working in the building industry than they do in manufacturing. However, Figure 3.1b indicates that it is the regions where industrial employment is highest (chiefly Lombardy, Piedmont and Liguria) which are decreasing their share of total national industrial employment. Central, northeastern and some southern regions are growing in importance, while other southern regions (Sicily, Calabria, Basilicata), Latium and Friuli possess a stable share, at least for 1961–81.

An analysis of the regional distribution of the value of industrial production is even more revealing of regional concentration (Figure 3.1c). Nearly 41 per cent of total industrial product originates in Lombardy and Piedmont, 58 per cent from the top four regions of Lombardy, Piedmont, Veneto and Emilia–Romagna. These regions also tend to have an above-average index of value-added per industrial worker.

Figure 3.2 shows that the northern dominance of industry holds for most of the major branches of manufacturing. Textiles are overwhelmingly concentrated in the five regions of Lombardy, Piedmont, Veneto, Emilia–Romagna and Tuscany (86 per cent of all textile workers). The same regions are also important for clothes and shoes, except that Marche comes in as a key region (especially for shoes) and some central–southern regions (Abruzzo, Apulia and Campania) also have significant employment percentages in this branch. The food and drink industry is more evenly distributed, reflecting the widespread distribution of demand, the small scale of most productive units, perishability and high transport costs for some food products, and the ubiquity of farming. In relative terms Emilia–Romagna, Campania, Umbria and Molise have the greatest specialization in food and drink industries; in the last two of these regions this is more a function of the lack of development of other branches of industry. By contrast vehicles and chemicals are much more regionally concentrated, the former in Piedmont which has exactly 50 per cent of all vehicles employment (mostly in the Fiat factories in Turin), the latter in Lombardy which has 39 per cent of all chemicals employment.

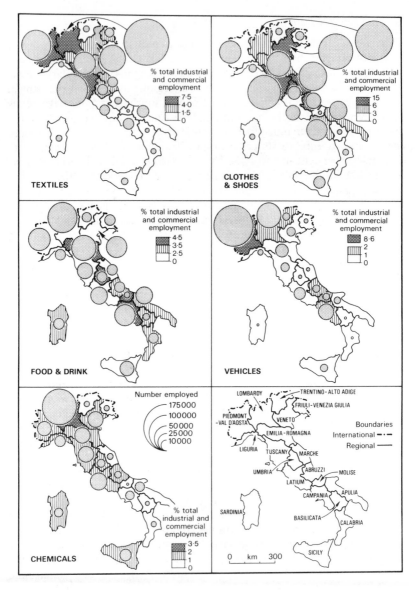

Figure 3.2 Employment in key industrial sectors, 1981.

3.4 Key sectors of Italian industry

The rest of this chapter consists of brief descriptions of several key branches of Italian industry: energy, transport and communications, food and drink, textiles, clothing and shoes, iron and steel, vehicles, 'white goods' and chemicals. Table 3.2 provides a broad comparative picture of the evolution of most of these branches in employment terms over the postwar period. Food and drink have tended to stagnate; textiles are the only industrial branch to consistently lose workers at each industrial census. On the other hand clothing and shoes, mechanical industries and transport equipment (including the important car industry) have exhibited continued growth in employment terms. The remaining branches — metallurgy (chiefly iron and steel), the working of non-metallic minerals, chemicals and rubber — show growth between 1951 and 1971, but decline from 1971 to 1981.

Table 3.2   Employment in the main branches of manufacturing industry, 1951–81

	1951	**1961**	**1971**	**1981**
Food and drink	357 982	398 656	380 761	387 499
Textiles	650 866	597 822	542 908	493 423
Clothing and shoes	411 547	513 390	587 966	636 231
Metallurgical industries	145 071	202 803	241 754	197 415
Mechanical industries	708 676	1 124 432	1 569 173	1 726 264
Transport equipment	188 215	237 976	334 659	413 323
Working of non-metallic minerals	206 668	319 474	324 345	319 341
Chemicals and hydrocarbon derivatives	167 451	234 516	268 151	264 057
Rubber	40,127	52 448	84 522	75 939

Source: ISTAT: *Censimento Generale dell' Industria, 1951, 1961, 1971, 1981.*

3.4.1 Energy

The restraining influence of Italy's lack of fuel and power resources on the country's economic development has already been noted. Meagre coal resources — anthracite at La Thuile in Val d'Aosta and Sardinian lignite — are now only desultorily worked. Shortage of coal reserves encouraged Italy to pioneer the field of electric power. The Alps and parts of the Apennines enabled widespread development of hydroelectric power but already by the

1950s most of the economically feasible sources of water power had been exploited. Emphasis then switched to thermal power stations and large thermal generating plants were built in each of the major urban and industrial centres. The rationalization of electricity production — before 1962 it was fragmented into 1200 private companies — also helped this process: ENEL (the nationalized electricity authority) now runs a wide range of power-producing facilities including hydroelectric stations, thermal electric plants, geothermal energy and nuclear power reactors. In 1960 hydroelectric stations produced 46.1 million kWh of electricity and thermo-electric stations produced 10.1 million kWh. Twenty years later the hydro power output was little changed at 47.1 million kWh whereas thermal electricity, including coal-, gas- and oil-fired power stations as well as geothermal sources (tapped at Lardarello in Tuscany) and nuclear energy, had jumped 12-fold to 120.3 million kWh (Colombo, 1980).

Trends in total energy consumption are no less dramatic and are a reflection both of postwar industrial development and of rising standards of living expressed in rising domestic energy consumption. Total energy consumption quintupled in the period 1955–80. Oil consumption expanded fastest, at least until 1973, followed by that of natural gas. Hydrocarbons supplied 23 per cent of energy needs in 1949, 55 per cent in 1964 and 84 per cent in 1980. However 99 per cent of oil, 92 per cent of coal and 52 per cent of natural gas requirements are imported. Domestic oil production has never lived up to its early promise: discoveries at Cortemaggiore by AGIP in 1949 and at Ragusa (Gulf Oil) and Gela (ENI) in Sicily in the mid-1950s have always had symbolic rather than real value, although fresh hope has been engendered by recent discoveries off the south coast of Sicily by AGIP in association with Shell.

The only really important domestic source of energy to be developed in recent decades is natural gas. Although some significant methane finds have been made in southern Italy — notably at Vallecupo and San Salvo (Abruzzo), Ferrandina and Pisticci (Basilicata), Crotone (Calabria) and Gagliano Castelferrato (Sicily) — the bulk of the output comes from the North Italian Plain. The largest finds have been located in the southeastern delta region, at Ravenna Mare-Sud in 1960, Casenatico in 1961 and Porto Corsini Est in 1963. More recently the main focus of exploration has shifted offshore to the shallow waters off Ravenna and Rimini (Pacione, 1979). A major gas project recently completed is the 2500-km 'Transmed' pipeline from Hassi R'Mel in Algeria to Minerbio near Bologna; finished in 1985, this will supply 12 300 million cubic metres of gas annually for the next 25 years.

One of Italy's major economic problems is how to sustain an industrial boom built on cheap imported oil now that this fuel has become so expensive (Pacione, 1976). Some oil-fired power stations are being switched to coal but this hardly constitutes a viable long-term solution, for coal is also expensive. Hydroelectric power has not expanded much since 1960, although some experts believe a 20 per cent increase could be achieved. To some the nuclear option seems an attractive solution (Fogagnolo, 1975). In the early 1960s Italy was in the vanguard of nuclear power development; indeed it was an Italian physicist, Enrico Fermi, who built the first atomic pile in the United States. By 1960 three small power stations had been built by Fiat, Montecatini and Snia Viscosa at Latina (Latium), Garigliano (Campania) and Trino Vercellese (Veneto); a fourth, much bigger, station was added in 1978 at Caorso on the Po. Since then the impetus has waned. Of the 'new wave' of four nuclear power complexes supposed to be built by 1985, on only one (at Montalto di Castro in Latium) has construction actually started. The other three have been blocked by local opposition, disputes over siting and the growing environmental lobby in the Senate.

3.4.2 Transport

Transport provides the second major infrastructural pillar for Italy's modern industrial economy, although the development of integrated transport systems has been hampered by relief and poor planning. Only one river, the Po, is navigable even for small vessels, and canal building has proved impossible outside the North Italian Plain.

The modern rail network extends to about 20 000 km, of which 80 per cent are controlled by the *Ferrovie dello Stato* (FS), the rest being run by private concessionaire companies. Figure 3.3a shows that the network is most dense in the North Italian Plain where there is a well-developed system of electrified double-track lines linking the major urban centres. Although the South appears from the map to be relatively well served by railways, there are important qualitative differences in the southern system — less frequent services, slower speeds and a much higher proportion than in the North of privately owned, narrow-gauge, single-track and non-electrified lines.

Compared to other European rail services, the Italian system has a high passenger but low freight usage. This can be partly explained by low passenger fares in the first case, and by the historic failure to integrate railway growth with industrial development in the second case (King, 1985). Since the early 1960s there has been a good deal of modernization of the railway system — electrification, double-tracking on important routes and improvement of stock. In 1967 Milan Rogoredo station became the southern terminus for the Rotterdam–Milan container service. A major internal container service operates between Milan and Naples. The quadru-

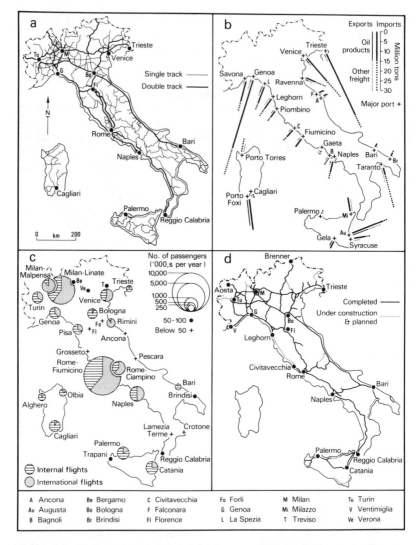

Figure 3.3 Transport and communications, c. 1980. a, Railways. b, Ports. c, Airports. d, Motorways.

pling of the Rome–Florence link in the 1970s allows speeds of up to 250 km/hr on the scenic route between these two prestigious cities. Finally, the FS has pioneered computerization of bookings and freight control systems within Europe. This has not, however, allowed the railways to shed much labour, and with over 200 000 employees the service is vastly overmanned.

The role of sea transport in Italian economic development extends back to the very earliest periods of the peninsula's economic history, for many modern ports have been in use at least since Roman times. Italy's 7400 km of coastline obviously favour coastal shipping and port proliferation. Shipping was crucial to the development of the infant nation in the latter half of the nineteenth century, compensating to some extent for the deficiencies of the railways at that time. At the time of unification the Italian merchant fleet was already the largest in the Mediterranean and the third largest in Europe after the English and the French. Genoa, Venice, Naples and Palermo were the major Italian ports at that time. The turn of the century, however, saw a downturn in the fortunes of Italian shipping as iron and steel replaced wood and sail, for Italy was short of iron and coal. By 1914 the Italian fleet had fallen to the position of sixth in Europe, a position it has retained ever since.

Post-1945 reconstruction of the Italian merchant marine has been guided by the IRI subsidiary Finmare. Coastwise shipping increased markedly in the 1960s and early 1970s, largely because of the growth and interdependence of coastal steelworks at Cornigliano (Genoa), Piombino (Tuscany), Bagnoli (Naples) and Taranto, the massive development of coastal oil refineries and petrochemicals complexes in the South, and the expansion of other coastal industries based on oil and natural gas. This recent industrial development has revolutionized the pattern of freight movements into and out of Italian ports, with the growth of one-product ports like Taranto (steel), Augusta and Poro Foxi (oil) challenging, at least in terms of tonnage handled, the more established and diversified ports of Genoa, Trieste and Naples (Figure 3.3b). Genoa nevertheless remains the major port of Italy, although Naples has more ships docking and handles more passengers. Naples is well down on freight, however: a reflection of the industrial weakness of the South. The second most important port for cargo handling is Trieste. Like Genoa's entrepôt function for Switzerland, Trieste also directs much of its freight to foreign hinterlands in Yugoslavia and Austria. Genoa's primacy rests on its multifunctional character, with a large and diversified cargo movement as well as important internal and international passenger links (Rodgers, 1958).

Freight handled by Italian ports increased by 7.7 times between 1952 and 1972, since when it has stagnated at around 300 million tons per year. The ratio of imports to exports by weight has remained remarkably stable over the past 30 years at about 3:1. Liquid bulk's share of total freight increased from 40.4 per cent in 1952 to 71.9 per cent in 1972, falling back to 67 per cent by 1980 in the wake of the oil crises. As with the railways, containerization is a growing trend. Container facilities are now present in all major ports. Attempts are being made to set up a container sorting terminal serving the whole Mediterranean basin at Cagliari on the south coast of Sardinia.

The port sector has been judged to be the most unsatisfactory part of the entire Italian transport system (Panunzio, 1978). Until recently responsibility for port administration was divided between the Ministries of Public Works and the Mercantile Marine, with the Cassa per il Mezzogiorno also playing a role in the South since 1950. Limited sums available for port development have been dispersed over too many ports (Italy has 144 recognized ports) so that vital strategic improvements at key ports have been neglected. Another problem has been the obstructive stance frequently taken by unionized port labour.

Italian airports (Figure 3.3c) suffer from many of the problems just noted for ports: excessive number, inefficient administration, lack of modernization, frequency of immobilizing strike action. Again the main problem is the plethora of organizational obstacles to getting investment to improve the key airports. Rome and Milan, with two airports each and a high percentage of international flights, have achieved reasonable working efficiencies, but much still needs to be done to improve certain important regional airports like Turin, Venice, Naples, Palermo and Cagliari. Air transport increased dramatically during the 1960s (freight by 10 times, passengers carried by 7 times), but the 1970s, with increasing labour unrest among airport staff as well as spiralling fuel costs, have seen the airline business in serious trouble. Since the disastrous year of 1975, when strikes paralysed air travel for long periods, there has been some rationalization. Alitalia has withdrawn from the fiercely competitive transatlantic market, while on the domestic front some little-used airports like Lecce and Comiso have been closed (the latter is now a NATO base), and routes hit by competition from new motorway links (e.g. Palermo–Catania, Naples–Bari) have been cancelled.

By far the most remarkable postwar transport development has been the spectacular growth of the road and motorway networks. Although many modern roads follow Roman routes the road network remained relatively primitive until the 1950s, particularly in the Apennines and in the South where many villages were served only by rough tracks. One of the early tasks of the Cassa per il Mezzogiorno was to improve the road network in the South and now most villages are served by tarred roads. In 1980 Italy had 295 000 km of roads, excluding motorways and urban streets. This figure represents a 72 per cent increase in surfaced roads since 1951.

Even more dramatic has been the expansion of Italy's motorway network to become the most extensive in Europe. Since the first motorway was built between Milan and the Lakes in 1925, the network has grown to over 6000 km, mostly built during 1955–75. The system has developed around a series of major axes, three running north–south and three east–west (Figure 3.3d). The major north–south axis, the backbone of the whole system, is the *Autostrada del Sole*, or 'sun motorway', which starts from the Swiss border at Chiasso and continues via Milan, Bologna, Florence and Rome to the tip of the peninsula at Reggio Calabria. Eventually it will be connected via a huge bridge to the Sicilian motorway network. The second north–south trunk starts at the Brenner Pass and continues down the Adriatic coast to Bari and Taranto. The third, with starting points at the Great St Bernard and Mont Blanc motorway tunnels above Aosta and the French border at Ventimiglia, is made up of motorways which form part of the dense Ligurian and Piedmontese lattice focusing on Genoa and Turin. Eventually this axis will extend via Leghorn and Civitavecchia to Rome. Of the east–west axes, the major one provides a continuous motorway link between Turin and Trieste serving the highly industrialized parts of the North Italian Plain. The other two are cross-Apennine links between Rome and Abruzzo and between Naples and Bari; these are vital routes linking the Tyrrhenian and Adriatic flanks of the southern peninsula, previously separated by forbidding mountains crossed only by winding roads and slow railways.

Toll income and the entrusting of much motorway building to private companies have freed construction and management from the shackles of the state budget and the delays of the state bureaucracy (Apicella, 1978). On the other hand, this system has allowed motorways to grow and proliferate in a haphazard way with some areas, like Sicily, overprovided and a lack of attention to intermode transport planning (the motorways closely duplicate the main rail network — cf. Figures 3.3a and d) and to relieving traffic congestion in urban areas. The situation has been aggravated by the general economic crisis set off by the sharp increase in the price of oil in 1973–74. This led to repeated increases in the price of petrol and to a sharp cutback in traffic growth forecasts, at least in the short term.

Along with the oil refinery and the petrochemical complex, the motorway is a symbol of the style of development embraced by Italy since the war — a model based on unbridled consumerism, unfettered personal mobility and soaring car ownership. In spite of its median economic position in terms of GDP per capita, Italy has one of the highest rates of car ownership in Western Europe, higher than those of the United Kingdom, The Netherlands, Denmark and Norway (of course part of this is accounted for by Italians' preference for small and cheap cars). Together with improved roads, the rapid evolution of the motorway network has played a primary role in revolutionizing the pattern of travel, to the detriment of the railways. It has also been instrumental in integrating the North with the South and the Tyrrhenian with the Adriatic. Another important effect of motorways has been the impact on industrial location, most dramatically seen in the mushrooming of hundreds of new factories along the Rome–Caserta stretch south of the Cassa per il Mezzogiorno's boundary for regional aid. Other areas where industrial development can be directly attributed to motorway development are S. Donato Milanese (near Milan), Prato (near Florence) and Bologna (Pacione, 1974a).

3.4.3 Food and drink

The processing of food and drink occurs throughout Italy, since in most instances it is advisable to carry out the processing as near as possible to the areas of production. In addition, large urban centres tend to attract food and drink industries, especially those requiring several ingredients. Since Italy imports some of its food requirements, food processing is also a feature of the larger ports like Genoa and Naples.

Employment in food and drink industries has remained fairly stable at just below 400 000 throughout the postwar period (Table 3.2). With only 200 food firms employing over 200 people, much of this employment is scattered in thousands of little enterprises in country areas. Village olive presses, flour mills, cheese plants, pasta factories, etc. still survive in spite of an inevitable trend to larger industrial units such as those processing sugar beet, wine and confectionery. Emilia–Romagna has a strong cooperative tradition in its food and wine processing sector, and in fact wine cooperatives have mushroomed in recent decades, especially down the Adriatic strip as far as Apulia, the region with the largest number. Foreign penetration of Italian food industries by American, British, Dutch and French capital has been a blow to national pride and the state holding sector has responded by supporting key Italian firms like Motta, Alemagna, Star and Cirio.

Apart from structural problems the Italian food industry has to operate within two fundamental constraints: the slow pace of agricultural modernization and the chaotic nature of the distribution system. Backward farming affects the food processers on the supply side. In spite of the rural exodus, enlargement of farms has not taken place. Italy is a heavy food importer, especially of meat and grains, and this does little to encourage an advanced processing industry. On the marketing side, merchants and other middlemen take an unduly large slice of food costs, while distribution is almost entirely in the hands of small retailers. Italians tend to prefer to buy fresh produce from small shops or market stalls. This, combined with a traditional liking for canned preserves like tomato paste and sardines, squeezes out the prospects for frozen food production and its marketing through high-turnover supermarket chains (Sicca, 1978).

The North Italian Plain, the area with the most productive agriculture as well as the biggest concentration of consumers, has most of the large processing concerns. Milan has the state-owned Motta and Alemagna food and confectionery factories; sugar processing plants are mainly found in the eastern Po Plain; and the packing and canning of fruit are important industrial activities in Veneto and Emilia. Outside of Milan, food industries are particularly important in Genoa, Verona and the string of towns along the Emilian Way — Parma, Reggio Emilia, Modena and Bologna. Parma hams and parmesan cheese are world famous, and no Italian city has a better epicurian tradition than Bologna. Along the Po axis Pavia, Lodi, Cremona and Piacenza have important dairy industries based on the rich pastures of the low plain; this is the zone of *provolone*, Gorgonzola and Bel Paese. The main dairy firm specializing in cheeses is Galbani, while Parmalat is one of Europe's largest manufacturers of packaged milk products.

Outside of the Northern Plain Campania is the most important food processing region (Figure 3.2). Apart from the packaging and despatch of fresh fruit and vegetables, this region specializes in the manufacture of tomato essences, preserves and pasta. Pasta factories are also widespread in Sicily, the classic region of hard wheat cultivation. Olive oil processing is mainly found in Apulia, Calabria and Tuscany. The manufacture of tobacco is a speciality of the provinces of Salerno (Campania) and Lecce (Apulia). In Umbria Perugia has a large chocolate and confectionery industry based around the Perugina company.

Italy produces more wine than any other country in the world, contributing one-quarter of global production. However, while Italian wine production has doubled since 1950, domestic per capita consumption, which rose during the 1950s and 1960s, has now started falling — by 15 per cent during the 1970s. The wine industry now concentrates on expanding the production of quality wines, especially since important new regulations on quality control were introduced in 1963. To date more than 200 wines have been given *denominazione di origine controllata* status — similar to, but in some respects stiffer than, the French *appellation controlée*.

3.4.4 Textiles

This is a branch of manufacturing in which Italy has enjoyed a strong reputation for centuries. Lombardy and Tuscany were leading centres of silk and woollen manufacturing in the late Middle Ages, and textiles were one of the key economic foundations of the cultural wealth of cities like Florence, Lucca and Venice. In the nineteenth century, too, textiles played a vital pioneer role in the revolution of industrial production. The cotton industry of Milan is generally regarded as the first instance of modern factory-based industry in Italy.

Regional specialization of the various textile branches became firmly established in the late nineteenth century and these regional concentrations, mainly in the Northwest, have persisted to the present day in spite of recent decentralization of some production into the northeastern and central regions. Como has long been the centre of silk production, now only a relict industry. For cotton the main centres are Gallarate, Busto Arsizio and Legnano, a trio of industrial towns northwest of Milan; also important is the Val Seriana northeast of Bergamo. The woollen industry remains concentrated at Biella (Vercelli Province, Piedmont), Prato (Florence Province, Tuscany) and at Schio and Valdagno (Vicenza Province, Veneto). The overall distribution of textiles employment is more concentrated in the north half of the country than is any other major branch of industry (Figure 3.2). Lombardy has 91 per cent of all silk factories and 65 per cent of all cotton factories; Piedmont has 46 per cent of all wool factories.

Most of the great textile companies — Lanerossi of Biella, Marzotto and Kossler–Mayer of Prato — had been founded before the First World War. Nevertheless the main structural characteristic of the textile industry has always been its very large number of small firms, 84 per cent employing less than 10 workers. Small firms are especially characteristic of the wool sector. Only in artificial and synthetic fibres do large firms dominate. Between the wars Italian firms like Châtillon and Snia Viscosa pioneered world rayon production, based on home-produced cellulose derived from cane, poplar and eucalyptus; since the 1960s, however, rayon has declined and been overtaken by hydrocarbon-based synthetic fibres, part of the petrochemical industry. Consistent with the overall lack of large firms is the fact that textiles is the branch of Italian industry least affected by public enterprise, which accounts for less than 2 per cent of employment, 3 per cent of gross production and only 5 per cent of fixed investment.

The textile industry suffered relatively little damage during the last war, and was able to profit in the early postwar years from the great demand for textiles and from the slow revival of its principal competitors in West Germany, France, Britain and Japan. After a short period of prosperity, however, the industry encountered a period of extreme difficulty with consistent decline, at least in terms of employment, over the period 1951–81 (Table 3.2). Part of this employment loss is explained by the shift of some processes into the chemical sector but it also reflects the stagnating output of basic cotton and wool products. Production of cotton yarn and cotton cloth was lower in the 1970s and early 1980s (annual output 154 000 tons of yarn, 114 000 tons of cloth) than it was in the 1950s (170 000 tons and 115 000 tons respectively). The decline in employment has been particularly marked in the cotton industry which lost 34.2 per cent of its workers between 1971 and 1981.

In the 1960s the textiles sector was affected by a number of factors, both internal and external, which threw the industry into a productive and competitive crisis. The world market was transformed by the entry of new cheap-labour countries in the Far East; raw material costs rose sharply (most wool and cotton for Italian textile processing is imported); and the emergence and development of many other profitable sectors of manufacturing industry (especially mechanical and electrical engineering) restricted opportunities for holding down labour costs in Italy (Picarelli, 1977). More specifically internal problems were the small size of the mills and the fragmented nature of the firms, the obsolescence of much of the plant, the high rate of absenteeism, the costliness and inefficiency of the distribution system and the lack of industrial diversification in the major zones of textile concentration (Botto, 1975).

3.4.5 Clothing and footwear

The decline in textiles employment is almost exactly matched by the growth of jobs in the clothing and footwear sectors so that the combined workforce in the textile and apparel industries has remained stable at around 1.1 million throughout the postwar period (Table 3.2). Exports have benefited from the creation of a fashionable image for Italian shoes and clothing and from the reputation of Rome, Florence and Milan as leading world fashion centres. The tardy development of supermarket chains in Italy has, however, limited sales of ready-made clothing and footwear on the home market; many Italians, especially the older generations, still prefer the services of the individual tailor, dressmaker or cobbler.

Knitwear has been the most buoyant branch of the clothing industry, expanding continuously between the 1950s and the late 1970s, sustained largely by penetration of European export markets, especially in West Germany and France. The initial development of knitwear manufacture took place in traditional textile centres like Milan, Turin and Biella. However, since 1961 this pattern has fundamentally changed. Although total knitwear employment, as recorded in the industrial censuses, grew by 43 per cent between 1961 and 1981, this took place not in the Northwest, where employment stagnated at around 63 000, but in regions like Veneto, Emilia–Romagna, Tuscany, Umbria and Marche where knitwear employment more than doubled from 46 000 to 94 000. By 1981 knitwear (including the much smaller hosiery branch) employed 180 000 workers in firms registered by the census, but to this number should be added another estimated 100 000 unenumerated domestic outworkers, for the knitwear industry is one of the major participants in the process of productive decentralization. Recent studies of the Emilian knitwear towns of Modena and Carpi show how the fragmented structure of the industry, divided into factories, workshops and outworkers, enables it to adapt sensitively to changing market conditions and opportunities (Brusco, 1982; Solinas,

1982). The knitwear and garment-making trades lend themselves easily to subcontracting; their multitude of specialized processes like knitting, stitching, finishing and buttoning can be carried out efficiently by under-paid female labour in artisan workshops or in the home. There is also a clear core–periphery structure to the industry with chains of low-paid rural outworkers extending out from the Emilian towns into the adjacent pro-vinces of the lower Po Plain (Mantua, Rovigo, Ferrara) and south down the Adriatic Apennines into Marche and Abruzzi.

The Italian footwear industry has many parallels with the knitwear sector: a prevailing structure of small firms and artisan-scale production (but less reliance on outworkers), a buoyant export market (accounting for 65–70 per cent of shoe production) and a growing territorial dominance in central regions at the expense of traditional northern centres. The footwear industry has experienced phenomenal growth in the postwar era. Employ-ment nearly doubled between 1961 (104 401) and 1981 (189 438), the most dramatic increases being seen in Veneto, Tuscany and Marche which now account for two-thirds of total footwear employment. In the Marche province of Ascoli Piceno 22.2 per cent of the employed population work in the footwear industry. By contrast, footwear employment in Lombardy, Piedmont, Liguria and Friuli–Venezia Giulia has declined by 20.8 per cent during 1961–81. Vigevano, in southern Lombardy, the traditional 'shoe capital' of Italy, still retains a certain importance, however. Also typical of the footwear industry is local product specialization, with individual towns or districts concentrating on, for instance, sandals, children's shoes, milit-ary footwear, skiing boots, etc. The staple product, however, is leather shoes and it is this which has spearheaded the export boom — 28 million pairs sent abroad in 1960, 173 million in 1970, 285 million in 1980. As with knitwear and clothing the main markets are in Western Europe (especially West Germany) and North America. Recently this export dominance has come under threat from the establishment of efficient shoe industries in other countries like Spain, Portugal, Czechoslovakia, Taiwan and Brazil.

3.4.6 Iron and steel

Lack of coking coal and the meagreness and dispersal of iron ore resources were fundamental handicaps to the early development of Italy's iron and steel industry. The island of Elba had the majority of iron ore, the rest coming mainly from the Alps and Sardinia. Before unification the industry was very small in scope; local ores were smelted in antiquated blast furnaces fuelled by charcoal, and iron goods, including weapons, were made in the Alpine valleys north of Como, Bergamo and Brescia. After unification and the introduction into Italy of the Bessemer converter (1860) and the

Martins–Siemens furnace (1870), the north Italian steel plants relied mainly on the French for technical expertise and supplies. As they began replacing imported fuel with hydroelectric power, they grew in size and importance, and by 1914 the Lombard steelmakers, led by Falck's new plant at Sesto San Giovanni near Milan, were operating autonomously and profitably. Nevertheless, on a national scale centrifugal locational forces had dispersed production to a range of disconnected sites: in Lombardy deriving first from the old Alpine iron industry and then linked to the expansion of engineering in and around Milan; in Liguria connected with the Genoese shipyards; in Tuscany in the vicinity of iron ore; at Terni (Umbria) because of government strategic policy; and in Naples because of plans to develop industry in the backward South. This fragmented development, together with the serious disadvantage of having to import coal, meant that the Italian iron and steel industry led a difficult life right up to the time of its reorganization following the Second World War.

When Italy joined the European Coal and Steel Community in 1951 it looked as if, without protection from the bigger and more efficient industries of France, West Germany and Belgium, the Italian industry would stagnate or decline. Precisely the opposite happened: within a decade Italian production of both pig iron and steel had doubled, and the momentum of increased production continued into the 1980s in spite of a dramatic drop in domestic iron ore production from 1.25 million tons in 1960 to 210 000 tons in 1980. Italian steel production doubled again during 1961–71 and grew by a further 40 per cent during 1971–81, by which time Italy accounted for one-quarter of the European Community's steel-making capacity. By 1983 Finsider, the public sector steel holding company, had become the second largest single producer in the world after Nippon Steel of Japan. This striking story of productive growth is all the more extraordinary because although the industry grew briskly in the boom years of the 1950s and 1960s, it achieved its present position by continuing to expand while rival European steel industries pared back production and employment under the weight of the recession. A key factor in Italy's increasing steel capacity was the construction of the giant Taranto works in the early 1960s. When its capacity was doubled a decade later to 10.5 million tonnes, it became the largest integrated steelworks in Europe.

The secret of Italy's postwar success in steel, a strategy embodied in the Sinigaglia Plan of 1950, has been the assembly of high-grade imported ore, much of it from North Africa, and relatively cheap US coking coal, in four large new or modernized integrated coastal complexes: Cornigliano near Genoa, Piombino near Leghorn, Bagnoli near Naples, and Taranto. According to Manuelli (1958), lack of raw materials was a positive advantage for Italy: the country could tap the cheapest ores and coals of the world

without the embarrassment of fixed investment in domestic supply industries — a complete reversal of the original locational values for the industry's growth. Moreover, Italian employment in the steel industry has
remained steady over the recent decade of economic crisis at around 95 000,
compared with declines of 66 per cent for the UK, 38 per cent for France
and 21 per cent for West Germany over the period 1974–83.

The dominance of Taranto, which has specialized in export orders, for
instance for oil pipelines to the Middle East, can be seen by comparing
production figures for 1980 for Italy's main plants. Out of a total national
output of 24.25 million metric tons of steel, half was accounted for by the
state-owned Finsider plants: Taranto 7.5 million, Piombino 1.4 million,
Bagnoli 1.1 million, Cornigliano 0.9 million and the inland sites of Terni 0.7
million and Dalmine (near Bergamo) 0.5 million. The private steel sector is
highly fragmented organizationally, although 40 per cent of productive
capacity is concentrated in high-technology (but small-scale) plants in
Brescia Province, specializing in steel rods.

The Italian steel industry weathered the world steel crisis of the mid- and
late 1970s, but succumbed in the early 1980s. Finsider has requested
massive government aid, for it now devotes the equivalent of 15 per cent of
is total turnover to servicing its huge debt (estimated at £16 billion in 1981).
Domestic demand for steel has fallen, while the world market is increasingly unbalanced by Third World competition. Most plants, Taranto included, are now working at 60 per cent capacity. Bagnoli is the chief loss
maker, but is kept open because of its location in an area of severe
deprivation and high unemployment.

The 1981 Steel Plan made some concessions to the unfavourable world
climate for steel, projecting reductions in the steel labour force of 8000
through natural wastage and early retirement by 1985 — redundancies
proving anathema. By 1983, however, EC pressure in Italy to further
reduce steel capacity and employment was almost insurmountable: 25 000
jobs had to be shed and either Cornigliano or Bagnoli shut down. Still
reluctant to issue redundancy notices, the Italian government cast round
for a way to cushion these blows. Cornigliano was sold off to a private
consortium which has cut production by one-third and laid off most of the
labour force. Bagnoli, now partially modernized, continues to limp along,
also with a reduced labour force. The revised Steel Plan of 1984 introduced
retirement at the age of 50 as the most painless way of cutting the steel
labour force by the required amount (Eisenhammer, 1985).

3.4.7 Vehicles

No other European country has embraced the automobile revolution with greater enthusiasm than Italy, although the sedate foreign driver or visiting pedestrian will be fairly appalled at the consequences. Italian car manufacture is one of the most brilliant success stories of Italian industry. In its early years, between 1899 (when Giovanni Agnelli founded Fiat) and 1914, it concentrated on luxury and sporting vehicles, deriving great prestige from winning famous races like the Paris–Peking in 1907; the Italian mass market at this time was limited by the poverty of the greater part of the country's population. The real success in terms of quantity of production came only after about 1950 when a succession of Fiat small cars exploited the ever-more affluent mass market, first in the North and then, since the 1960s, in the South. Considerable export successes were also achieved. Annual production of Italian cars rose 10-fold between the early 1950s (100 000 per year) and 1963 when the total surpassed 1 million. Further growth took place to 1.8 million in 1973, since when annual production dropped and then stabilized at around 1.4 million during 1975–80.

In 1981 274 000 people worked in the vehicle manufacturing industry. There is heavy concentration of this employment in the North (Figure 3.2), especially Turin, but since Alfa's shift to Naples in 1968, Fiat too have opened up scattered productive facilities in the South, for instance at Cassino (southern Latium), Termoli (Molise) and Termini Imerese (near Palermo). Fiat's dominance among vehicle production remains strong; today the firm accounts for about 80 per cent of total car production and 90 per cent of total vehicle production. The company also now controls Lancia and Autobianchi (both car firms) and the Iveco commercial vehicle enterprise.

Turin can with some justification be called 'Fiat city' for the car firm thoroughly dominates the city's economy, making it a company town on the grand scale. Fiat has 23 plants in Turin (not all of them in the vehicles sector) employing 140 000 workers; probably as many again work in Fiat's supply industries in the city (rubber, glass, plastics, components, etc.), thus making two workers out of every three in the city either directly or indirectly dependent on the motor giant.

In contrast to Fiat, which can be considered as Italy's most potent symbol of industrial private enterprise, Alfa Romeo, the country's second biggest car giant, is state owned under the IRI umbrella. Alfa Romeo's base is in Milan but it was the first major car company to 'go south' when, in 1968, it started constructing its Alfa Sud plant at Pomigliano d'Arco near Naples. This venture also marked an important product switch for the company, diversifying away from sports cars and fast saloons into the 'popular' car sector. Unfortunately the Alfa Sud project has encountered many problems and, in spite of generous regional incentives, has failed to make a profit in any one year since it started operations in 1972. Amin (1982) diagnoses the failure of the Alfa Sud plant in its timing, for it was built just at the time when, because of the labour struggles of 1969–70, the large-scale, integrated, production-line style of manufacturing (the method adopted by Alfa Sud, replicating the model already in existence in the Alfa plant in Milan) could no longer be made to work. After 1970 labour rebelled against such demeaning regimentation and Alfa Sud's labour productivity record has been consistently low, just as its absenteeism and incidence of stoppages have been consistently high. When the Napoli football team are playing an important home fixture, the entire production line can be stopped!

The location of Alfa Sud in the South brought both moral and economic pressure on Fiat to follow suit. Indeed criticism of Fiat for not helping to develop the South had been mounting for some time. Fiat's move to the South came three years after Alfa's and, crucially, after the 'hot autumn' of labour unrest. Fiat was thus able to learn from the Alfa Sud mistake. In fact in its new plants set up in the South in the 1970s Fiat revealed a sharp awareness not only of how to benefit from regional incentives but also of how best to exploit the new labour situation (Amin, 1985). Instead of gravitating to urban areas with established, and militant, industrial working classes, Fiat opted for more conservative rural areas with high unemployment, creating a scatter of medium-sized plants in a range of locations. This multiplant strategy, which also includes plants abroad, prevents a sudden strike from being able to paralyse the entire production system, for key products like gearboxes or engines can be obtained from more than one source.

Fiat has also adopted two other strategies to weaken the power of labour. First, it has pioneered the use of robots for labour-intensive tasks like welding. Second, especially in and around Turin, it has decentralized many of its subprocesses and components to subcontracting firms. There are an estimated 8000 supporting satellite firms which are in various ways subordinate to the main industry; Fiat determines the supply of these firms' products, the level of prices and, by implication, the investment and staffing levels. These changes in technical strategy and in management–labour relations also help to explain Fiat's historic victory over its workers and trade unions in the 1980 right-to-work march.

3.4.8 White goods

At the lighter end of the engineering spectrum, the growth in the manufacture and export of domestic electrical appliances, especially washing machines and refrigerators, has been another postwar industrial success. In 1960 Italy imported half its domestic appliances. Ten years later the Italian white goods industry had grown to become the second largest in the world after the USA, exporting nearly two-thirds of its output. Further growth occurred in the early 1970s but since the world recession the industry has faced a number of problems, including the slackening off of spending on such consumer durables and the saturation of the European market. For the past 10 years most of the purchasers are no longer being supplied for the first time, and the replacement market is heavily dependent on levels of disposable income. Annual production of refrigerators fell from 4.5 million in 1976 to 3.4 million in 1980, washing machine output has stagnated at around 3.3 million units per year, and unsold stocks have built up at the factories. Large portions of the white goods workforce of 67 000 have been temporarily laid off and two of the biggest names — Ignis of Varese and Zanussi of Pordenone — have recently been the subject of foreign take-overs. Nevertheless the Italian domination of the European domestic appliance industry remains strong; Italian products account for 38.5 per cent of refrigerators, 39.1 per cent of freezers, 33.5 per cent of washing machines and 22.5 per cent of dishwashers (King, 1985). However, as with many other Italian industrial products which thrived on exports in the 1950s and 1960s, white goods now face fierce competition from those of cheap labour countries in Eastern Europe and the Far East.

3.4.9 Chemicals

Like white goods, chemicals are a relatively late addition to the Italian industrial family, growing rapidly to become a major employer and income earner only in the postwar period. Table 3.2 reveals remarkable employment growth between 1951 and 1971, followed by slight retrenchment by 1981.

The industry's historical origins lie in fertilizers and explosives. The Montecatini Company, founded in 1888 to run copper mines in Tuscany, pioneered the production of copper sulphate, an important fungicide for vines. During the Fascist period important state holding interests were established in hydrocarbons and chemicals when AGIP was created to prospect for oil and gas and to develop associated industries. After 1953 ENI spearheaded state involvement in hydrocarbons and petrochemicals. Under Enrico Mattei ENI rapidly became one of the biggest oil and chemical concerns in the world.

The Italian chemical industry consists of two distinct fields: basic or primary chemicals, including synthetic fibres and plastics; and secondary or fine chemicals, including paints, drugs and cosmetics. Large firms dominate the first of these two groups, with Montedison (formed by the merger of Montecatini with Edison in 1965) being larger than all other primary chemical firms put together. The fifth largest chemical firm in

Europe and eighth in the world, Montedison is second only to Fiat as a private enterprise in Italy. By contrast, secondary chemicals are highly fragmented: 3700 of the 4000 firms have less than 20 employees and only 10 have over 1000 workers.

The spatial structure of the industry partly reflects the very different organizational and size characteristics of the primary and secondary branches. Basic chemical production, with about 100 companies and 160 plants, has followed the shift of oil refining into the Mezzogiorno and there has been significant southward decentralization of petrochemicals, rubber and fertilizers, although the employment impact of these new industries has been relatively limited because of their highly capital-intensive nature. On the other hand the fine chemical industry is still concentrated in northern regions like Lombardy, Veneto and Emilia–Romagna. Lombardy alone accounts for 40 per cent of national chemicals employment (Figure 3.2) with Milan as the main focus (26 per cent of the national total).

Over the long period 1951–73, chemicals had the highest rate of growth of output of any Italian industry — more than 10 per cent per year. Exports of chemical products grew even faster, at an annual average of 14.2 per cent. Italy's strong investment in chemicals, accounting for 18 per cent of total industrial investment during 1951–73 — more than any other major European country — paid handsome dividends: by the mid-1970s the Italian chemical industry vied with the British for the position of third largest in Europe after the West German and the French (Bracco, 1976).

The discovery of large quantities of methane in the lower Po Plain was the most important raw material factor aiding this phenomenal postwar growth. Sleepy Ravenna, isolated from its Byzantine maritime heyday by the advancing Po delta, became a chemicals boom town: a new port was excavated in the deltaic mud, improved communications put the town in touch with the Lombardy industrial area, and ANIC built a major synthetic rubber complex as well as factories manufacturing artificial fibres, resins and fertilizers.

The second factor boosting the postwar development of the chemical industry was the Cassa-induced creation of several petrochemicals complexes in the South, tied to the coastal oil refinery sites which in turn were close to the main Mediterranean oil routes. Between the late 1950s and the early 1970s several key refinery and petrochemical sites thus developed in the Mezzogiorno. The main ones were Montedison's plants at Brindisi and at Priolo (Sicily), and the ENI/ANIC complexes at Gela (Sicily) and in the Basento Valley (Basilicata). As well as base chemicals these plants developed substantial manufacturing capacity in plastics and synthetic fibres. The entry on the scene in the early 1960s of SIR (Società Italiana Resine) with its massive integrated petrochemicals complex at Porto Torres on the north coast of Sardinia did much to upset the competitive balance of Italian petrochemicals. Sardinia made further bids for petrochemicals supremacy in the 1970s by hosting new plants at Cagliari (Rumianca and Saras Chimica) and in the Tirso Valley in the centre of the island (ENI–Montedison).

Already, however, signs of the petrochemicals crisis were looming. Overambitious, politically inspired and uncoordinated expansion of petrochemicals capacity made the sector more vulnerable than any other branch of industry to the oil-price jolt of 1973–74. By 1975 output in the chemical industry had fallen by 9.6 per cent, made up of an 18.1 per cent decrease in base chemicals and only a 0.3 per cent drop in secondary chemicals. The worst affected field was synthetic fibres, down by 29.5 per cent. At the same time the sale price of base chemicals fell by 23.4 per cent, while labour costs in the industry rose by one-quarter (Bracco, 1976). Huge losses were made by the main petrochemicals firms and one of them, SIR, collapsed in 1979, eventually being sold off to the American Occidental Petroleum in 1981. The image of the petrochemicals industry was badly tarnished by allegations of financial and political corruption over access to development funds. More dramatically catastrophic was the dioxin explosion in 1976 at the Swiss-owned Ichmesa chemical plant at Seveso near Milan. The ghost of Italy's worst pollution disaster has yet to be laid for, quite apart from the death of vegetation and animals, the contamination of soil and buildings and the recriminations over responsibility, the human repercussions have still to be fully evaluated.

FOUR

Urban Issues

4.1 Introduction

Italy is a highly urbanized country by any standards. Today most Italians live in urban areas with 53 per cent living in settlements of more than 20 000 inhabitants (the official threshold for urban places) and 29 per cent in cities of over 100 000. However, the numerous towns and cities represent a great variety of urban situations, from ancient to modern, from small country town to burgeoning metropolis, and from dynamic expansion to crumbling decay. No other country can boast such a magnificent urban heritage going back over two and a half millennia. Yet really large cities have been slow to emerge. Italy has no dominant, long-established metropolitan area comparable to Paris or London. No city counted more than 1 million people before the 1961 census. Now there are four — Milan, Turin, Rome and Naples.

Since the early 1950s rapid urbanization has occurred, but it has been more intense in the North because of migration from the South. The decade of most rapid urban growth was 1951–61 when the urban proportion of the total population climbed from 41 to 48 per cent — a net addition to the urban population of 4.4 million persons (Calabi, 1984). However, over-rapid and poorly planned urban growth in the big cities resulted in many social inadequacies as well as heightening the contrasts between exploding urban agglomerations and depopulating countrysides and between more and less developed areas of the country. These are not new problems, as a brief look at Italian urbanism in the past will reveal.

4.2 A long tradition of urbanism

The Etruscans and the Greeks brought urban civilization to Italy. Although much has still to be learned about the form and nature of Etruscan towns, it is thought that the urban traditions of Etruria (the region between the Arno and the Tiber where the 12 cities of the Etruscan nation were organized into a loose federation) were passed on to the Romans; the origin of the Seven Hills of Rome as a cluster of villages grouped around the Forum owed much to Etruscan overlords. Etruscan cities, like their Roman successors, were conceived as distinct entities from the very beginning, with clearly defined quarters produced by the intersecting streets of the *cardo* and the *decumanus*. As the Etruscans expanded their domain northwards to the Po Valley and southwards to Campania, their model of city development was extended to other parts of the peninsula. Like Etruria proper, their Campanian territory was divided into 12 small city-states, of which Capua was very likely the leading city. Greek influence was limited to the South where there was a dense scatter of coastal Greek colonies, some of which ultimately grew to exceed the influence of Athens itself. In the fifth century BC the population of Syracuse, thought to exceed 250 000, made it probably the largest city in the world at the time.

City builders *par excellence*, the Romans greatly developed the urban framework of the peninsula. Seventy new colonies were founded, mostly in the North and Centre, many as ports along the Tyrrhenian coast. Even more numerous were the native centres which the Romans developed into colonies of urban status — 42 in Umbria alone. The Italy of Augustus was thus heavily urbanized. Rome itself had nearly 2 million inhabitants and there were a dozen other cities with at least 100 000 inhabitants each. Most of the larger towns of modern Italy are of Roman if not pre-Roman origin, and several preserve the gridiron Roman street plan — Turin is a good example.

Italians tend to be profoundly conscious of their Roman urban heritage but they are, not unnaturally, more aware of the good than the bad. Triumphal arches, basilicas and the palaces of the rich reveal little of the real quality of life in Ancient Rome which, for the masses, involved residence in overflowing tenements and exploitation by a leadership lacking in social awareness or responsibility. Even the layout of Roman towns was pedestrian when compared to the organic imagination and sensitivity of the cities of Ancient Greece. The public buildings were monumental in size but functional in appearance. A clear comparison with the urban style of the Fascist period can be made. Both revelled in monumentality and hyperorganization, convinced that their empires would last forever. But both failed: their cities became empty demonstrations of soullessness, their art sterile and secondhand (Gutkind, 1969).

Whereas in Western Europe urban life did not generally survive the Dark Ages, many Italian towns preserved their continuity as agricultural, trade and ecclesiastical centres. The well-developed if ponderous machine of Roman urban administration was made use of by the barbarians and endured by sheer weight of momentum. Many of the northern cities survived the perils of the period because of the inherent richness of their surroundings or because of their importance as route centres, rising repeatedly after successive sackings. Such were Milan, Pavia, Verona, Padua and Ravenna.

Renewed population growth occurred after the tenth century. The rise of the universities, notably at Bologna, Padua and Pisa, and the economic stimulus of the Crusades were contributory factors in this expansion. New city walls were added, often one series in the eleventh century and another around 1300. Coastal cities, on the other hand, were more vulnerable. While some, like Naples, Taranto and Messina, have persisted since Greek times, many important Etruscan, Greek and Roman ports declined and ultimately disappeared through piracy, malaria and silting; today their ruins are notable archaeological treasures, as at Paestum.

From the twelfth century onwards republican city-states flourished in north and central Italy; in the early thirteenth century more than 200 self-governing urban republics stretched from the Alps to the borders of the Kingdom of Naples (Waley, 1978). By modern standards most were small or medium-sized towns, the chief exception being Venice, ruler of a great maritime empire. South of Rome colonial regimes and powerful monastic lineages discouraged city-republic growth.

As Italy's commercial revolution gathered pace in the late Middle Ages the smaller city-states were replaced by the more despotic rule of the *signori*, concentrating urban power in the hands of wealthy families such as the Florentine Medici. Nowhere else in Europe were the dominant cities so large, effectively dwarfing other types of town. Foremost of all was Venice, predating and outliving all Italian rivals, its prosperity uniquely geared to maritime trade. Seldom has a city exploited its geographical advantages more skilfully. Then arose Milan, Florence, Lucca and the maritime emporia of Genoa and Pisa. In these and other towns an incipient industrial revolution was occurring with wool, silk and iron industries prevalent. By 1400 Venice had a population of 200 000 and Milan, centre of arms and metal manufactures, was only slightly smaller. Florence, Genoa, Naples and Palermo all had populations of around 100 000.

The great city-states asserted their ascendancy not only in the political and economic fields but also, and perhaps above all, as agents of cultural dissemination. The big communes emulated each other by employing the best artists and architects of the time in the erection and decoration of churches and other splendid public buildings. Politically the Renaissance was the nadir of Italy as a state but culturally it was a period of architectural creation that produced, in Florence, Siena and many other places, townscapes of worldwide fame in terms of the history of architecture and urban design. The seemingly unsystematic 'picturesque' appearance of mediaeval Italian towns has often been misinterpreted as a lack of order and functional clarity. In fact, the more irregular the town, the more detailed and comprehensive the building rules. Siena, situated on its three hills, produced the most exact bylaws for its complex layout and construction (Gutkind, 1969).

As the Renaissance matured, new ideas on urban form emerged. As life became increasingly secularized and a scientific outlook heavily charged with geometry replaced the old symbolism and spiritualism, a revolution in city planning took place. The key was the introduction of perspective into the spatial arrangements of buildings and townscapes. Unlike the mediaeval city which grew by accretion around an originally modest nucleus, the ideal city of the Renaissance was conceived from the start as a unit that was not supposed to grow beyond its intended size. Renaissance city planners were influenced by the geometry of Roman towns and the survival of gridirons in cities like Lucca and Florence, but they imposed circles, spider webs and polygons over what they saw as the excessive rigidity of the Roman grids. Utopian designs abounded between the fifteenth and the seventeenth centuries, of which the Venetian city of Palmanova, built in 1593, is the best extant example. Yet most Renaissance urban planning was expressed in individual buildings or squares rather than complete cities. The Piazza SS Annunziata in Florence has been described as perhaps the perfect Renaissance square — classic in proportion, 'space at rest' (Gutkind, 1969). Also worthy of note, although they have a more complex architectural history, are Piazza San Marco in Venice and the Piazza del Campidoglio, designed by Michelangelo, in Rome.

With the latter we move into the Baroque, the last great period of Italian urban planning, in which the restful balance of Renaissance squares and streets gave way to movement, expansion and a search for spatial infinity. As square and circle gave way to oval and rectangle a theatricality emerged in urban forms, paralleled by a penchant for fanciful detail seen in the fountains of Bernini or the elaborate façades of thousands of Italian churches. Two of the most harmonious creations of the period were the southern cities of Lecce (Apulia) and Noto (Sicily); in both, the honey-coloured local building stone provides an excellent foil for the Baroque extravaganza. Back in Rome, the Piazza and Scala di Spagna (early eighteenth century) and the Piazza del Popolo (early nineteenth century) are magnificent individual examples of Baroque city planning. Bernini's re-modelling of St Peter's Square also dates from the Baroque period; the grandeur of this Vatican open space is unsurpassed in the whole of Christendom.

Remarkable though the Baroque period was for giving so many present-day Italian cities their predominant architectural flavour, the movement must be exposed for what it was — the pompous expression of the ruling minority. Like Ancient Rome, Baroque Rome was a place of splendour and misery, of showpieces without social responsibility. The grand avenues (now the main traffic arteries) driven through the amorphous mass of congested mediaeval alleys paid scant attention to the much-needed renewal of these rundown residential quarters. This sharp contrast persists today as an important feature of the Italian urban scene. The grand boulevards with their banks, fine shops and smart bars lead the eye away from the hovels and tenements that hide, immediately behind, in a rabbit warren of alleyways and courtyards.

Such, then, have been the major phases of urban growth until the modern period of industrialism dating from the mid-nineteenth century. The significance of this long tradition of preindustrial urbanism should not be overlooked. From classical times to the Baroque the vision of urban society as the ideal form of life was ever present. Unlike other European countries, in Italy the emergence of a well-established hierarchy of urban centres preceded industrialization, and the variety and complexity of preindustrial urban forms have a powerful influence on modern urban planning.

By the mid-nineteenth century the development of a railway network and the slow spread of new industries encouraged a generally haphazard growth of many cities beyond their mediaeval walls and an increase in building densities within the old cities themselves. However, since unification Italy has seen less obvious correlation between industrialization and city growth than have most North European countries such as Great Britain and Germany. Naples was the only Italian city on a par with European capitals in the nineteenth century (it had more than 400 000 inhabitants in 1861), yet this city has never been highly industrialized.

Rapid urban growth in the late nineteenth century was limited to the capital and certain large northern cities. Rome grew from 244 500 in 1871 to 423 950 by 1911, Milan from 261 085 to 490 085, respective increases of 73 and 88 per cent over the 40-year period. Milan's growth was related to its emergence as Italy's dominant commercial and industrial city during the last two decades of the nineteenth century, and in particular to the development of the electrical and engineering industries, while Rome's expansion was linked closely to its function as capital after 1871. Turin's growth was more uneven. This city experienced strong growth in the first two-thirds of the nineteenth century, reaching 218 000 by 1864. Loss of capital city status slowed Turin's growth after 1870 but it then accelerated again towards the turn of the century as the motor car industry became established; by 1911 the population had reached 415 000. Naples, on the other hand, experienced no late nineteenth-century industrial revolution. The population of this southern city stagnated at below half a million: by 1911 five cities had overtaken it.

The irregular pattern of nineteenth-century urbanization was complemented by a lack of attention to town planning. This failure was due to the continuing dichotomy between theorists, who stressed aesthetics rather than the need to cope with the growing working-class districts of towns, and engineers who concentrated on single buildings and other construction ventures without any broad social perspective. The old cities were seen as historical centres where redevelopment should be limited, the suburbs as the areas where new building technologies could be tried without, however, any reference to the need to house the new industrial working class who, by and large, remained encamped in the old city centres. Any initiatives that were set in motion were piecemeal and often the result of specific circumstances, such as the Naples cholera epidemic of the early 1880s which gave rise to the 1885 Naples Act to clear parts of the old city, or were related to political exigencies such as the successive shifts in location of the capital — in both Florence and Rome central city redevelopment accompanied the transfer of capital status (Calabi, 1980, 1984).

The two decades of the Fascist period stand out as a distinctive phase in the history of urban development in Italy. The direct impact on the physical development of existing urban centres was limited to certain specific cases such as central Rome, where large areas of the historic centre were demolished, and Turin, Bologna and Brescia where parts of the old town were destroyed to make way for new streets, office blocks, schools, banks and railway stations. The Fascist government 'presented' all municipalities with one or more monumental *Case del Fascio* (Fascist Party headquarters). This was also the era of municipal master plans and of planning competitions. In the space of 10 years between 1927 and 1937 there were more than 1000 town layouts designed for 50 competitions, yet less than a dozen reached the stage of formal approval — a colossal waste of effort (Astengo, 1952). Nor did such competitions produce good work: Albertini's victorious master plan for Milan was, with its 178 drawings and plans, a graphical arabesque of streets, squares and gardens without the least thought for the realities of urban life — no facilities, no zoning, no recognition of the city's existing residential social geography.

Much more important, however, was Fascism's struggle against the growth of cities. Any influx to the cities was seen as a destabilizing trend which would threaten the ruthless establishment of order. Opposition to urbanization became the regime's official policy, with laws passed in 1928 and 1931 to limit the growth of cities by controlling inmigration. However, despite this legislation the country's major cities experienced rapid growth in the interwar period. Between 1931 and 1936 (the two censuses taken in the Fascist period) the main towns grew by 2.1 per cent per year, surpassing the previous highest rate of 1.9 per cent during 1901–11. Milan, symbol of industrial development and 'urban danger', reached its highest ever growth rate in the 1930s. Rome also grew massively, due partly to the expansion and centralization of the state bureaucracy there. The smaller towns and villages, on the other hand, decreased in population. These results, disconcerting for the Mussolini government, can be partly explained by the non-enforcement of the 1928 and 1931 anti-urban laws. Although these laws gave prefects unprecedented powers to curb city growth, few actually bothered to enforce them (Treves, 1980).

A 1939 'catch 22' law, which established that the acquisition of residence in urban areas was only possible for those who already had a job in the town, but which also stated that residence was necessary to have a job, only operated for a year before war broke out. Ironically, the 1939 law remained in force for 15 years, so that this particular anti-urban measure had a greater significance in democratic than in Fascist Italy. It did not stop the mass movement to the cities of the reconstruction period, but it made it a clandestine activity and greatly increased the social cost and the human suffering of those involved.

4.3 Postwar patterns of urban growth

Figure 4.1 shows the distribution of towns and cities in Italy with an indication of their relative size at the 1981 census. The map includes all regional and provincial capitals and any other towns with more than 100 000 inhabitants. The inset shows metropolitan areas, to be discussed later.

The map shows that several lines and clusters of major towns have developed, especially notable being those on the northern and southern sides of the Po Plain and in the Arno Valley in Tuscany. Few sizeable towns are to be found in the Alps, the Apennines and Sardinia. South of Rome, with the exception of Naples, Bari, Messina, Catania and Palermo, provincial capitals tend to be much smaller than those in the North. Sicily and Sardinia have no important towns that are not coastal.

An important regional contrast also exists in respect of the nature of Italian towns. Urbanization in the North has been fairly closely accompanied by the development of modern industry and commerce. The major exceptions to this statement have been the tourist and resort towns of the Ligurian, Tuscan and Adriatic Rivieras, such as San Remo, Viareggio and Rimini. Southern urbanization, on the other hand, has been largely preindustrial. Many southern towns of 10 000–50 000 inhabitants are only glorified dormitories for the farmers who work in the surrounding countryside; these 'peasant cities' or 'agro-towns' are especially common in Sicily and Apulia, regions where the rural heritage of peasant landlessness and feudalism lingered longest (Blok, 1969; King and Strachan, 1978). Overcrowded, squalid and poor, these southern towns are a world apart from those of the North, which are more comparable in character to the more industrialized cities of Western Europe.

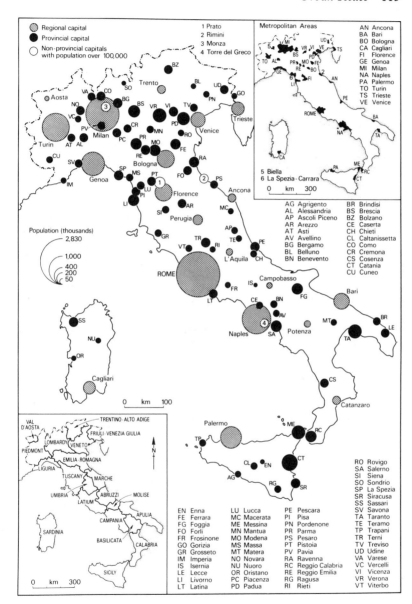

Figure 4.1 Towns, cities and metropolitan areas, 1981.

The progress of urbanization since the end of the war has been very rapid, especially in the North. In 1951 there were 22 Italian cities of greater than 100 000 inhabitants; by 1964 there were 36 and by 1983 there were 50. Since 1961 four cities have had over 1 million inhabitants; together they account for 12.1 per cent of the national demographic total (1981). Italy has changed from the 'country of the hundred cities' to the 'country of the four metropolises' (Fried, 1967).

Table 4.1 shows the pattern of urban growth at intercensal periods between 1951 and 1981 for the 11 largest Italian cities. All these cities contained at least 250 000 in 1951 and at least 350 000 in 1971. In fact there is a pronounced gap in the urban ranking below Bari and Venice; the twelfth city, Messina, having 220 766 in 1951 and 255 980 in 1981.

All 11 cities grew fastest during 1951–61, slowest (including many in decline) in 1971–81. In spite of the fact that the 1939 law discouraging rural–urban migration was not repealed until 1954, the decade 1951–61 was clearly the boom period for postwar urban growth, especially in Rome and the big northern cities of Turin, Milan and Bologna. In fact, over the country as a whole, 91.4 per cent of the 1951–61 intercensal population increase of 2.9 million was concentrated in the provincial capitals which accounted for 27.2 per cent of the Italian population.

It is important to realize that during the urbanization boom of 1951–61 different urban growth mechanisms were at work in different parts of the country and for different size categories of towns (Archibugi, 1965). The 13 largest cities (those above 250 000 in 1961 — the 11 in Table 4.1 plus Messina and Trieste) divided into two major groups. First, there were southern cities whose growth was almost entirely due to natural increase, with stagnant or even negative migratory balances (Naples, Bari, Messina, Catania, Palermo). Second, there were northern cities whose growth reflected exactly the opposite circumstances — high inmigration and stagnant or even negative natural change (Turin, Milan, Genoa, Bologna, Florence). Of the three remaining cities, Rome grew rapidly because of both high natural increase and high inmigration, Venice grew slowly because of a combination of weak inmigration and slight natural increase, whereas Trieste stagnated because of zero natural growth and zero net migration.

During the succeeding decade, 1961–71, all the top 11 cities continued to grow but at rates markedly inferior to those of 1951–61. Only Rome and Bari maintained most of their momentum; in the others the growth rate was halved or even cut by three-quarters. However, in many of the smaller regional and provincial capitals of the South (mostly in the range 50 000–200 000) growth was faster in 1961–71 than in 1951–61, due to their continuing high birth rates combined with the start of localized rural–urban migration.

During 1971–81, following a 'counterurbanization' trend now well established in many European countries, most of the larger cities lost population. The greatest proportional losses were recorded in the main industrial cities of the North. Turin, Milan and Genoa, famous cities of the industrial triangle, each lost 5–7 per cent of their populations; similar losses were sustained by port cities like Venice, Trieste, La Spezia and Savona, all overdependent on declining shipbuilding and oil industries. In southern cities like Naples and Catania the decline registered in total population is all the more remarkable considering the high rate of natural increase. Naples, for example, experienced a net loss of population of 16 091 in spite of a natural growth of 107 961 people over the decade. Catania, with a natural increase of 41 228, nevertheless lost 21 527 overall.

The three cities which continued to grow during 1971–81 (see Table 4.1), albeit at a reduced rate compared to previous decades, are all important administrative centres, their expansion assured by the proliferation of tertiary employment, unaffected by northern industrial decline. Rome, it is true, grows but slowly now although Palermo, capital of Sicily, and Bari, the regional city for southeast Italy, still have some momentum. This pattern is also borne out by many of the other, smaller administrative towns of southern Italy, especially the 'new' regional and provincial capitals created around 1970, such as Catanzaro (+ 16.6 per cent), Isernia (+ 19.7 per cent) and Oristano (+ 11.6 per cent). In fact in the whole of southern Italy, together with the adjacent regions of Latium and Umbria, only 3 out of 41 provincial capitals lost population during 1971–81. These were Naples, Catania and the old hilltop city of Enna in Sicily. By contrast, in the North (Lombardy, Piedmont, Liguria, Trentino, Veneto and Friuli) 23 out of 33 provincial capitals lost population. Anomalies, such as the 8.5 per cent growth in Pordenone, can be explained by reference to specific circumstances — in this particular case, the growth of the Zanussi 'white goods' industry.

All the data on urban size and growth discussed above are subject to one major shortcoming. In Italy population figures are recorded and published by commune. For big cities, the boundary of the commune may not correspond to the edge of the built-up or urbanized area, which may have spread beyond the boundary into the territory of adjacent communes. The cases of Rome and Milan illustrate this problem perfectly. Rome commune has an enormous territory (1508 sq km) which contains not only the entire city but also a wide surrounding rural zone extending to the coast and including other settlements, such as Lido di Ostia, which are completely detached from Rome itself. The area of the commune of Milan, by contrast, is only 182 sq km, and this territory is, and has been for some time, completely urbanized. Factories and housing have spilled over into many

Table 4.1 Demographic evolution of Italy's major cities, 1951–81

	1951	1961	1971	1981	% change 1951–61	% change 1961–71	% change 1971–81
Rome	1 651 754	2 188 169	2 781 993	2 830 569	+32.5	+27.1	+1.7
Milan	1 274 245	1 582 534	1 732 000	1 634 638	+24.2	+9.4	−6.0
Naples	1 010 550	1 182 815	1 226 594	1 210 503	+17.0	+3.7	−1.3
Turin	719 300	1 025 822	1 167 968	1 103 520	+42.6	+13.9	−5.5
Genoa	688 447	784 194	816 872	706 300	+13.9	+4.2	−6.9
Palermo	490 692	587 985	642 814	699 691	+19.8	+9.3	+8.8
Bologna	340 526	444 872	490 528	455 853	+30.6	+10.3	−7.1
Florence	374 625	436 516	457 803	453 293	+16.5	+4.9	−1.0
Catania	299 629	363 928	400 048	378 521	+21.5	+9.9	−5.4
Bari	268 183	312 023	357 274	370 781	+16.3	+14.5	+3.8
Venice	316 891	347 347	363 062	332 775	+9.6	+4.5	−8.3

Source: ISTAT: *Annuario Statistico Italiano*, 1962, 1982.

adjacent communes which have, in consequence, seen their populations leap upwards.

There is, therefore, no official figure for the population of 'Greater' Milan, 'Greater' Turin, etc., nor for any of the other cities whose built-up areas have invaded adjacent communes. It is, however, possible to intuitively reconstruct the total urban agglomeration by the painstaking use of maps and census data. If this is done some rather different figures emerge. Milan and Florence continued to grow, both by about 3 per cent during 1971–81, the Neapolitan agglomeration grew by 8 per cent, but Turin dropped by 2 per cent. The evidence for counterurbanization is thus far from clear.

While no official data exist on the size of continuously built-up urban areas, there are figures on wider metropolitan areas. These are defined as functionally specialized and linked urban systems of at least 110 000 total population and with at least 35 000 workers gainfully employed in non-agricultural activities (Cafiero and Busca, 1970). Metropolitan criteria yield another perspective on the relative importance of Italian urban areas for while Rome, the largest individual city, has 3 million inhabitants, metropolitan Milan counts nearly 6 million and Naples 3.6 million. In 1971 the 32 metropolitan areas contained 43 per cent of the Italian population, having grown from 15.5 million in 1951 to 23.2 million in 1971, an increase of nearly 50 per cent (Table 4.2). The non-metropolitan population, meanwhile, fell slightly from 32 million to 30.8 million. Forecasts made in 1970 by Cafiero and Busca that by 1981 the Milan 'megolopolis' would contain 8–8.5 million and that the Rome and Naples metropolitan areas would each contain 4–4.5 million seem to have been overambitious. Calculations based on 1981 census data are not yet available but given the stagnation of many big cities since 1971, metropolitan areas are unlikely to have grown by very much. Figure 4.1 (inset) shows the remarkable concentration of the metropolitan areas in northern Italy. South of Florence they are widely spaced and all coastal.

4.3.1 The role of migration

Although there are significant differences in rates of natural increase — chiefly due to the cities and metropolitan areas of the South having a higher birth rate than those in the North — the key component of urban growth and decline is migration. The period 1951–71 saw a massive rural–urban transfer of Italian population. Much of this movement was fairly localized, intraregional and even intraprovincial, but ISTAT sources also indicate that since 1945 a huge South–North drift of around 3 million people has taken place. Most of these interregional migrants settled in Rome and in the big industrial cities of the North. Archibugi (1965) calculated that, of the

Table 4.2   Metropolitan growth, 1951–71

	1951 population (000s)	1971 population (000s)	Change (000s)	% change
Metropolitan areas in:				
Northern Italy*	7 221.4	11 034.0	+3 812.6	+52.8
Central Italy†	3 553.0	5 715.1	+2 162.1	+60.8
Southern Italy‡	4 730.7	6 436.5	+1 705.8	+36.1
All Italy	15 505.1	23,185.6	+7 680.5	+49.5
Non-metropolitan areas	32 010.5	30 839.6	−1 170.9	− 3.7
Italy total	47 515.6	54 025.2	+6 509.6	+13.7

Source: Rodgers (1978).
* Milan, Turin, Genoa, Alessandria, Biella, La Spezia–Carrara, Brescia, Vicenza, Verona, Padua, Venice, Udine, Trieste.
† Florence, Leghorn, Rome, Bologna, Modena, Reggio Emilia, Parma, Ferrara, Rimini, Ancona.
‡ Naples, Pescara, Bari, Taranto, Reggio Calabria, Messina, Catania, Palermo, Cagliari.

1.55 million people who moved from communes of less than 50 000 inhabitants to bigger communes during 1951–61, nearly 1 million ended up in Rome, Milan and Turin.

Patterns of Italian rural–urban migration have evolved in a complex time, space and scale perspective (Golini, 1983). Initially, in the nineteenth and early twentieth centuries, the industrial cities of the Northwest depended on migration from their surrounding agricultural regions. Turin drew particularly from the western Alps and the Monferrato Hills, Milan from the farming districts of southern Lombardy. Later, northern industries' recruitment drives switched to the northeastern regions of the country, tapping especially the vast labour reserves of rural Veneto, always a traditionally poor and overpopulated region. Since the late 1950s, the North's main labour reserves have been found in the South.

Milan, Turin and Rome have thus pulled in migrants from all over Italy. While the first two have drawn in workers destined mainly for industrial labour, Rome's service-based economy has attracted people from a broad range of backgrounds from the parliamentarian and university professor to the taxi-driver and bootblack. The middle-range cities of 100 000–500 000 have tended to be objectives for mostly intraregional movement. Thus Florence attracted mostly Tuscans, Bologna mainly Emilians, etc., although in both cases the neighbouring rural regions of Marche and Umbria were also heavily involved as supply areas. Towns and cities of less than 100 000 inhabitants have been sustained mainly by local migrants (Gentileschi, 1976).

4.3.2 Southern migrants in northern cities

The massive migration of southerners into northern cities and metropolitan areas has resulted in a high level of ethnic and cultural heterogeneity, eroding these cities' earlier social and political cohesion. Although many southern migrants have a strong desire to become assimilated into the northern urban scene, having undergone, even before departure, a kind of anticipatory socialization into urban life through television and the media, the realities of occupational exploitation, segregated housing and ethnic stereotyping have prevented this integration from happening. Anti-southern prejudices were fanned by the scale of the new arrivals who were everywhere treated as social inferiors, common terms for them being *marocchini*, 'little Moroccans', or *terroni*, 'earth-grubbers'.

In addition to prejudice and discrimination showered on them by the local population, the integration of southern immigrants is more objectively blocked by their occupational characteristics and educational backgrounds. Using data from a survey in Milan, Bielli (1973) shows that southern migrants are far more concentrated in unskilled, insecure and dependent employment than are native Milanese. They also have more restricted occupational mobility, at least in terms of moves related to career improvement, and lower educational qualifications; for example, whereas 19.7 per cent of local-born Milanese workers have no post-primary school qualification, the figure is 43.7 per cent among migrants from southern towns and 66.4 per cent among those from rural areas of the South.

Further problems awaited the migrants in the field of housing. Most migrants settled in two main urban zones — either the inner city or the peripheral shanty town. Fofi (1970) provides vivid documentation of the Turin case. Enterprising and unscrupulous locals bought up delapidated tenements in Old Turin and rented them at extortionate rates to migrant workers from the South. Another tactic was for local flat dwellers to crowd several camp beds in a spare room and, by overcharging the migrants, pay off their entire rent. By these mechanisms the most delapidated inner-city neighbourhoods came to be dominated by migrants and characterized by appallingly high population densities and deteriorating living conditions.

In Milan and Rome it was more common for migrants to settle in peripheral slums. The Milanese *corea* — named after the Korean War which had brought shanty settlements to the notice of the Italian public during the 1950s — was produced by a process of land subdivision manipulated by urban fringe farmers and middlemen who divided former agricultural land into house sites for sale to migrant families. The new owners scrounged for building materials, provided the labour themselves, and the end-product was an unplanned sprawling shanty town devoid of all public services such as electricity, sewers, shops, schools, clinics or bus services (Mannucci, 1970). Local planning officials ignored such phantom settlements for fear of bankrupting council budgets. Similar problems existed — and still largely exist today — in the periurban *borgate* of Rome.

By about 1970 there were signs that the big industrial cities of the Northwest had reached saturation point with respect to their capacity to absorb southern migrants. The former receiving cities of Milan, Turin and Genoa were themselves becoming the staging points for outmigration, both to their immediate hinterlands as industry became decentralized, and abroad as rural and southern migrants gained some skills in the city and then 'traded up' by moving into Europe.

As a result of these changes the typical new arriver in the 1970s and 1980s has somewhat different characteristics to his or her forbears of earlier decades (Douglass, 1983). No longer is he likely to be the head of household seeking to establish a new life for his family in the urban milieu. Rather, he or she is likely to be young, single and in possession of a marketable trade or skill. Members of the 'second wave' can count on the help of kinsfolk established during the 'first wave'. The urban environment is now less hostile; 30 years of 'southernization' have damped down the raw prejudices of the earlier years.

Now, the southerners' places at the bottom of the hierarchy are taken by foreign immigrants, the vast and partly invisible army of illegal workers from Third World countries who work in domestic service, hotels, restaurants and the more menial service occupations and who are to be found in all the big cities of the North as well as in Rome, Naples, Bari and Palermo.

4.4 Postwar urban planning

Italy's urban planning framework has coped inadequately with problems of rapid postwar city growth, immigrant ghettoes and shanty towns. Indeed the shameful extent to which such malaises persist is a testimony to the failure of town planning, although certain extenuating circumstances exist. The Second World War paralysed the building industry and left 500 000 dwellings in ruins and 250 000 severely damaged. Multiple occupation and subletting were, perforce, common features of the immediate postwar period. The 1951 census gave an average figure of 1.35 inhabitants per room for the country as a whole (1.21 in the North, 1.86 in the South) with 750 000 dwellings being shared by more than one family, and 220 000 families living in dwellings coyly referred to as 'inappropriate' (in practice these were caves, cellars and shacks). The national housing deficit was estimated at 2.5 million dwellings.

The government's response was to stimulate private sector construction with minimal direct intervention by the public authorities. In the big cities planning restrictions were relaxed to allow more intensive land use than that prescribed in existing legislation. Heavy subsidization of the private building sector by grants and soft loans led to an escalating boom in the construction industry. Between 1951 and 1955 an average of 150 000 dwellings were built per year, rising to 380 000 per year during 1961–65, after which the rate of increase was checked by economic recession. Only a small, and decreasing, proportion of the new dwellings were built by public housing authorities financed directly by the state.

Much postwar urban reconstruction and development have been framed within the 1942 Town Planning Act which set out a hierarchy of planning levels. *Piani Regolatori Intercomunali* (PRI) were to be drawn up by groups of municipalities acting as one planning consortium, *Piani Regolatori Generali* (PRG) were the standard commune-level master plans and *Piani Regolatori Particolareggiati* (PRP) were more local-level plans drawn up within the framework of approved PRG. Because of the war and the years of reconstruction the 1942 Act was not applied until 1954 when the major city councils were charged with the responsibility of devising their own plans. According to Calabi (1984) the 1942 Act was qualitatively on a par with most planning acts approved in Europe in the early postwar period, but in practice it was rendered ineffectual by the economic and political forces which shaped the Italian development process in the 1950s and 1960s. The economic boom, tumultuous rural–urban migration and rampant speculative building brought sweeping changes in the urban morphology of the country's major cities and posed new planning problems. Administrative chaos and political corruption were less readily acknowledged but they are widely known to plague Italian planning, especially in the South where the ruling class is largely made up of building speculators and high-level bureaucrats (Ginatempo and Cammarota, 1977). Congested and disorganized suburbs sprung up around most cities — huge, tightly packed blocks of flats containing residential densities at least 10 times higher than suburban areas in most British or American cities. Moreover, much of this development was illegal and it almost always lacked public services such as schools, shops, parks or transport links. Sometimes even sewers, water and electricity were lacking.

The 1970s brought rather more successful attempts at controlling the urban growth process. The 1971 Housing and Town Planning Act gave local authorities new powers to expropriate sites for state-subsidized housing projects, for public service infrastructure and for inner-city conservation and improvement. This legislation was reinforced by the National Framework Act of 1972 and the Regional Government Act of 1977 which progressively introduced regional authority responsibility for planning, urban renewal and housing provision. This new responsibility is of great importance, since it means that the regions must establish plans on inter-commune and regional scales which will serve as a framework for smaller-scale plans (Evans, 1979).

The 1977 round of planning legislation reflected the period (1975–79) when working-class participation in the government was at its strongest. The long-awaited *Legge Urbanistica*, also known as Law 10 or the Bucalossi Law (after the Minister of Public Works who pushed it through), was a reformist law intended to solve the contradictions in previous legislation and was part of a package of housing and development measures designed to benefit the poorer classes. At first sight Law 10 appears to be one of the most advanced pieces of development planning legislation in Western Europe: no form of development can be carried out without the 'concession' of the local governing authority; such concession is only given when the property falls within the areas scheduled for development within the commune master plan (the PRG) and its three–five-year zonal implementation programmes; the concession establishes time limits for the completion of a development, never more than three years; a property owner in the development area has to develop his land; a development charge of 5–20 per cent of the building costs accompanies the concession, and in addition the developer has to bear the costs of infrastructure and facilities. The extent to which these provisions in practice meant the nationalization of development rights was hotly debated; the problem was the ambiguity of the term 'concession'. In 1980 the Constitutional Court ruled that the right to development had not been nationalized but several other ambiguities remain unresolved. One important facet of Law 10 remains: the multiyear implementation plans are an important mechanism for controlling development, although they have the side-effect of sharply differentiating land values, leading to skyrocketing inflation of land in the delimited areas (Calavita, 1983).

4.5 The housing crisis

In practice, these efforts to create a rational urban planning framework have done little to solve one of Italy's most pressing social problems: the chronic shortage of certain types of housing. The major housing needs are concentrated in urban areas. A 1976 survey found that more than 7 million dwellings — nearly half the total housing stock — were in a state of disrepair, with nearly half of these in a state of serious delapidation. Another survey carried out three years later confirmed these figures, noting a slight increase in the percentages of housing in a state of disrepair or unfit for habitation in major urban areas (Padovani, 1984).

Added to the problem of physical decay is the phenomenon of overcrowding, again most serious in urban areas. The incidence of house sharing is on the increase. Shared households comprised 8 per cent of the total in 1961 and 1971, rising to 11 per cent at the 1981 census. The number of families on the waiting list for public housing is close to one million, yet only about 25 000 public dwelling units are built per year. Recent estimates indicate that in order to eliminate overcrowding it would be necessary to rehouse, either through new construction or rehabilitation, one-fifth to one-quarter of Italian households (Padovani, 1984).

Table 4.3 charts the evolution of Italian dwellings as recorded in the four postwar censuses, including some information on overcrowding and facilities. The overall statistical picture is one of steady improvement. The 1951 census revealed a lot of overcrowding in dwellings that often lacked the basic amenities. From this situation of widespread deprivation the country has apparently reached a point where standards at a national scale compare fairly favourably with those of most other advanced European countries. The numbers of dwellings and rooms have increased much faster than the overall population, the average size of dwelling has increased from 3.26 to 3.96 rooms, the 'overcrowding index' has decreased to 0.79 persons per room, and provision of facilities such as water and electricity is close to 100 per cent.

How can the paradox of considerable, and accelerating, growth of accommodation combined with continuing overcrowding and deprivation be explained? One factor to bear in mind in the population–housing equation is the faster increase in the number of households in relation to population growth, reflecting a complex social transformation of the traditional Italian family. However, the key to answering this question lies in the structural contradictions in the Italian building industry and in the wide differences in housing conditions between the social classes (Ginatempo, 1979). While the poorer sections of the urban population are corralled in decaying city-centre tenements or banished to peripheral estates and shanty towns, the middle- and upper-income groups have engaged in a fair degree of 'opulent consumption' in the housing market, occupying houses or apartments that are substantially bigger than their real needs and participating in the growing European phenomenon of second-home ownership. The real growth in the number of dwellings has come in the 'unoccupied' category, which has roughly doubled in size at each successive intercensal decade (Table 4.3). During the most recent period (1971–81) occupied dwellings increased by 14.7 per cent, unoccupied by 103.7 per cent. Roughly half the unoccupied units are reckoned to be second homes,

Table 4.3 Census data on housing, 1951–81

	1951	1961	1971	1981
Total number of dwellings (000s)	11 410.7	14 213.7	17 434.0	21 852.7
Occupied dwellings (000s)	10 756.1	13 031.6	15 301.4	17 509.1
Unoccupied dwellings (000s)	654.6	1 182.0	2 132.5	4 343.7
% dwellings unoccupied	5.7	8.0	12.2	19.9
Rooms per dwelling	3.26	3.33	3.67	3.96
Persons per occupied room	1.35	1.13	0.94	0.79
% dwellings classed as overcrowded	39.0	27.6	14.9	12.1
% dwellings classed as 'improper'*	2.3	1.3	0.5	0.4
% dwellings with piped drinking water	35.1	60.6	85.0	98.7
% dwellings with internal bathroom	10.4	28.4	63.1	86.5
% dwellings with electricity	80.9	93.8	98.1	99.5

Source: Tagliacarne (1974); Dandri (1978); Padovani (1984).
* Caves, cellars, shanties, etc.

common particularly in coastal and mountain areas. The rest are made up of houses abandoned by emigrants (widespread in rural areas) and by dereliction (common in inner-city districts, especially in southern towns), and of the large number of newly built units which remain empty through speculative anticipation of increasing prices or rents.

The phenomenon of housing waste reflects the divorce between housing production and housing need, and the separation between investors and builders. Since the building industry cannot obtain the necessary means of investment from direct sales, the main sources of capital are banks and other financial institutions such as insurance companies. Because of the high costs of the building industry and because of the need, dictated by the investing institutions, for maximizing rates of return, builders increasingly favour large-scale accommodation geared exclusively to high-income purchasers (Ginatempo, 1979).

4.6 Urban struggles

With the exception of Rome where there has been a long tradition of urban activism since the early liberation period of the 1940s (Della Seta, 1978), the contradictions in the field of housing lay dormant until the 1960s when the class struggle intensified and the economy faltered. It became increasingly evident to the working class that living conditions in the cities had deteriorated; the expectations raised by the 'opening to the Left' had not been met. By the late 1960s the poorer classes were involving themselves directly in campaigns for better housing and more social services. Rent strikes, squatting and demonstrations were the main forms of protest.

This crucial period in Italian urban life is described in detail by Angotti (1977). The upsurge started in Milan when, in January 1968, hundreds of public housing tenants went on a rent strike to protest against a 15 per cent rent increase. This was the beginning of one of the largest and most militant tenant movements, not only in Italy but in the Western world: by October 1972 35 000 families had joined the rent strike. Action soon spread to other cities. In the spring of 1968 30 000 people demonstrated for housing reform in Florence. In the summer there were squatters in 11 new council house blocks in Turin. By the autumn squatting had begun in Rome and spontaneous actions ensued in most major cities. The pressure mounted and culminated in the general strike of November 1969 when 20 million people signified their support for housing reform.

The organizational and political background to the housing struggles reflects a complex and shifting set of involvements. Since the chaotic housing situation mirrored the complexities and privations of work, it was not surprising that trade unions were active in campaigning directly for more, better and cheaper housing. This was especially the case in the large industrial cities where, on average, only one-quarter of families own their own dwellings (nationally the proportion is over one-half). The late 1960s, therefore, saw the trade union movement 'socialized', moving out from the factory to the city and the neighbourhood (Calavita, 1983). The political pattern of involvement is divided by Marcelloni (1979) into three phases. During the initial phase (1968–70) the struggles were directed by PCI militants, the PSIUP and dissenting Catholics. Occupation of dwellings occurred mainly in older and abandoned blocks in public ownership. The second phase occurred in 1971–72 and was characterized by a split between the old and the new Left. The Potere Operaio (Workers' Power) and Lotta Continua (Continuous Struggle) groups which had been active in the factories during the 'hot autumn' moved out to involve themselves in urban issues and in work with marginal populations. They employed a strategy of confrontation, for instance in the defence of occupied buildings, and strongly criticized the PCI, which was progressively distancing itself from such direct action, as a traitor to the working class. They also extended the squatting campaigns to embrace new and empty private constructions. The third phase (1972–73) saw the birth of the first *comitati di quartiere* (neighbourhood committees). This development occurred when the previous militant struggles were neutralized, in particular by the Housing Act.

The nature of the housing struggle also varied between northern and southern cities. In the North the rent strikes involved industrial workers, first as individual tenants and later with union support. Large demonstrations of solidarity occurred. For example, in Milan in 1972 50 000 workers marched in sympathy with people who had occupied empty housing but had been evicted by the police, and in Turin strikes were held in support of such squats. In contrast, in Rome and in southern towns there was very little participation by industrial labour and workers' groups in the housing struggles. In Rome the squats were carried out by more marginal elements of the population and their actions had more impact, particularly when they were occupying new private dwellings rather than old or abandoned public housing.

The sense of urgency about housing faded for a while during the early 1970s, but mass action was renewed in 1974. During that year there were several national strikes promoted by SUNIA (the main tenants' union, with 200 000 members) and supported by the trade union and cooperative movements. Between January and March 5000 new private dwellings were occupied by squatters in Rome, and similar occupations occurred in Milan, Florence, Naples and even Communist Bologna. Occupations, evictions and reoccupations followed in a continuous cycle of conflict. The conflict assumed new dimensions in the 'battles of the poor' — incredible states of siege between families officially assigned to public housing and those in occupation. Meanwhile, owners of private housing formed vigilante squads and employed armed guards.

Midway through 1974 the Communists commenced their attempt to reassert their popular control through the trade unions and by launching a campaign for 'participation'. A ferment of committees arose in many Italian cities as the process of decentralization got underway. New neighbourhood committees were able to supplant grass-roots groups in most cities. After their successes in the 1975 regional and 1976 municipal elections the PCI could legitimately claim that they had eliminated extremism in favour of responsible and democratic struggle. On the housing front, pressure for reform continued, but in a less direct form, being filtered through the bureaucratic procedures of the new local councils. In some cities occupations switched to empty dwellings in the historic centres: here the objective was to persuade councils to block these buildings' imminent destruction by speculative developers in favour of a policy of rehabilitation for 'social housing'. Unlike the peripheral squats which were remote from the everyday experience of the bourgeoisie, these central occupations, accompanied by slogans and red flags, more directly touched the consciousness of middle-class city dwellers because they passed these buildings every day.

Housing struggles fell off appreciably after 1976, ceasing to act as a political force. With the exception of urban terrorism and various fragmented groups of unemployed youths and anarchists which have little by way of a constructive message, urban protest is, for the time being, a thing of the past.

4.7 The problem of the historic town centres

Italy has the privilege of possessing an urban heritage unequalled by any other European country. Yet the priceless patrimony of mediaeval and Renaissance towns and town centres has been a major casualty of government inertia in urban policy, allowing private interest free reign to destroy and redevelop. From the early years of the Republic through the Fascist years to the postwar period, demolition was regarded as the best way to 'improve' overcrowded and decaying city centres. The late nineteenth century saw long arteries cut through the mediaeval cores of the major cities. Such schemes, originally carried out for aesthetic and sanitary purposes (and now the main traffic arteries), have often destroyed older quarters of considerable historical interest and have caused a remodelling of site values with speculation in land and buildings along these 'axes of the bourgeoisie' (Bethemont and Pelletier, 1983). The names of these arteries — Via Garibaldi, Via Mazzini, Corso Vittorio-Emmanuele — are redolent of the Risorgimento and are a symbolic stamping of a uniform *Italian* model on the varied tapestry of pre-unification townscapes. The same mixture of functionalism and speculation is encountered in the urban planning of the Fascist era, which profoundly modified some Italian cities in the interwar years and during the reconstruction period. Speculation certainly outweighed ideological and aesthetic principles in the destruction of some of the most beautiful villas of Rome, including the magnificent Villa Ludovisi for a shopping precinct.

For many years the mutilation of the traditional Italian townscape was accepted as the inevitable reverse side of the development coin. Before the early 1970s relatively few voices were raised in alarm over the desecration of the historic city centres; such protesting voices as there were came from a small band of architects, journalists and small cultural groups such as Italia Nostra. However, over the past 10–15 years, an emerging consensus among urban analysts seems to be in favour of abandoning the metropolitan slant of the *Progetto 80* and replacing it by the promotion of medium-sized cities and by the rescue of the *centro storico* or historic town centre (Corna Pellegrini and Zerbi, 1983). It is clear that cities which failed to participate in the economic miracle of the North during the 1950s and 1960s, or in the forced industrialization of the South in the 1960s and 1970s, also managed to avoid the systematic destruction of their cultural fabrics. Cities such as Perugia and Urbino moved forward more slowly and less spectacularly than, for example, Ferrara and Pavia in the North, or Taranto and Gela in the South, all of which have suffered considerable despoliation and congestion over the past 25 years. The towns of central Italy have been most successful in preserving the genius of mediaeval design. In addition to the factor of economic stagnation, we should not forget the influence of topography, for hilltop cities have little contiguous space in which to expand. Their *centri storici* are thus well preserved, modern development being diverted away by a bypass or a railway station to an axis in the valley below. It is, perhaps, no accident that now, as Italians rediscover their taste for the quality of life, central Italy should be the *locus classicus* for the current wave of diffuse industrialization which improves the region's economic standing without fundamentally disturbing the settlement pattern.

Another powerful instrument in the desecration of Italian urban life is the motor car. Historically its influence has no doubt been more incremental than physical redevelopment of the urban fabric, but its impact — on the eyes, the nose and the ears, and on personal liberty and safety — is nevertheless enormous. Italian traffic is no respecter of pedestrian crossings, while pavements are there to be parked on, not walked along. Noisy motorbikes, holes drilled in their silencers to maximize the decibels, have become the symbol of teenage *machismo*. The *centri storici*, with their graceful piazzas and narrow streets, are perfectly adapted to the pre-motor (or non-motor) age. They are the very essence of Italian urbanism, providing the perfect setting for the *passeggiata*, ritualized public behaviour and the art of outdoor conversation. How sad that they should be ruined by vehicular traffic, with car parking filling the squares and 'the townscape served up on a thick lining of car roofs' (de Wolfe, 1963).

Recent years have seen a partial reappraisal of the value of the *centro storico*. Tourism provides one economic justification for preserving the old cores, while in the larger cities especially, historic and formerly rundown districts are becoming gentrified: the flight of the working class, often stage-managed by urban administrators and planners, is replaced by the invasion of the professionals with an eye for the picturesque and the ancient.

The legislative background to the rehabilitation of the *centri storici* has already been mentioned. The 1971 Housing Act gave local authorities powers to expropriate sites for inner-city conservation and improvement; the initiatives of the Bologna town council played a pioneer role here. A number of special acts were subsequently passed for the financing and planning of inner-city rehabilitation in other cities; sometimes these followed natural disasters, such as floods at Venice or earthquakes at Ancona and Naples. New procedures were approved in 1978. Communes acquired the power to prepare plans for rehabilitation which included areas for conservation, improvement, redevelopment and changed land use. Such areas may include single buildings, blocks of housing and areas of service buildings. It is now recognized that there is positive economic value in conservation, over and above the historic and cultural value of old sites and structures (Bardazzi, 1984).

4.7.1 Urban renewal in Bologna

The city of Bologna has played a key role in Italian urban renewal policy. Angotti (1977) claims that Bologna is the first industrial city in the Western world to have a central area renewal programme that aims to preserve the historic and social character of the urban environment by not displacing low-income people from their homes. The theoretical basis of the Bologna policy is the notion of the city, with all its buildings and services, as a 'public good' (*bene pubblico*) and not a place for speculation and private profit. On a practical level, the policy's success is due to a basic political commitment by the city's Communist administration to reinforce the social foundations of the central core by improving the physical environment, increasing the level of services, controlling rents and promoting democratic participation in decision-making. Surveys carried out as part of the 1969 city master plan enumerated a rich heritage of seventeenth-century artisan housing interwoven with a multitude of religious and aristocratic buildings. Arcaded pavements ensure separation of pedestrians and traffic and provide shelter from summer sun and winter rains. The majority of the accommodation was, however, substandard with 80 per cent of families living in rented units, 60 per cent of which lacked a bath or shower and 68 per cent heating. There was also a noticeable lack of accessible public open space.

Restoration plans designated old and redundant churches to serve as community centres, providing space for schools, daycare centres, meeting halls, theatres, etc. Rehabilitation of housing started in the mid-1970s. Large or corporate real estate holders have had their property expropriated, with compensation at well below market prices. Small property owners (with up to three apartments) who did not wish to sell to the city were obliged to sign a long-term contract with the council which guarantees the status of their tenants, limits rents and provides for low-interest loans to cover renovation expenses. Different restoration policies are based on the distinction between the building as a work of art, where historic and aesthetic value dominates, and the building as an element in urban design, where its function and relationship to the overall urban environment are valued. Individual buildings are treated by either 'scientific' or a 'conservational' restoration. Scientific restoration requires historical research to discover the original form and use of the building, the intention being to restore the building to its original state, accommodating its original function (or the modern equivalent) without making structural changes. Conservational restoration does not necessitate the removal of all later modifications or preclude structural alterations; an example would be the provision of modern housing within the shell of a seventeenth-century building.

In the *centro storico* of Bologna residential units are typically located on deep, narrow building lots with two blind walls running the full depth, windows at front and back and occasional skylights. The units are two or three storeys, with ground-floor usage in commercial hands, usually for retail outlets, workshops or stores. The housing forms an entire four-sided tenement block, with a variety of interior spaces for light and air. Such blocks were identified as potential suitable housing for working-class families as well as providing more flexible units for students, single persons, old people and young couples. Each restored block thus has a variety of apartment types to cater for the modern social and household mix. The arcaded ground floor retains its shop or professional function. An entrance way connects directly to the interior yard, a central stair block and common service areas accommodating central heating plant, laundries, restaurants for students and elderly, daycare centres and nurseries. All plans and proposals are discussed at neighbourhood level. While renovation work is carried out, tenants are moved to temporary accommodation nearby. Rents are fixed at existing public housing levels, about 12 per cent of income.

Bologna's progressive municipal policy clearly demonstrates that city-centre housing can be rehabilitated without removing people and destroying working-class neighbourhoods, and that the historic integrity of the environment can be maintained and used for the benefit of the community as a whole. While the case of Bologna demonstrates that the housing question must be confronted first at the political level, the success of the city's Communist administration hangs less on the doctrine of Marxist socialism than on competent administration, local public involvement and pragmatic fiscal management (Fried, 1971).

4.7.2 Venice: a city struggling to survive

No account of Italian urban problems would be complete without reference to the sinking of Venice, for many the most magical city in Europe. The problems of Venice are probably beyond the capabilities of one nation to

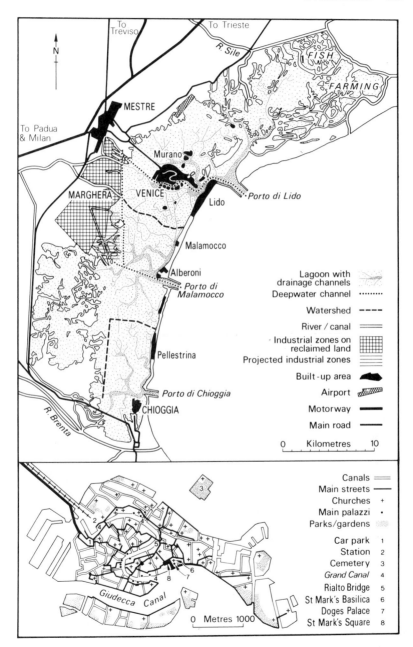

Figure 4.2 Venice and its setting.

solve, so the city is fortunate in that its uniqueness can command the concern of the world. Venice thus illustrates a fundamental question: how much is Western society prepared to sacrifice to preserve the glories of its past?

Founded in the fifth century as an island refuge of Roman culture amid the collapse of the Empire, Venice became a republic in the ninth century and for 500 years was the most powerful state in Europe. Later it became immortalized in the mid-eighteenth-century paintings of Canaletto. Although Cosgrove (1982) has argued that there is much that is mythical about the symbolic landscape of Venice — particularly the utopian appeal to nineteenth-century romantics of its 'perfect union' of politics, society, place and water — there is no doubt that the city is one of the very great historical and architectural treasures of the world. Its urban landscape presents a remarkable visual harmony, in spite of the lack of uniform planning or of a dominating architectural style; the well-known Doge's Palace and the Piazza San Marco defy stylistic classification.

Figure 4.2 shows the geographical setting of the island city in its lagoon. The original builders of Venice set ground level only a few centimetres above the highest tide marks. Most buildings were built on foundations of wooden piles driven into the mud — 6000 to support the Rapallo Bridge alone. From the earliest days the Venetians were preoccupied by the extent to which the wellbeing of the lagoon depended on avoiding the build-up of silt at the river mouths. They eventually diverted all silt-bearing rivers away from the perimeter of the lagoon. Meanwhile the seaward defences, narrow strips of land framing the lagoon, were strengthened from the fourteenth century on, culminating in the great sea-walls of the eighteenth century, completed only 15 years before Napoleon took the city in 1789.

The city plan is one of bridged islets (Figure 4.2). Each islet forms a community with its own patron saint, church, central square, palace and noble family. The most splendid buildings are to be found facing Piazza San Marco and along the Canale Grande, but there are dozens of other palaces and churches as well as the mass of proletarian housing that fills in the townscape.

The problem of Venice is really twofold: the physical problem of decay, inundation and pollution, and the human problem of population loss and an uncertain social future. The human problem is partly related to the physical problem, although demographic loss has been a common phenomenon in Italian *centri storici* since 1945. Although in most people's minds the physical problem is the more dramatic, this can be (and is being) solved, given the appropriate technology and financial backing. The social issue, less well known, is more intractable.

Physically the city is suffering the effects of four separate phenomena: the sinking of the ground, the rise of sea level independent of this sinking, the pollution of the lagoon and atmospheric pollution. A few simple facts bring some of these phenomena to life. Sea level has risen 33 cm over the past century. In 1908 a tide of 1.1 m above normal flooded one-tenth of Venice; in 1961 a tide of the same height flooded 36 per cent of the city. The homes of 10 000 people living at ground level are flooded regularly. Such regular inundation by polluted salt water is not only damaging structurally, it is also psychologically harmful, inducing a feeling of hopelessness about the city's future and leading to outmigration, particularly of younger people (Pacione, 1974b).

The worst flooding disaster, that of November 1966, resulted from an unfortunate coincidence of a rapid Alpine thaw, heavy rain, high tides and southeasterly gales. The city was flooded to a depth of nearly 2 metres. Although a disaster of such magnitude has not been repeated, minor flooding has become more regular and high tides retain their peaks for longer.

The Venetians themselves have played a major role in creating the problems with which they are now confronted. The sea defences have been neglected and are in poor condition. The massive postwar growth of industries (about 200 concerns) on the mainland at Marghera has caused both atmospheric and lagoonal pollution, while extraction of water and methane gas from beneath the soil has been a major factor causing the sinking. Modifications of the lagoon's physiography by land reclamation for industry and the airport, by the creation of large diked fish farms and by the dredging of deep channels to allow ships access to the industries (especially oil tankers to feed the Porto Marghera petrochemicals plant) have altered the hydrological balance, impairing the gentle natural tidal scour which flushes out the lagoon through its three entrances (Figure 4.2). The wash created by increased, and faster, boat traffic attacks the stonework of the city, causing extensive erosion of water-level coursing. When the water flows over the Istrian stone and marble of the building foundations it is sucked by capillary action into the brick walls to a height of about 3 metres. Such repeated wetting causes the stucco to flake off and the brickwork to rot. Further damage is done by the harmful chemicals emanating from industries on the landward side of the lagoon.

After the 1966 floods and subsequent UNESCO reports, private organizations from a variety of nations raised more than £3 million. Most of this has been earmarked for the repair of specific buildings and works of art, especially important churches. Under the aegis of the Venice in Peril fund, individual countries are made responsible for specific renovation projects. While this is an encouraging illustration of the worldwide concern over the plight of Venice, such a system of international aid results in only piecemeal restoration with no attention to the root causes of the problem.

In 1973, after many years of discussion, the Italian government passed the Law for Venice which released £200 million for saving the city. Together with other monies from the United Nations, this was to be used for building an aqueduct to supply the industries of Marghera, new sewage systems, flood prevention schemes, research into tidal surges and above all for restoring the damage to the city. A ban on artesian water extraction has almost solved the sinking problem, reducing the rate from 6 mm to 1 mm per year. But continued dithering meant that most of the 1973 allocation was never spent. The Venice town council was made up of a plethora of political parties unable to agree on an effective policy and on which of the many schemes proposed (subterranean repressurization, sluice gates, caissons, etc.) the money was to be spent. A further source of conflict was the Communists' insistence that, following the Bologna model, priority be given to reclaiming housing for low-income families.

It was not until the 1980s that real progress was made. In 1982 the Italian government gave the final approval for construction of a system of caissons across the lagoon entrances. By late 1984 the funding for this — £258 million — had passed through the country's Senate, and a 'Venezia Nuova' consortium of 27 of Italy's biggest engineering and contracting firms is lined up to carry out the work. The steel caissons will be built across the three inlets and will function in a similar way to the recently completed Thames Barrage. Each barrier will consist of a string of hollow cylinders which will normally rest in rubberized cradles on the lagoon bed. With advance warning of a tidal surge, never less than 6 hours, the cylinders can be pumped full of air so that, within 1 hour, they hinge up to form a barrier. It is estimated that they will need to be erect for only 34 hours per year on average, so their interruption of shipping and of the normal interchange of water between the lagoon and the sea (important for flushing out Venice's sewage) will be minimal.

With the exception of effective pollution control, the technical problem of saving the destruction of Venice is thus close to solution. Greater uncertainty, however, surrounds the city's future as a social entity. The preservation of historic Venice just for scholars and dilettantes, with only a dwindling number of ordinary Venetians to give life and purpose to the city, would be a partial victory. Indeed it has been suggested that to check the influx of the sea without stopping the outflow of the population would be to save Venice from the fate of Atlantis while condemning her to the destiny of Disneyland (O'Riordan, 1975).

Population drift from the island city to the mainland has been going on since the sixteenth century. Between 1951 and 1981 the population of the island halved from 167 000 to 83 000. The Venetian commune's *terra firma* districts of Mestre and Marghera now contain 250 000 people, most of whom have settled in the postwar period, drawn in from old Venice and from rural Veneto by the prospect of industrial jobs and modern housing.

Building restoration has continued to focus on major monuments rather than ordinary housing although one scheme, the Campo Ruga, a poor area originally inhabited by shipyard workers, has made progress. Generally, however, a shrinking, ageing population is unwilling to renovate big, decaying houses, or is unable to pay the higher rents demanded after renovation has taken place. Any attempt to reduce the outflow of native islanders and tempt back some of those who have already left is highly dependent on control of house prices and rents; otherwise the city will pass increasingly into the hands of rich outsiders searching for a personal piece of Venice's history along the more fashionable streets and canals. With Milan only $1\frac{1}{2}$ hours away by motorway and with Switzerland, Austria and southern Germany all fairly close, an increasing trend is for second-home ownership by non-Venetians. Certain footloose activities, such as cultural, business and educational organizations, are also being drawn to Venice by the advantages of life in a historic city without the curse of the automobile.

Moves to more intensively exploit the tourist industry are limited by the destructive nature of tourism itself. Venice's mayor, Mario Rigo, has described the tourists as locusts who descend on the city for a few hours in an indiscriminate invasion, showing no real love or appreciation for the city. Of course it is true that tourism provides a good deal of employment and income for the residual population, supporting the renting of rooms, the provision of services such as restaurants and hotels, and the commercialization of artisan industry such as the Murano glassmakers, but wholesale reliance on tourism also turns the city into a museum to be opened up at Easter and locked up in October.

FIVE

Agriculture and the Transformation of the Rural World

5.1 Introduction

Italy's contemporary self-image as a predominantly urban country under-plays the importance of the rural environment. Italian agriculture's rich and venerable history confers a certain nobility on rural life, with the yeoman farmer considered as the ideal citizen and patriot, but this is small compensation for agriculture's progressive loss of rank compared to other economic sectors. This loss of rank is the outcome of continuous failure in the struggle to compete for factors of production — land, labour, entrepreneurship — which are captured mainly by industry and the tertiary sector. Italy's partial catching-up of other European countries in the fields of industry and services has been achieved by plundering the resources of agriculture, depriving it of its youngest, most able workers, usurping much good land close to urban markets, and appropriating many of the most plentiful sources of water. At the same time rural Italy has had to give up the regulations protecting most of its staple crops against the competition of its European Community partners and is exposed, practically without defence, to the damages of pollution caused by industry and towns. Small wonder that agriculture is held to be a victim rather than a beneficiary of Italian economic development (Lacci, 1973).

Over the 50 years from 1931 to 1981 agriculture has gone from employing more than one-half of the Italian working population to employing just over one-tenth. The most rapid rate of loss of agricultural employment was during 1951–71: from 42.2 to 17.6 per cent, or from 8.3 million to 3.2 million workers (Table 5.1). This provides spectacular evidence for the evolution not only of agriculture but of the whole of Italian society. The exodus from agriculture took place with an intensity unknown in most other European countries. This was because the industrialization and urbanization processes were much more rapid than elsewhere: late to start, they had much ground to make up.

In 1930 when about 9.4 million people were engaged in agriculture there were 4.2 million farm holdings. In 1961 when the number of farmers and

Table 5.1   Evolution of agriculture, 1930–82

	1931	1951	1961	1971	1981
Persons employed in agriculture (000s)	9422	8261	5693	3243	2239
% total working population in agriculture	51.7	42.2	29.1	17.2	11.2
	1930		**1961**	**1970**	**1982**
No. of agricultural holdings (000s)	4196		4294	3607	3284
Area of agricultural land (000s ha)	26 252		26 572	25 064	23 579
Average holding size (ha)	6.3		6.2	6.9	7.2

Sources: ISTAT: *Censimento Generale della Popolazione, 1931, 1951, 1961, 1971, 1981.*
ISTAT: *Censimento dell' Agricoltura, 1930, 1961, 1970, 1982.*

farmworkers had dropped to 5.7 million, there were still 4.3 million farms. By 1982, the most recent agricultural census, the number of agricultural workers had slumped to 2.2 million but the number of farms had only shrunk to 3.3 million. The reduction in land under agricultural use, meanwhile, has been even more slight: 26.3 million ha to 23.6 million ha (Table 5.1). This lack of match between the drop in agricultural employment and the restructuring of the land was due to two main factors: an increasing number of holdings employing only one person — made possible by the greater availability of farm machinery — and the increasing dominance of part-time farming.

5.2 Evolution of the agrarian landscape

Of all European and Mediterranean countries, Italy's rural landscape is the most humanized: the product of three millennia of agricultural settlement and development. Neolithic towns and villages studied in the Apulian Tavoliere indicate well-developed settled agriculture but the archaeological evidence on crop types and farming systems is as yet thin (Delano Smith, 1979). The Greek agricultural colonization of southern Italy was seen as the systematic development of a classical land of promise. The Greeks established a triad of land use which has held remarkable permanence: olives on thin soils and rocky slopes, vineyards on pediments rich in subsurface water, cereals on the plains where winter rains made possible a seasonal use of otherwise parched land. The modern view from the Greek temples at Agrigento in Sicily exemplifies the durability of this pattern perfectly. Roman colonization was also basically agricultural — land conquered by the sword but subjected to the plough. In the modern agrarian scene, centuriated field patterns, areas of specialized crops and varied breeds of livestock are all traceable to the Roman heritage.

Barley and wheat were the predominant cereal crops of Greece and Rome respectively. For more than 2000 years the wheatlands of Sicily, the Tavoliere and the Sardinian Campidano have produced regular surpluses of high-quality grains, especially hard (durum) wheat (Delano Smith, 1979). The Greeks also introduced the vine and the olive, characteristic tree crops of Italian agriculture down through the ages. Roman olive farming reached its zenith in the second century BC and the olive groves of Lucca have maintained a reputation for fine oil ever since. Rome was the first civilization to mass-produce vineyards, vintages becoming differentiated as the vine spread southwards along with the establishment of Roman villas. It is significant that modern Italian wine specialities are not very different from those of the classical locations. Other tree crops introduced by the Romans were the fig, apple, cherry and lemon. In central Italy the Romans perfected the interculture of grain and tree crops — the *coltura promiscua* so characteristic of modern Italian farmscapes.

The Arabs, who colonized Sicily and restricted parts of the mainland South from the ninth to the eleventh centuries, introduced further agrarian elements, notably terracing, irrigation technology and a range of new crops including the mulberry, apricot, carob, cotton, alfalfa, rice and probably the sweet orange. Some of these species later became regionally specialized, such as mulberries in the North Italian Plain and oranges in Sicily.

Although an ancient practice, irrigation has been a potent force shaping Italian agriculture's increasing productivity. Irrigation serves three main purposes: it lengthens the growing season, improves yields and extends the range of crops that can be grown. Some of the north Italian city-republics fostered irrigation in the twelfth and thirteenth centuries in response to the growing demand for food by a rapidly increasing urban population. Religious orders, such as the Benedictine houses in the twelfth century and later the Cistercians in Lombardy, developed an extensive system of irrigation channels fed by the rivers and springs of the upper plain. These spread water over the low-lying meadows, increasing the quality and frequency of the hay yield and allowing cattle to be fed on green crops virtually throughout the year. By the fifteenth century rice was being widely planted as an alternative cereal on land which was irrigated and periodically flooded. Vast hydraulic works were completed in the decades following unification. The Cavour Canal, built in 1866 to irrigate 150 000 ha in the western Po Plain, initiated the policy of direct state control. Other notable late nineteenth-century schemes were the Alto Veronese and Agro Veronese canals, deriving their water from the Adige to irrigate 366 000 ha. In the twentieth century most spectacular progress has been made in the eastern Po Plain where plans to irrigate 500 000 ha are near completion, and in the South where a target of 360 000 ha has been set. Despite this widening distribution, irrigation is still concentrated in the Po Valley, whose great river system provides 70 per cent of all the water used for irrigation in Italy.

Reclamation of marshland has also played an important role in the evolution of the agrarian landscape. Between the sixteenth century and the early twentieth century reclamation work — *bonifica* — was almost entirely concentrated in the Po Plain. A notable exception was the Val di Chiana in Tuscany, whose early stages of reclamation were planned by no less a person than Leonardo da Vinci. In the period 1861–1915 330 000 ha of the North Italian Plain were drained compared to only 2000 ha of reclamation achieved in the South. From the Tuscan Maremma southwards, coastal plains had been deserted since the collapse of Rome; ill-drained and malarial, they were little used except for the grazing of sheep and water buffaloes. Early *bonifica* legislation, such as the key Baccarini Law of 1882, suffered from three major defects: excessive concern with isolated technical problems of lowland areas rather than with the integrated needs of drainage basins, mountains and plains; the neglect of the social dimension of the rural economy; and neglect of the South where soil erosion and malaria (2 million sufferers between 1887 and 1920) were rampant (Houston, 1964).

Fascist legislation attempted to remedy some of these problems. The notion of reclamation was widened to include mountain streams, irrigation, settlement and malaria eradication — *bonifica integrale*. Progress in the 1930s was rapid, prompted by unemployment and political considerations. Many ambitious schemes were started such as the Maccarese in the Roman Campagna, the Sele Plain near Salerno and the Fertilia and Arborea schemes in Sardinia. By far the most prestigious of Mussolini's reclamation projects was the Agro Pontino (Pontino Marshes) which converted, regardless of cost, 75 000 ha of marshes and dunes into a model agricultural colony of 3000 farms, mostly tenanted by Venetian war veterans (Gentilcore, 1970). Still, however, the problem remained of concentrating on the more spectacular schemes of lowland drainage while neglecting proper watershed management and erosion control. Few of the interwar land reclamation and settlement schemes were complete by 1939 but their initiation made postwar projects easier and they provided a model for the settlement planning associated with the 1950 land reforms. These reforms, considered in more detail later in this chapter, provide the final phase in the evolution of the Italian agrarian landscape, their distinctive regimented rows of newly built farmhouses a unique addition to the country's rural scene.

5.3 Rural land use and agricultural production

For the student interested in the geography of Italian agriculture, a useful starting-point is a look at the beautiful land-use maps published by the Touring Club Italiano between 1956 and 1968. Although the maps are rather dated now, and although, at a scale of 1:200 000 (1 cm to 2 km), the fine detail of small terrace plots and *coltura promiscua* cannot be recorded, they nevertheless provide a striking visual testimony to the fascinating regional specialisms of Italian farming: examples are the bright pink of the tree-farming of the Apulian littoral, the splash of yellow for the wheatlands of central Sicily, or the dominant pale blue of pastoral Sardinia.

The 90 per cent of Italian territory occupied by agriculture or forest can be divided into four broad categories of rural land use: arable or sown land, comprising a variety of field crops from cereals to market gardening; tree or orchard crops including vines; pasture land; and forest (Cole, 1968). To a certain extent these categories overlap. Tree crops such as olives and other fruit trees can either be grown on specialized plots or they can be mixed with field crops or pasture; such trees may serve as field boundaries or be grown in rows among the arable or meadow. Ecologically the two-tier cropping system of *coltura promiscua* fits in well with the Mediterranean climate; the field crops, mainly autumn sown, depend on the moisture in the topsoil provided by the winter rains, while the tree crops can survive the summer drought on water stored in the subsoil. As well as cereals and vegetables, field crops can include plants grown solely for animal fodder such as lucerne and grasses; sometimes sown land is therefore pastured but normally livestock in such areas is stall fed. Although there are some areas of rich permanent meadow in the North Italian Plain, most permanent pasture is poor-quality unimproved grazing on hillsides where cultivation is not possible or worth while. The fourth category, forest, embracing 6.35 million ha, is a flattering term for what is often degraded scrub and maquis, commercially very poor. Areas of good-quality timber are to be found mainly in the Alps, though chestnut forests are widespread in the northern Apennines and the Calabrian Sila. The North Italian Plain, Apulia and the southern half of Sicily are practically devoid of woodland.

Just over one-third of the agricultural and forest area is under field crops. Areas where the arable proportion of rural land use is well above average include the whole of the Po Plain, the Adriatic coastal belt between Rimini and the Gargano, and central and southern Sicily. Tree crops (3 million ha) comprise 11 per cent of the agricultural and forest area; Apulia is the outstanding region for specialized tree crops on account of its concentration on both vines and olives, but other areas of note are Asti Province in the North (vines), western Sicily (vines), and southeastern Sicily (vines, olives and almonds). The most important expanses of natural pasture are to be found in the Alps, Sardinia and the high Apennines.

5.3.1 Field crops

Of the total sown area about 40 per cent is under fodder crops, 36 per cent is under wheat, 10 per cent under maize and the rest under a range of relatively minor crops — in order of area occupied, barley, sugar beet, beans, oats, rice, potatoes and tomatoes. Area is only a crude guide, however, for some of these crops (sugar beet, potatoes and tomatoes) yield heavily and are quite important in production terms.

If fodder crops are excluded, cereals are the main branch of arable farming in Italy. Wheat is grown on two-thirds of the cereal area but accounts for only about one-half the weight of grain harvested. The wheat area reached its maximum extent, 5.1 million ha, in the late 1930s under Mussolini's 'Battle for Wheat' campaign. Over the postwar period the area has steadily diminished to around 3.3 million ha by the early 1980s. Yields remained low — below 15 quintals (q) per ha — until well into the postwar period. Since the 1960s they have risen appreciably to their current level of 27 q/ha, partly as a result of a withdrawal of wheat from low-yielding marginal areas. Nevertheless current yields are lower than those in all central and northern European countries, but higher than those of Italy's Mediterranean neighbours — Greece, Spain and Portugal. Yields of wheat, and most cereals, are two to three times higher in the North Italian Plain than in the South.

As Figure 5.1 shows, wheat is grown widely in Italy, being unimportant only in the three regions (Val d'Aosta, Liguria and Trentino) with an almost total lack of level or gently sloping land. Although not immediately obvious from the map, Italy's main wheat belt extends down the Adriatic regions of Italy, reappearing in central Sicily; generally it corresponds to rolling hill country of medium fertility. Two main types of wheat are grown. Soft wheat, formerly predominant but since 1980 occupying less than half the total wheat area, is grown throughout the country and is destined for bread, pizza, biscuit and cake making. Hard or durum wheat, the basis for pasta products like spaghetti and lasagne, is grown almost entirely in the southern half of the country.

Maize occupies just over one-quarter of the area of wheat although its mean yield, around 60 q/ha, is over twice as high. Imported American hybrid varieties, grown mainly in the North, are much more high yielding than the so-called 'native' stock, *nostrano*, now grown only in the South. Grain maize is used both for human consumption, especially to make polenta, a favourite dish of the Veneto, and as animal feed. The main region

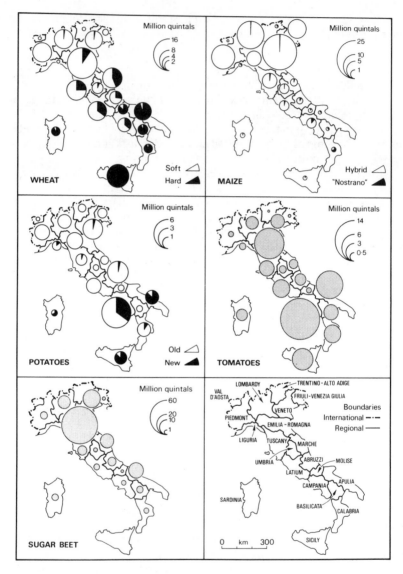

Figure 5.1 Regional pattern of production of major field crops (annual average 1980–83).

of maize production is the northern Po Plain, increasing in importance, along with precipitation, eastwards into Veneto and Friuli where it accounts for one-third of the arable land. It is also grown in the more humid parts of the Centre and South, notably Tuscany, Umbria and Campania, but is largely absent from the far South and islands (Figure 5.1). Other cereal crops are of more localized importance. Rice is highly concentrated in the Lomellina, a low-lying district of the northern plain bordered by the Po, Adda and Dora Baltea rivers. Oats are mainly grown in the drier, less inviting parts of the peninsula, while barley is confined to mountain areas in Trentino, the Apennines and Sardinia.

The remaining field crops can be grouped under four headings: vegetables, salad crops, industrial crops and flowers. All of these occupy much smaller areas than the cereals but they are of higher value per unit area, require a more intensive labour input and are therefore often associated with areas of dense rural population. Of the vegetables, beans are a basic item of the rural diet in many parts of the country. Both broad beans, a traditional peasant staple, and green beans are grown widely in the peninsula. Potatoes are also grown in all regions (Figure 5.1), although both area and production have declined rather sharply over the past 20 years. Campania, Apulia and Sicily have an interest in exporting early varieties; within Italy potatoes are not such a fundamental item in the diet as they are in central and northern Europe. Vegetables such as cauliflowers, carrots and onions and salad crops such as lettuces and peppers are common in market gardens outside major towns and cities; again the possibilities of early season cropping, often under glass or plastic sheeting, are increasingly being exploited by farmers in the southern regions. An important crop for both domestic use and export (usually canned) is tomatoes, a speciality of Emilia–Romagna and the Naples area (Figure 5.1). Between the early 1950s and the early 1980s the area of tomato cultivation has increased by 50 per cent and production has quadrupled. The most important industrial crop is sugar beet, half of which is grown in the Emilia–Romagna part of the recently reclaimed Po delta. Hemp is also grown in the lower Po Valley, tobacco is a speciality of Lecce Province in Apulia and the plain of Battipaglia near Salerno, and a little cotton is grown in southern Sicily. The growing of flowers is a distinctive feature of Imperia Province, hard by the French border.

5.3.2 Tree crops

The specialized cultivation of tree crops occupies nearly 3 million ha in Italy, of which vines and olives account for about 40 per cent and 35 per cent respectively. All tree crops are also grown alongside field crops in *coltura promiscua*; indeed the mulberry is cultivated almost entirely in this way. Vines and olives are increasing slowly in specialized culture, but decreasing in mixed cultivation as peasant-farmed hill land goes out of production. Nevertheless the production of wine and olive oil has respectively doubled and trebled over the postwar period, although olive oil output is subject to wide fluctuations according to weather conditions. Italy produces more wine than any other country in the world, and only Spain produces more olive oil.

Figure 5.2 shows that an appreciable quantity of wine is produced in all of Italy's 20 *regioni*. Although it grows well on deep-soiled lowlands, the vine in Italy is essentially a hill crop, often grown on terraced slopes where field crops cannot easily be cultivated. Each district aims at being self-sufficient in wine, though the quality of such local produce is often poor — a much higher degree of cooperation is necessary among growers to standardize the product and market it effectively, including exporting in the face of French, German and Spanish competition. In spite of the vine's ubiquitous cultivation, there are, nevertheless, 'wine deficit' regions such as Lombardy, and 'wine surplus' regions such as Apulia and Sicily. The heavier wines come mainly from the South. Apulia sends most of its wine for blending or for making vermouth. The dark, sweet Marsala wine from western Sicily has been exported by English traders since the late eighteenth century. The lighter wines, such as the sparkling Asti Spumante from the Monferrato Hills near Turin and the well-known products of Veneto (Bardolino, Soave, Valpolicella), tend to be northern. In spite of having the well-known Chianti district, Tuscany is not one of the major regions for specialized viticulture; its vines are grown mainly as part of *coltura promiscua*, although there are a few large vine estates (Flower, 1978).

Table grapes are an increasingly important submarket of viticulture. In Apulia over one-third, and in Abruzzo nearly one-half, of grapes picked are reserved for eating; but in other regions the proportion is very small. Sicily is the only region to have an interest in the production of dried vine fruits.

After wheat and vines, the olive tree is the third traditional source of rural sustenance in Italy south of the Po Plain. In the words of a Sicilian proverb, 'a life spent digging is worth nothing if you plant no olive trees' (Maxwell, 1959). The peasant family's jar of oil is like their life-blood, an essential element in cooking, dressing and flavouring. Planting olive trees is a long-term investment for they take 8–10 years to bear fruit and their yields are erratic. Some orchards are centuries old, the ancient trees developing characteristic twisted, gnarled profiles. In fact, the olive is the classic Mediterranean tree crop, perfectly adapted to the climate of the region, the long summer drought being necessary to build up the oil content of the fruit. Like the vine, the olive is primarily a hill crop and is especially

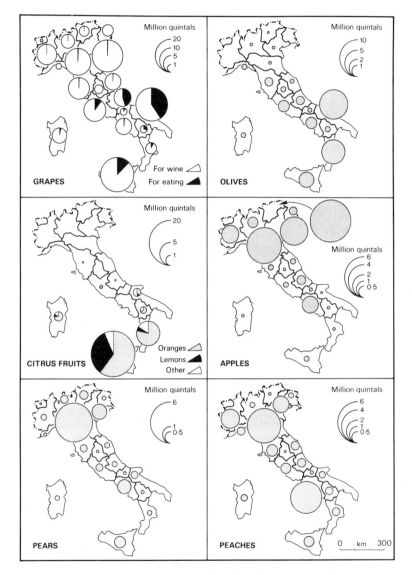

Figure 5.2 Regional pattern of production of major tree crops (annual average 1980–83).

widespread in the rocky limestone areas of Apulia and Sicily and among the steep slopes of Calabria. It is, however, much more sensitive than the vine to late and severe frosts which can be lethal. With few exceptions, such as the sheltered microclimates of the Italian lakes and the Ligurian Riviera, olives are only grown south of Tuscany and Marche. Apulia is the largest producer (Figure 5.2), accounting for 45 per cent of production, followed by Calabria, Sicily, Campania, Latium, Abruzzi and Tuscany.

Citrus fruits are an important southern crop, their distribution controlled by their sensitivity to frosts. They are highly valued because a small area can produce a high cash return and absorb a lot of labour. Over the period 1950–83 the specialized citrus area has grown steadily from 69 000 ha to 170 000 ha, while production has leapt from 9 million to 35 million quintals. Sicily accounts for 60 per cent of all citrus fruit production in Italy, Calabria and Campania for most of the rest (Figure 5.2). Within these regions cultivation is confined to certain sheltered lowlands where soils are good and irrigation water plentiful. A distinction can be drawn between traditional areas of spring and well-fed irrigation, such as the Sorrento Peninsula, the Gioia Tauro Plain in Calabria, the Conca d'Oro behind Palermo and the lower slopes of Etna, where terrace plots and farm holdings are small, and newer areas of recent large-scale irrigation (the Metapontino coastal strip southwest of Taranto, the Plain of Catania, the Campidano) where plantations are newer, larger and more rationally laid out. Lemons predominate in traditional areas in Sicily and Calabria, mandarins in newer plantations in Apulia. Oranges, somewhat less vulnerable to frost, are more widely distributed and are grown at higher elevations. On Etna, for instance, oranges form a distinct belt above the coastal strip of lemons; above the oranges come vines and then finally deciduous fruits like pears and cherries (Clapperton, 1972). In spite of being named after the northern town of Bergamo, the cultivation of bergamots, a citrus variety grown just for its perfume, is confined to the southern tip of Calabria.

Deciduous fruits have a wide distribution in Italy, although two regions are the main producers: Emilia–Romagna produces most peaches, pears and plums, while Campania leads in cherries, apricots and nectarines. In apple production Emilia–Romagna is just pipped by Trentino (Figure 5.2). Nut production occurs mainly in Campania (hazelnuts) and Sicily and Apulia (almonds). Figs are grown widely in gardens and hedgerows. The carob, a tree more characteristic of the eastern Mediterranean, is grown for animal fodder in Sicily and Apulia while the mulberry, whose leaves are used for raising silkworms, is a familiar tree along the field boundaries of the Po Plain.

5.3.3 Livestock

While the numbers of cattle and sheep have remained stable over the past 30 years, the numbers of goats and equines (horses, donkeys, asses, mules) have declined and the number of pigs has more than doubled. The greater size and value of cattle (equivalent to roughly six head of sheep, goats or pigs) means that the 9.2 million cattle are roughly three times as important to the rural economy as the 19.5 million head of smaller animals; this should be borne in mind when interpreting the distribution maps in Figure 5.3.

Cattle are concentrated in the North, dominating the livestock side of farming in both the Alps and the North Italian Plain. Milk and meat production based on maize, forage crops and intensive hay cultivation are well developed on the large and medium farms of Piedmont, Lombardy and western Emilia. These farms are technically of a high standard and processing and marketing are well organized, mostly through a sound cooperative structure. Dutch breeds are preferred by the larger producers, but Alpine and Swiss breeds are also represented. Liquid milk has a ready market in the northern industrial towns and in Rome, but two-thirds of the output is processed for butter and cheese. The butter is entirely for domestic consumption but some cheeses, such as Gorgonzola, Parmesan and Bel Paese, are exported. Dairying is a much more isolated activity in the Centre and South where cattle (chiefly Tuscan and Marche breeds) are also regarded as work animals. Italy also has around 50 000 buffalo, pastured on marshy coastal areas in Tuscany and Campania; their rich milk goes to make *mozzarella* cheese.

Pig distribution, like that of cattle, is primarily northern, with particular concentration in Lombardy and Emilia–Romagna, whose sausages and hams have a high reputation. Pigs are also reared throughout the country for home and local market consumption. The keeping of the family pig, ritually slaughtered at Easter, is a peasant tradition still widespread in country districts.

Sheep, on the other hand, are much more numerous in the South (Figure 5.3), the island of Sardinia containing one-third of the Italian total. Traditional practices and patterns of transhumance are fast disappearing (Patella, 1978). In Sardinia the distinctive hard *pecorino* cheese is made from sheep's milk. Wool is destined largely for mattresses and felts; the large-scale wool textile industries of Tuscany and the North rely on higher-grade imported fibres. In general lamb is available only at Easter when the surplus young animals from the lambing season are sold off. Goats and equines are not shown in Figure 5.3 but their distribution is markedly southern, reflecting their link to a residual peasant mode of farming and, in the case of

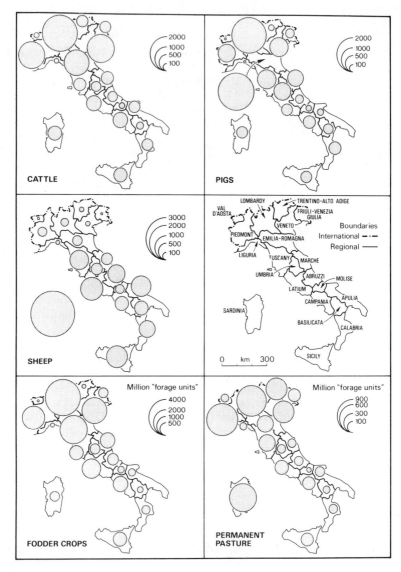

Figure 5.3 Regional distribution of livestock (1981) and of forage (annual average 1980–83).

goats, over half of which are found in Sardinia, Calabria and Basilicata, to a poor pastoral environment.

The distribution of livestock is related to two main sources of fodder: field crops such as maize, lucerne and rotation grasses, and permanent natural pastures. The main area for arable fodder is the North Italian Plain, whereas permanent pasture dominates the cattle-farming area of the Alps and the sheep- and goat-grazing regions of the peninsula and Sardinia (Figure 5.3).

The livestock sector is the main problem area of the Italian agricultural economy. Rising living standards and changing dietary habits have created a growing demand for animal products to which Italian livestock farming has been unable to respond (Venino, 1976). In 1951 total domestic meat production stood at 7.9 million quintals, roughly equal to domestic consumption. By 1973 production had risen to 23 million quintals but consumption had climbed to 34 million quintals. A similar pattern was evident in milk: the 1951 output of 66 million quintals of dairy produce covered internal demand, but not so the 1973 production of 93 million quintals, for consumption had risen to 114 million quintals. Per capita consumption of beef and veal rose from 7 kg in 1951 to 26 kg in 1973, of poultry meat from 2.5 kg to 17 kg. Such deficits have had to be met by imports of meat and dairy produce on such a scale as to severely embarrass the balance of payments. Indeed Italy has become the world's foremost importer of fresh meat and live cattle. Since 1973 the pace of demand growth has slackened, while production has continued to rise slowly; the trade gap remains wide, however.

5.3.4 Mechanization

Only recently has Italian agriculture become at all mechanized, and even then only in certain areas. Over large parts of the country the widespread use of machinery is precluded either because of the physical limitations of steep slopes and tiny, fragmented plots, or because of the nature of the agricultural enterprise — tree crops and peasant mixed farming being unsuited to the use of big machines. Elsewhere, on the other hand, the use of machinery has been encouraged by the diminishing availability and increased cost of labour due to the agricultural exodus.

ISTAT data on farm machinery show that the number of tractors increased from 57 000 in 1950 to 250 000 in 1960, 630 000 in 1970 and 1 million in 1980. A small and only slowly increasing proportion of these are to be found in the South: 13 per cent in 1950, 15 per cent in 1960, 17 per cent in 1970, 20 per cent in 1980. But the signs are that this proportion will increase rather more sharply in the future, for Barbero (1972) has argued, on the basis of the low degree of usage of tractor capacity, that mechaniza-tion in the North has been pushed too far. Furthermore, tractors are made available to a large number of farms in the South through contract arrange-ments; in a region where small farms predominate this is probably a more efficient use of such machinery than if all farmers had their own machines. Much more widespread in the South are various two-wheeled hand-operated machines like rotavators which are more suited to cultivating the land on small plots or on fields where mixed forms of cropping prevail (e.g. working the land between rows of vines or citrus trees). If, therefore, the use of fuel for agricultural machinery is taken as the criterion of farm mechanization, southern regions like Apulia and Campania compare favourably with most northern regions because of their widespread use of such appropriate small-scale technology.

5.4 Land tenure: the farmer's straightjacket

From the physical and economic aspects of farming we pass to the social ones. Interposed between the farmers and the land they work are the legal constraints of land tenure, some of which survive from Italy's colonial and feudal past. The mediaeval structure of lord, vassal and serf survives today as the hierarchy of landowner, tenant and labourer. Land tenure is still of central importance to any analysis of Italian farming and rural social change since most country dwellers still maintain some contact with the land, even if they are no longer principally employed in the agricultural sector (King and Took, 1983).

5.4.1 Evolution of land tenure and rural classes

Whereas both commercial estates and stable, peasant-farmed property (owned or rented) have long been established in the North, in the peninsula and the South the situation is rather different. Sharecropping — called *mezzadria* after the practice of dividing all farm produce into half shares for the landowner and share-tenant — is, or rather was, a form of tenure practised throughout central Italy. Tuscany was its core area, from which it spread to other central regions, mainly Emilia, Umbria, Marche and northern Abruzzi. Its inception dates back more than 800 years and it was applied on a relatively large scale throughout the newly established com-munes of the late Middle Ages as a means of breaking up the feudal system into family-sized units (Peruzzi, 1965).

In the South the feudal estates or latifundia survived longer. In the Maremma, the Apulian lowlands, the Calabrian Marchesato and central Sicily, vast landholdings survived into the early postwar period; and with them persisted many quasi-feudal forms of behaviour and social relations, including an overwhelming sense of deference to the landowners. Mostly, however, the dissolution of feudalism in the South in the eighteenth century transferred the ownership of the land not, as in France, into the hands of the peasants, but into those of the rural middle class (Rossi-Doria, 1958). The peasants were left disinherited, disillusioned and desperately poor.

A mammoth 15-volume inquiry into land tenure and land ownership carried out by the Istituto Nazionale di Economia Agraria during 1946–47 (for an excellent English summary see Medici, 1952) revealed in minute detail the skewed ownership of agricultural land and the variety of oppressive tenure contracts operating in different parts of the country in the early postwar period. On a national scale 0.2 per cent of the landowners (those with more than 100 ha) monopolized 26.4 per cent of the agricultural land, while at the other end of the spectrum 93 per cent of the smallest landowners (those with less than 5 ha) shared just 30 per cent of the land. Many agriculturalists were, of course, totally landless; the South contained 2 million day-labourer families whose livelihood was precarious in the extreme. At the local level of individual communes, hundreds of villages were discovered where virtually all the worthwhile farmland was in the hands of a single noble family, on whom the village population was, therefore, totally dependent. In the Sardinian village of Urzulei, for example, two large landholdings accounted for 97.6 per cent of the commune's agricultural area, the remaining 311 ha being divided among 387 properties, an average of only 0.8 ha each.

The polarity of landownership defined the polarity in rural social status. Moss and Cappannari's (1962) study of a Molisan village provides a representative case study whose results can be generalized over hundreds of similar communities in the South and in Sicily just prior to their transformation by postwar emigration and development policy. At the top of the social pyramid were a small number of landed gentry. These were the *signori* (lords), the *baroni* (barons), the *galantuomini* (gentlemen), the *persone benestanti* (well-to-do people), defined by their noble birth and tradition of landownership. Visible manifestations of their status were their large *palazzi*, their dress, their mannerisms and style of living. Since 1950 the landed aristocracy has declined in power, but relict noble families still exist in many rural communities, clinging to a way of life more eighteenth than twentieth century in character. The second stratum, roughly one-tenth of the population (but tending to increase over the past 30 years), was the *borghesia* class made up of professionals (doctors, lawyers, teachers, administrators) and small businessmen (merchants, shopkeepers, artisans, truckowners, etc.), many of whom reinforced their local prestige by owning some land. Next came the *contadini*, the peasants who either owned, rented or sharecropped land and who therefore possessed *some* rural status. In Moss and Cappannari's village they made up one-third of the population. Finally, at the bottom of the pile, and constituting over half the population, were the landless — the *braccianti* (day-labourers), the shepherds and the charcoal burners — many of whom suffered a further reduction in their status by living outside the village, and therefore outside the recognized social system, in huts or in barracks attached to the *masserie* (the country headquarters of the old latifundia). Where they were linked to an extensive monoculture of wheat, unemployment for much of the year was unavoidable for the *braccianti* (Dickinson, 1955a). Each morning they would assemble at dawn in the local piazza in the hope that they might be hired for the day. Those taken on were paid a few hundred lire for a day's hard toil under the broiling sun. In winter, if it rained when they got to the fields, they were sent home without any pay.

Nor was this picture of a highly stratified society constrained by tenure boundaries found only in the South. Silverman (1970) has characterized the *mezzadria* tenure of central Italy as no more than a legalized system of rural exploitation. The landlords constituted the upper stratum in the class organization of the countryside, the *mezzadri* tenants the lower, with the village artisans forming a small middle stratum. Landlords and tenants were the cores of the two major classes and the *mezzadria* share relationship was the key point of class interaction. As well as providing all the labour and half the working capital — contributions fixed by the *mezzadria* contract — the tenant family frequently had extra obligations to the landlord such as food offerings, supply of firewood, doing the laundry and cleaning his stables. The traditional *mezzadria* was thus a pervasive patron–client relationship in which the peasant gave all his economic obligations, and more, as well as his loyalty and deference for the landlord's reputation and honour.

Rural social conditions in northern Italy were certainly less exploitative, a fact not unconnected with the better tenurial status of the peasantry, a history of peasant solidarity and organization (especially in Emilia–Romagna) and the existence of many large and medium-sized commercial farms. Even here, however, conditions varied from one district to another. The Alpine zone has long been a region of peasant holdings combined with communal ownership of the high pastures. In Lombardy efficient and intensive commercial farming provided more than 200 days of work per farm worker per year — the best in the country. By contrast the Emilia–Romagnan and Venetian sections of the Po Plain contained a great concentration of agricultural unemployment, much of it resulting from immigrations of labour for land reclamation work in the late nineteenth century. A narrow range of crops — mainly sugar beet and maize with few tree crops or livestock — provoked marked seasonal unemployment with an average of only 120 days of work per year (Dickinson, 1955a).

5.4.2 Land reform

It was against this background of rural unemployment, landlessness and an oppressive social structure that the 1950 land reform was passed. But the political context is also vital if the significance of the reform measures is to be properly evaluated. In the years following the collapse of the Fascist state many promises of land reform were made but frustration set in as Parliament spent its time in lengthy debate over bills that merely purported to effect reform. Many parts of rural Italy, especially in the South, went through a period of workers' agitation, occupation of the land by the landless, and repression by the police and by field guards employed by the big landowners to protect their estates. The Communist Party tried to organize this rural protest and turn it into an effective political and even revolutionary movement. Peasant protest was most desperate in the Calabrian Marchesato which contained Italy's greatest inequality of land ownership; seven or eight big landowners controlled the lives of 200 000 persons living in an area of about 2500 sq km (Arlacchi, 1983). In a lunar landscape of denuded clay hills the landless labourers — almost all the population — lived in squalid villages in conditions of appalling poverty and wretchedness. It was in one such village that the trigger for the land reform was sprung. A group of peasants marching on an estate were blocked by the police who fired on the crowd, killing three persons and wounding many more. The outcry was nationwide and it was clear that a quick solution had to be found to defuse the situation. The Christian Democrat government rushed through a law to break up the Calabrian estates (the *Legge Sila*); later in the same year (1950) the *Legge Stralcio* extended the reform to certain other parts of the country, while a separate law was passed in Sicily.

In all, the eight land reform districts, each administratively distinct, covered 28 per cent of the national territory. Six of the districts and more than 80 per cent of the land involved were in the South; the land reform was thus primarily a southern policy (Figure 5.4), designed to operate in the areas where latifundia were most widespread. Of the two non-southern districts, the Maremma, stretching between Pisa and Rome, was in fact rather 'southern' in character with a mixture of latifundia and *mezzadria* estates, while the Po delta, due partly to its recent reclamation, contained a large concentration of militant landless labourers.

Land was expropriated according to a complex formula based on area of landholding, taxable income and intensity of cultivation. The aim was to expropriate most land from large uncultivated or inefficiently operated

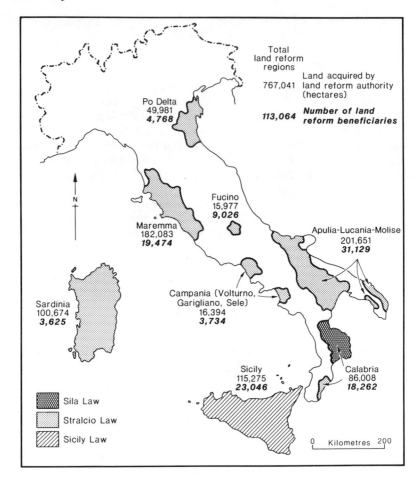

Figure 5.4   Land reform regions.

latifundia; intensively cultivated 'model farms' could be spared. Expropriated landowners could retain one-third of their land for their own use; for the rest they were paid compensation based on their own tax returns (thus those who had undervalued their land for tax evasion purposes got lower compensation). Altogether the eight land reform agencies acquired 767 000 ha (including some state land), 681 000 ha of which were eventually assigned to 113 000 beneficiary families. Assignments took two forms:

complete farms (5–20 ha each, depending on land quality and population pressure) for beneficiaries with no land; and 'quota plots' of 1–4 ha for those who already owned a bit of land. The beneficiaries paid for their land in up to 30 annual instalments. They were also obliged to become members of new agricultural cooperatives set up in reform districts. The Ministry of Agriculture, supported by the Cassa per il Mezzogiorno in the southern reform districts, was charged with the responsibility for providing all the necessary physical and social infrastructure for the previously underused land. This involved a vast programme of land transformation — destoning, deep ploughing, irrigation, building of farmhouses and service villages, supply of water, electricity, etc., as well as provision of technical assistance and training.

Although the land reform, by parcelling out the estates and by land improvement works, allowed much more labour to be absorbed on the land than under the latifundian regime, in most areas there was nowhere near enough land to satisfy all the landless. Applications for land greatly exceeded the number of plots available. This further strengthened the network of patron–client relationships, creating ritual ties between peasants and aspiring beneficiaries on the one hand and local political leaders and reform agency bureaucrats on the other. Since the reform was a DC policy, it certainly favoured peasants belonging to that party, as well as strengthening the government's electoral base in rural areas, stemming the Communists' advance (King, 1973b).

The land reform's most remarkable effect was to transform the empty landscape of the old feudal estates into a dense network of self-sufficient small farms whose rectangular boundaries and regimented rows of pastel-painted homesteads drew heavily on Fascist models of land settlement of an earlier generation. Such paternalistic planning was not devoid of mistakes, however. As early as 1956 a parliamentary report acknowledged several difficulties: farms set up on holdings that were too small to be economically viable; the purchase for the reform of land of the worst quality, rocky, muddy, and far from villages and roads; the failure to exclude many unsuitable assignees; the insufficient size of houses and stables; and the failure to ensure that land reclamation proceeded in step with land redistribution (Milone, 1957).

Economic data on the reform do nevertheless show impressive gains in some areas. As tree crops matured and livestock enterprises became established throughout the 1950s, per hectare incomes grew by upwards of 7 per cent per year, significantly higher than the national rate of increase. An econometric evaluation of the irrigated reform holdings of the Metapontino demonstrated that they had a high productive potential when planted with citrus and other tree crops (Dean and De Benedictis, 1964). A visit to this area today shows that this potential has largely been realized: this is Italy's 'little California'. Citrus fruits, peaches, table grapes, strawberries, salad crops and flowers provide formerly poor peasants with decent incomes, and the original reform cottages have been greatly extended and modernized. Positive productive effects have also been achieved on the Volturno, Garigliano and Sele riverine plains in Campania, in the Po delta and in the irrigated parts of Sardinia.

But there are other areas where the land reform has been less successful. In dry farming districts of the Maremma, the Marchesato and the Apulian Tavoliere a regime of wheat, vines and mixed livestock farming barely suffices to support a family. Accordingly there has been much abandonment, emigration and amalgamation of holdings into more viable units. In Sicily the reform has been little short of a fiasco — sabotaged by the Mafia and rejected by the peasant 'beneficiaries'. In this region landowners were allowed to divide up their estates among family members to avoid expropriation, while the meagre amount of land redistributed was of such poor quality and so remote that most of the new farmhouses have never been lived in; they are now empty shells scattered about the island in forlorn little clusters (Blok, 1966).

While the land reform was fairly successful (Sicily excepted) in reducing the power of the landed elite and in elevating the status of a section of the *bracciante* and small peasant classes, it has not really succeeded in creating a new rural social structure or mode of life. Socially the reform is more notable for what it destroyed than for what it created. The reform's dispersed settlement pattern broke up established village communities and made social interaction difficult, especially for females tied to the farmhouse. The paternalism of reform agency personnel discouraged peasant independence. Beneficiaries had their old feudal ties cut, but these were replaced by rigid obligations to the reform's administrators (Franklin, 1961). On the demographic side, the tightly planned fixed network of uniform small farms provided no flexibility for fluctuating family sizes or population growth, so that off-farm migration has had to take place in all but the most favoured areas, turning the reform holdings into part-time enterprises.

It must also be stressed that the land reform has not been a general reform; it was applied only to areas where large estates were dominant and where land concentration was marked in 1950. Political necessity dictated that the landless labourer class should be the main beneficiaries of the reform, while Christian Democrat ideology determined that these landless workers should be transformed into small owner-farmers. Even within the reform districts, the small and medium *borghesia*, who still draw part of their income parasitically from the renting out of land, have been left untouched. Such landowners, large in number and close to the values and institutions of Italian society, were electorally too important to be expropriated. The vast majority of Italian peasants oppressed by their tenurial position, including those living in the *mezzadria* regions of Emilia, Marche, Umbria and eastern Tuscany, those living in the upland districts of the South and those working in the zones of intensive farming along the Tyrrhenian coast and along the Bari littoral, have been unaffected by the land reform.

5.4.3 Recent trends in land tenure and land ownership

Recent changes in agrarian structure have to be evaluated within the framework of definitions of tenure and farming types adopted by ISTAT, the primary source of statistical data on such changes. Four main tenure types are recognized:

1. *Family farms*, whereby the farmer is effectively his own boss and farms, together with other members of his family, the land he either owns or rents.
2. *Commercial or 'capitalistic' holdings* operated by wage labour on which the owner performs only managerial duties, not manual labour.
3. *Mezzadria* estates on which the tenants have small to medium-sized holdings on stable tenancies, together with a farmhouse provided for them.
4. *Other types of tenure*, comprising insecure tenancies and sharecropping arrangements.

The brunt of agrarian structural change has been borne by the decline of categories (3) and (4) (Table 5.2). The *mezzadria* sector was losing an average of 20 000 families per year during the 1960s and has now all but disappeared except in the Marche where the sharecropping tradition still survives. Its shrinkage has been hastened by a series of early postwar legislative measures which shifted the original 50:50 share progressively in favour of the tenant and by a 1978 law which forbade the signing of any new *mezzadria* contracts. The fourth category, never very important except in a few southern regions, has declined equally quickly. With commercial holdings retaining their relative importance over the period 1961–77, the *mezzadria*'s decline has been mainly compensated by the increase in the importance of family farms, especially in terms of area.

The above description of changing tenure patterns is only partly satisfactory, for two reasons. First, the family farm sector, which in 1977 accounted for nine-tenths of holdings and nearly two-thirds of land, is so dominant that it obliterates many real variations in the character of farming. Second,

Table 5.2 ' Land tenure, 1961–77

Tenure types		1961	1970	1977	% data 1961	% data 1970	% data 1977
Family farms	No.	3 485 968	3 119 299	2 359 334	81.2	86.5	89.6
	Area (ha)	13 218 337	14 370 712	14 284 564	49.7	57.3	64.0
Commercial holdings	No.	330 060	287 325	184 665	7.7	8.0	7.0
	Area (ha)	9 158 660	8 991 879	7 082 351	34.5	35.9	31.8
Mezzadria farms	No.	316 549	130 393	71 293	7.4	3.6	2.7
	Area (ha)	3 125 536	1 259 023	757 797	12.1	5.0	3.4
Other types	No.	161 347	70 245	18 780	3.7	1.9	0.7
	Area (ha)	1 069 132	442 604	185 401	4.0	1.8	0.8
Total	No.	4 293 924	3 607 262	2 634 072	100.0	100.0	100.0
	Area (ha)	26 571 665	25 064 218	22 310 113	100.0	100.0	100.0

Sources: ISTAT: *Censimento Generale dell' Agricoltura, 1961, 1970*.
ISTAT: *Annuario Statistico Italiano, 1981*.
Note: 1977 data are from a sample survey.

the distinction between categories (1) and (2), the 'family' and the 'capitalistic' farms, is very blurred. For instance, many of the so-called capitalistic estates (defined on the criterion of being operated by wage-labourers) are former peasant smallholdings in hilly and mountainous areas which have been abandoned by their peasant owners and are now operated desultorily with part-time hired labour. Barberis (1971) estimates that these probably account for most of the 264 000 farms of less than 50 ha operated with wage labour recorded in the 1970 agricultural census. Such holdings are hardly 'commercial' or 'capitalistic'. On the other hand, the category of family farms masks an increasing heterogeneity of economic types ranging from smallholdings on which all the labour requirement is provided by the farmer and members of his immediate family to larger economic units, including many over 50 ha, on which the majority of labour is hired — these enterprises are not classified as commercial holdings because the farmer still provides *some* of the manual labour requirements of the holding. As the predominant family farm sector becomes increasingly modernized and commercialized, a larger proportion of the farm units will inevitably fall into this ambiguous 'family-commercial' bracket.

The main structural problem of Italian farming is undoubtedly the continued dominance of small farms. Three-quarters of Italian farms had less than 5 ha according to the 1970 agricultural census. A study of the Upper Agri Valley in Basilicata revealed that nearly 80 per cent of the farming units were less than 1 ha in size (Lane, 1980). The national mean farm size, 7.2 ha, has increased only slightly since 1930 when it was 6.3 ha. Small farms of less than 10 ha, or even less than 5 ha, may be viable if they concentrate on intensive, specialized crops such as flowers, citrus fruits or market gardening; but the undercapitalized mixed smallholding has no real economic future in a country of Italy's general level of development. This type of farming only survives because of the advanced age of most farmers and their sentimental reluctance to part with inherited land.

Small as they are, Italian farms are often composed of several separate parcels of land. This fragmentation hinders their efficient running because of the difficulties of organizing production in many scattered locations and of travelling back and forth. The 1961 agricultural census, which contained detailed tabulations of farm fragmentation, recorded a mean of four plots per holding, but over 300 000 farms consisted of 10 parcels or more. These data show the extraordinary degree to which fragmentation of land has been carried in Italy. Yet, although the problem has been recognized for at least 50 years, no effective methods to control it have been devised, except laws limiting subdivision of farms in areas of reclamation and land reform.

5.5 The Common Agricultural Policy and Italian agriculture

As noted in Chapter 2, Italy joined the Common Market with high hopes. As far as agriculture was concerned, it was assumed that: competition with the more efficient agricultures of partner countries would speed up modernization in Italy's farm sector; continued exodus of labour from agriculture would permit substantial structural adjustments leading to a pattern of farm sizes more similar to those existing in other member countries; increase in labour productivity engendered by technical progress and structural change would elevate agricultural incomes to approximate those of other economic sectors; and there would be considerable possibilities for expanding the production and export of Mediterranean crops to cancel out imports of cereals and livestock (De Benedictis, 1981).

Twenty years after the first market and price regulations for farm products were put into practice, it is clear that not only were these expectations overly optimistic, but in many respects Community policies have actually made matters worse by initiating or accelerating trends in the opposite direction to that anticipated. By supporting mainly north European agricultural products like cereals, meat and dairy produce, the price and market mechanisms of the Common Agricultural Policy (CAP) worked against the interests of Italian farmers whose Mediterranean crops, with the exception of durum wheat and olive oil, received no guaranteed price support. Thus, poor farming districts in central and southern Italy have become profoundly disadvantaged, receiving in some cases only one-fifth of the CAP aid showered on privileged areas of already rich farming in the Low Countries, France and West Germany. An EC commissioned report (Cesaretti *et al.*, 1980) on the impact of the CAP on Italy showed, on the basis of several indicators, that most Italian regions deteriorated in terms of their relative position vis-à-vis the Community average over the period 1965–77. While most southern Italian regions had agricultural incomes of around 40 per cent of the EC average in 1965, by 1977 Molise had slumped to 27 per cent and Basilicata to 33 per cent. Regional disparities in agricultural performance also widened within Italy. Taking the criterion of agricultural value-added per worker (Italy = 100), the range increased from 53 (Basilicata): 172 (Lombardy) in 1965, to 42 (Molise): 189 (Lombardy) in 1977.

During the 1970s, following the Mansholt memorandum of 1969, the CAP devoted more attention to structural measures. Two 1972 directives aimed to reduce the EC's farm labour force by giving incentives to young farmers to retrain for other jobs and to elderly farmers to retire. Also in 1972, funds were allocated for the modernization of farms on condition that an approved farm development plan was completed within six years and provided that the aid recipient was a full-time farmer. Later, regionally specific measures were introduced: in 1975 the hill-farming subsidy for farmers in environmentally difficult upland areas; and in 1978 the 'Mediterranean package' which included the development of farm advisory services and irrigation in the Italian Mezzogiorno.

In spite of the greater relevance of these structural measures and of their greater regional sensitivity, Italian agriculture has continued to miss out. Various reasons account for this (Podbielski, 1981). First, these 'guidance' measures have amounted to only about 5 per cent of total CAP expenditure and, although Italy has obtained 30 per cent of these allocations since 1973, the absolute amount is still too small to make much impact. Second, some of the measures continued to favour the better-off farmers and failed to respond to the special conditions of backward and difficult farming environments. For instance, it has proved well-nigh impossible for a small and poor farm operating in the hill districts of the Italian South to work out a realistic programme for farm improvement within six years, while the criterion of full-time farming for obtaining modernization aid does not fit an area where part-time farming is a significant and even necessary component of the agricultural scene. Third, Italian delegates in Brussels have failed to make a sufficiently forceful and coherent case for Italian farming: the contrast with the French attitude is striking. On the home front, procedures for getting access to CAP funds are slow and cumbersome because of a multiplicity of decision-making and fund-allocating agencies at national, regional and local level. Product payments and special aids for farmers have often taken years to come through, while evidence exists pointing to widespread corruption in the allocation of funds for the olive and tomato sectors.

The enlargement of the EC to include three more Mediterranean countries with farm production patterns and structures very similar to those of Italy will exert more competitive pressure on Italian agriculture. It is also doubtful, once the transition periods for Greece, Spain and Portugal are over, whether the present support level of some Mediterranean products will remain compatible with the availability of Community financial resources. Recent conflicts in Brussels over the finance of the CAP allow little room for hoping that the CAP can be reformed to Italy's advantage.

5.6 The changing social context of rural life: peasants no more?

A generation ago Italy was basically a peasant country. Over the past 30 years outmigration, economic development and the penetration of modern communications into the countryside have changed the character of rural life. There has, in fact, been much debate as to whether these changes have transformed the Italian countryside to such an extent that the modern rural milieu represents a 'clean break' with the past, or whether the changes have merely occurred within pre-existing social and agrarian systems, elaborating and modifying but not radically altering or destroying them. The title of Joseph Lopreato's (1967) book *Peasants No More* is highly indicative of the former view. According to Lopreato the peasants of southern Italy, even 20 years ago, were no longer peasants in the old sense of being subject to abject poverty, servility and hopelessness. Emigration enabled them to break their bonds, and several years later they were able to return financially better off and with greater social prestige. But Lopreato's is a highly particular view and is countered by plenty of evidence documenting the survival of peasant farming not only into the 1960s but even into the 1980s. Cosmetically modernized but not fundamentally changed by the Green Plans and later policies, peasant farming remains as a contracting but nevertheless important structural component of Italian agriculture. However, rather than regarding the peasant sector as a kind of residual sector which has somehow failed to catch up with the modern, capitalistic sector, the persistence of precapitalistic productive and social relationships in most parts of rural Italy can be interpreted as an essential functioning part of the country's capitalistic development, both agricultural and industrial. Mottura and Pugliese (1980) suggest that the poor peasant farmer and rural labourer classes have been preserved as a scattered pre-proletarian 'industrial reserve army': a source of cheap labour to feed industrial expansion and a residual cushion — they use the term 'sponge sector' — to soak up industrial unemployment at times of industrial recession, as over the past decade.

5.6.1 Part-time farming

Although part-time farming is often thought of as a marginal or transitional feature of agriculture, there is plenty of evidence in Italy to suggest that it is not only a permanent, structural feature of rural life but also increasing steadily in importance. It is, moreover, a highly complex and diverse phenomenon, exhibiting different characteristics and performing different functions in different parts of the country.

Part of the reason for underappreciating the role of part-time farming in Italy is its statistical elusiveness. According to the 1970 agricultural census one-third of farm operators, or 1.2 million persons, are part-time farmers — defined as having their principal economic activity (in terms of labour commitment) away from their farms. Two-thirds of these part-time farmers work in non-agricultural jobs, one-third on the land of other farmers. This, however, takes no account of farmers who perform off-farm work which takes up fewer days per year than their farm labour. The same census indicates that 60 per cent of peasant farms absorb less than one person's labour per year. If we take into account the average characteristics of the rural family unit, namely its large size and its cohesion, it is clear that part-time farming must be very widespread. Recent estimates by the Istituto Nazionale di Sociologia Rurale suggest that it could involve about three-quarters of all farm holdings and that it increased strongly during the 1970s (Pieroni, 1982).

It is also a mistake to regard part-time farming as inversely correlated to agricultural prosperity. In fact the highest incidences of part-time farming encompass provinces that are poles apart in this respect: Varese and Como on the highly industrialized northern fringe of the Po Plain, and Potenza in the poverty-stricken southern Apennines. Clearly the nature of off-farm employment for part-timers reflects the characteristics of the local economy and labour market (Mottura, 1980). In the North Italian Plain and in the lower Alpine valleys the 'second job' might be a secure job in a factory. In the highlands of the South, if supplementary work is to be found at all, it is likely to consist of precarious and unskilled employment, probably in a variety of short-term and irregular labouring jobs. In the northern Apennines of Emilia and Marche, where part-time farming has been intensively studied, other possibilities exist. Here the sharecropping tradition has long involved the supplementary development of artisan activities. Recently these have matured into small industrial concerns and there has also been a strong development of outwork circles for farm-based females working in the knitwear sector. From rural areas within commuting distance of the Adriatic Riviera tourism draws many younger family members down to find work on the coast; much of this work is seasonal and can be easily integrated with part-time work on the family farm.

Contrary to the popular image of part-time farming as a residual, inefficient form of agriculture (which it certainly is in some areas, particularly in the South), research in the Marche has shown it to be rational and efficient when viewed within the overall context of the region's economy (Cavazzani, 1976). Not surprisingly, part-time farms are smaller and carry more people per unit area than full-time farms. Part-time farms also tend to concentrate more on subsistence production and less on livestock. However, they contain more machines (partly to accommodate the reduced availability of labour) and more investment capital. Part-time farmers with holdings of at least 10 ha tend to be younger, better educated, more innovative and more disposed to joining cooperatives than their full-time counterparts.

5.6.2 Rural exodus

Like part-time farming, the drift from the land can only be fully understood within the context of the evolution of the entire Italian economy. It is not just an agricultural phenomenon but needs to be related to the postwar industrialization of Italy and the availability of work opportunities in other countries. Thus rural depopulation started much earlier in the North, where urbanization and industrialization also commenced earlier, than in the Centre and the South. Detailed studies of mountain depopulation in the Alps were made as early as the 1930s (Toniolo, 1937), but from Emilia and Tuscany southwards the rural haemorrhage only became a major and consistent phenomenon in the 1950s, continuing for about 20 years until the 1970s. Exceptions were those areas where land reform, land reclamation and irrigation allowed an increase in the density of the farming population.

The character and strength of the exodus reflected first government policy towards agriculture but later changes taking place in other sectors of the economy (Mottura, 1980). Thus, in the period between 1951 and 1958, when government agricultural spending was geared mainly to sustaining the farm unit by land reform and the financing of large-scale reclamation and irrigation projects, the drop in agricultural employment — 19.2 per cent — did not fundamentally alter the overall structure of farming. The peasant remained the predominant figure, and the rural exodus reflected more a rise in temporary off-farm employment (in building or forestry work for instance) than a complete withdrawal from agriculture. During the 'miracle' years (1958–63), by contrast, the drift from the countryside reached its peak (27.9 per cent loss of agricultural employment) and was due above all else to the rising demand for industrial manpower in the North. The workers who were sucked, this time permanently, out of agriculture, were those with the most unstable employment, the lowest incomes and the most onerous tenure contracts, mainly *braccianti* and sharecroppers. From the end of the miracle to 1974 the significance of the rural exodus changed once more. During this period the 'attraction effect' of the availability of industrial and service sector jobs was joined by a growing 'repulsion effect' that stemmed from changes in the agricultural sector and in rural society. Rising standards of education led people automatically away from farming, while the agricultural sector itself underwent a process of restructuring, including rapid mechanization; thus the resulting expulsion of manpower went ahead independently of the falling demand for labour in Italian industry. Finally, in the 10 years since 1975, the most conspicuous phenomenon has been the gradual slackening of the rural exodus, to a point where the trend has actually been reversed. In common with many other rural regions of Western Europe, a process of rural repopulation has been set in train which is beginning to rectify some of the demographic losses of the past.

It needs to be stressed that agricultural exodus and rural exodus are not the same thing. Even during the height of the flight from farming the former was more than four times as great as the latter: the exodus has been much more vocational than territorial (Barberis, 1968). Nor has the massive exodus from agriculture (6 million people left farming between 1951 and 1981) produced corresponding adjustments in farm structure. Labour mobility has not been accompanied by land mobility. In many cases this is because transfer out of agriculture involved only some members of the farm family; but even when entire families have left, the land is often retained as a precaution against future unemployment, as a hedge against inflation or just through plain sentimentality.

Demographically the rural exodus removed up to 40 per cent of the population of many rural districts during 1951–71. The selectivity of the outmigration has led to the progressive ageing of the residual rural population, at least up to 1971, and to a consequent decline in rural fertility rates. Especially in upland districts where outmigration has been most intense, farming has passed almost entirely into the hands of elderly peasants and females. Many farming households now consist of a solitary middle-aged or elderly couple whose offspring have migrated elsewhere. Such household units are clearly incapable of reproducing themselves on the land. According to the 1970 agricultural census only 14.5 per cent of farm administrators are under 40 years of age, compared to 36.1 per cent who are over 61. Elderly farmers are particularly concentrated in mountain areas; younger farmers are more common in lowland areas and on part-time holdings.

The sociological impact on the communities left behind has been interpreted in various ways. Initially it appeared that the rural exodus functioned as a demographic and political safety valve, removing the innovators and the political activists, preserving social and political stability (Moss and Cappannari, 1962). At a later date, when migrants' urban and industrial experiences in the North and abroad were fed back to the rural areas, the old rigid structures of privilege and inherited wealth began to break down. New attitudes and behaviours have taken root, even among those who have never been away. For instance, the young village woman no longer wishes to marry a farmer and live in her village of origin; her ambition is to marry a man who will take her away to live in the city and perhaps enable her to work in a factory or office (Alberoni, 1970). Ultimately, then, outmigration initiates a process of social decomposition in which the old community structures crumble away.

Economically, outmigration turns the residual rural society into a subsidized community heavily dependent on remittances, pensions and social welfare. An ageing population requires increasing amounts of medical help, pensions and other forms of welfare. Remittances from abroad contribute at least 10 per cent of the value-added in many rural areas; to this must be added internal migrants' remittance transfers which are not recorded. In a region like central Sicily, studied in detail by Reyneri (1980), the decline of the only economic activities producing saleable goods — agriculture and handicrafts — transforms the local economy from one of production to one of consumption, sustained only by various kinds of external subsidy. The subsidization of the rural South is further discussed in Chapter 6.

5.6.3 Rural rejuvenation

Over the past 10 years or so, demographic and migratory trends in rural Italy have changed. Golini (1983) interprets the slackening and the reversal of the rural exodus in terms of the changing interaction between the economic system and the attitudes and values of individuals. The changing character and location of industrial production appear to be having a significant role in the reversal of the relationship between the rural exodus and urbanization. Changing production technologies and strategies for utilizing labour are contributing to a decentralization of industrial processing into small firms, many of which are located in rural areas. Maximum decentralization occurs in certain branches of the clothing and footwear industries where 'cottage industry', carried out in rural homes, produces articles requiring much labour and little technology. At the individual level, for those able to make and act on a choice, there is clearly in train a rejection of urban life. The reasons for opting for a rural rather than an urban existence are difficult to quantify and possibly even to express, but they probably include all or some of the following: a reaction against the noisy and oppressive urban environment; the quest for private space and an environment closer to nature; the rejection of dwellings that are standardized and tightly packed; the desire for better interpersonal relationships; and the fear of urban crime and social unrest.

Rural repopulation reflects different circumstances in different parts of the country. In the North village growth is common around, but separate from, the major metropolises, and in tourist areas of the Alps. In the Northeast and Centre the processes of productive decentralization and diffuse industrialization are leading to rapid rural population growth in regions like Friuli, Emilia and Marche. In the South rural population revival is more a function of the decline in emigration combined with a continuing high rate of natural increase. However, net outmigration continues, albeit at a reduced level, from interior upland districts of the South and islands.

Most of the rural inmigrants are not going back to farming; instead they contribute to the progressive industrialization and tertiarization of the rural economy. Improved services in the countryside (better roads, buses, sewers, power, etc.) and increased levels of car ownership mean that an 'urban' lifestyle can now be enjoyed in rural areas. Nevertheless rural repopulation is not unrelated to the changing composition of the agricultural labour force. Some rural immigrants take up part-time farming or buy land to rent out or use themselves for hobby farming. Thus there was a slight increase in the number of independent farm workers during the 1970s made up of a marked rise in part-timers and a slight fall in full-time independent farmers (Mottura, 1980).

While these rural demographic trends provide an obvious counterpoint to the declining metropolitan growth described in Chapter 4, it is perhaps too early yet to speak of a complete counterurbanization process, for the national aggregate of 6000 communes with less than 5000 inhabitants continued to lose population between 1971 and 1981. The most rapid population growth is in fact taking place in communes with between 10 000 and 100 000 inhabitants which represent the large village–medium-sized town stratum (Golini, 1983).

5.6.4 Return migration

Another demographic factor of relevance to the changing social and economic structure of rural areas is return migration from abroad. Most of Italy's vast numbers of foreign emigrants have originated from rural areas and it is to their home villages that nearly all intend to return. Their potential impact on rural social processes and economic life is thus considerable.

A first point to note is that, although return migration has only recently been recognized as a possible instrument of economic policy, it is not a new process in rural Italy. Historical studies (e.g. Caroli, 1970) speak of the return of overseas emigrants from North and South America as early as the turn of the century and of the powerful social impact of these rich *Americani* in villages of the South. Thus an ideology of emigration and of return migrant behaviour has been established for several decades. The ideology is one of leaving poor and returning rich; of building a fine new house; and of beneficent but often ostentatious behaviour — donating money to the church and other 'worthy' local institutions, being generous and generally acting as if one has 'seen the world'.

Over the past 20–25 years returns from West European countries have been the most important — from West Germany, Switzerland, France, Belgium and the United Kingdom, in descending order of importance. These intra-European migrants have inherited some of the return ideology

of the earlier *Americani* but they also have their own distinguishing characteristics. Generally they have been abroad for shorter periods of time and
they are younger when they return. The majority are thus economically
active, unlike the predominantly semi-retired *Americani*. On their return,
their impact is very much a function of the economic structure of the region
in which they settle. In the northern region of Friuli–Venezia Giulia
returnees since 1970 have been very fortunate in returning to an economy
which is booming; the vast majority quickly found work in the construction
sector and in small and medium-sized enterprises in various craft and
industrial trades (Saraceno, 1986). The situation is very different in the
more backward areas of the South where shortage of work opportunities
makes life very difficult for returnees. Returned migrants have generally
not been successful in getting jobs in the new industries of the Mezzogiorno,
in spite of their industrial experience abroad and their desire to work in this
kind of job (Vigorelli, 1969). Many returnees are forced back into agriculture as their only safeguard against unemployment and sinking back into
the poverty that originally led them to migrate. Others decide to establish
small service sector enterprises like shops, bars, hairdressers or taxi
businesses. In stagnant rural areas such services are now in oversupply so
that many must become marginal and eventually fail.

Regional government policies to encourage returning migrants to invest
their often considerable accumulated capital in enterprises which would
have a more lasting beneficial effect on the local economy — such as
intensifying agriculture or setting up small industrial firms — have been
dismal failures. It appears that migrants are unwilling to risk their savings in
such ventures and are mistrustful of official help. They are also unwilling to
cooperate with their fellows, for instance in forming agricultural cooperatives or limited companies, partly because the migrants' ideology is an
individualistic one of personal sacrifice and individual success and achievement (Signorelli, 1980). The idea of the returning emigrant as an agent of
rural economic development is thus largely a myth.

Returning migrants from abroad also suffer some difficulties of social
reintegration, none more so than the migrant children born and educated
abroad who are unable to adapt to the cultural, linguistic and employment
situations of a village and a country of which they have had little first-hand
knowledge or experience. After growing up in Dusseldorf, London or Lille,
adaptation to life in a remote southern hill village can be very painful.

5.6.5 *The changing character of rural areas*

In the past most country dwellers were peasants of one kind or another, and
most of those who were not were connected in some way with farming as

merchants, artisans making agricultural tools, millers, land agents, etc. The rural population of today is more and more divorced from life in the fields. It comprises urban office and factory workers for whom the advantages of lower housing costs and the cohesion of the family are sufficient for them to continue living on the family farm, and intellectuals and executives who prefer to live in a pleasant rural environment now that life in Italy's large towns has become so crowded and noisy. Various phenomena — migration and return, productive decentralization into rural areas, expanding commuting hinterlands, improved communications — have reduced the significance of the rural–urban dichotomy by encouraging interpenetration between the urban and rural worlds. Now, more than two-thirds of country dwellers are not employed in land-related jobs as Italy moves progressively towards a non-agricultural rural society.

Around major cities commuting has become increasingly important over the past 20 years as people have been willing to live further and further from their work. Milan sucks daily workers in from a wide section of the western Po basin while in the Alpine valleys west of Turin daily travel has now replaced the permanent residential shifts of earlier decades. Roman commuters have almost completely colonized the countryside of central Latium, especially the scenically attractive hill districts inland.

The increasing impact of tourism and leisure on Italian rural areas is another recent change. The effects of tourism have been clear for some time in areas of celebrated beauty and in towns of major cultural and historical interest. Now the phenomenon is spreading so that areas which have experienced heavy outmigration in the past are now retaining their populations, and even attracting new inmigrants. Two main types of area are involved; both are developing primarily under the impetus of domestic tourism and the leisure boom linked to increased affluence, personal mobility through increased car ownership and the desire for second homes in a different environment from that of the primary residence. First, there is the attraction of coastal districts with access to the sea. Hitherto undeveloped rural coastal areas are attracting population and settlement in a fever of mostly uncontrolled and unplanned building speculation, which is unfortunately ruining formerly attractive sections of coastline. Second, a significant growth has occurred in tourist zones in the mountains. Skiing regions are found mainly in the Alps but are also scattered in more restricted locations elsewhere, for instance the Abruzzian Gran Sasso, the Calabrian Sila and Aspromonte massifs and the upper slopes of Mount Etna where 'weekends on the snow' have become fashionable among the better-off sections of the population. 'Snow tourism' is but one aspect of the positive valuation of the mountains, however. In summer, highland areas above about 700 metres are much appreciated by lowland town dwellers for their fresh air and cooler temperatures. Attractive upland landscapes, such as those of Tuscany and Umbria, have been greatly affected by the second-home phenomenon whereby old farmhouses and village dwellings are renovated by rich outsiders. In some rural districts one-third of the building stock may now be in the hands of non-locals. Such an invasion has mixed blessings for the local rural populace: it provides some work in the construction and renovation trades and provides some support to local shops and services, but it drives up property prices and causes a certain alienation.

Even in rural areas which remain remote and peripheral, untouched by tourism or any form of industrial development, important social changes are taking place. The existence of mass culture, the modern consumer economy and Italian bureaucracy have affected all parts of the countryside, however physically isolated they may be. Television, which knows no barriers of relief or distance, has been the main diffusion agent of mass popular culture. Remittances, welfare payments and hire purchase arrangements are the mechanisms by which a consumer economy can be underwritten in such economically stagnant areas. At the same time, an expanding bureaucracy responsible for administering welfare and local social and economic policy becomes an increasingly dominant constituent of local society, in many ways replacing the former landed elite and *borghesia* as controllers and allocators of resources (Weingrod and Morin, 1971). The villages and small towns of Italy now contain significant numbers of bureaucrats — personnel connected with trade unions, agricultural cooperatives, banks, irrigation consortia, development agencies and welfare offices. They are the new 'patrons' and the new 'brokers'. Many of the bureaucratic organizations have party affiliations — especially the unions and the cooperatives — so that the countryside is becoming not only bureaucratized but also politicized.

SIX

Regionalism, Regionalization and Regional Development

6.1 Introduction

Regional variation has been a constantly recurring theme in all the previous chapters of this book. There are regional contrasts in industrial and agricultural patterns just as there are in urban development and style of political activity. The recency of nationhood and the frequent insensitivity of central government to regional issues have meant that regional identities have remained strong. The process which transformed Italy from a stagnant to a dynamic industrial power evolved differently in time and space. Prior to unification the South, then the Kingdom of the Two Sicilies, held its own, with Naples the largest urban and industrial centre in the peninsula. In the post-unification era, however, nascent industrial modernization concentrated mainly in the North: a spatial trend fostered both by 'natural' location factors and early government policy. The South was left behind. As a result the problem of the Mezzogiorno has been a constant negative feature of Italian economic development throughout the past 125 years, and especially since 1945. Economic dualism, to use a term first widely used in the Italian context by Vera Lutz (1962), is woven into the fabric of Italian economic life. On the surface it reflects the contrast between the progressive regions of the North with their technologically advanced industrial giants like Fiat and Pirelli, and the backwardness of a South still characterized by tiny workshop industries and peasant farming. But really the dichotomy runs deeper, both historically and structurally. Some elements of the North–South schism were laid down in the period prior to unification; in the Middle Ages, for instance, the splendid epoch of the city-republics in the North and Centre was an era of feudalistic colonialism for the South. Since unification the lesson has been clear: if classical economists in their optimism used to trust that automatic market mechanisms would eradicate the imbalances between developed and underdeveloped areas, the Italian economic history of the past 100 years has shown that imbalances become, over time, aggravated rather than cured if left to *laisser faire*.

6.2 Frameworks for regional analysis

North versus South is only one, albeit the most fundamental, of a number of possible divisions of the Italian territory (Figure 6.1a). This simple divide places the Centre with the North and the islands of Sardinia and Sicily with the South. A commonly used threefold division is that into continental, peninsular and insular (Figure 6.1e). Continental Italy, consisting of the Po basin and the Alps, is sometimes referred to as *Alt'Italia* or 'High Italy', and the area south of Rome as *Bass' Italia* or 'Low Italy'. ISTAT employs a threefold macroregional division into North, Centre and South, sometimes dividing the North into Northwest and Northeast and the South into mainland South and Islands (Figure 6.1b, c). Recently Bagnasco (1981) has refined the ISTAT divisions somewhat into the three 'regional formations' of Northwest, Northeast–Centre and South (Figure 6.1d). The Northwest (Piedmont, Val d'Aosta, Lombardy and Liguria) is characterized by large-scale industry, an urban way of life and a large and well-protected working class. The Northeast–Centre has historically played the role of labour supplier to the Northwest but since the 1960s has emerged as a dynamic area, with economic growth founded on the expansion of small businesses and light industries. The third regional formation is the South, for long the major underdeveloped part of the country, with a weak economy and a social system dominated by patronage and rigid hierarchies. We return to Bagnasco's 'three Italies' later in this chapter.

Another ISTAT regionalization, used mainly for the publication of settlement and population data and for agricultural statistics, is based on altitude and morphology with divisions into mountain, hill and plain districts (Figure 6.1f). Table 6.1 shows that there has been a long-term drift of population from mountain regions to the plains and coastal strips. In 1871 the mountains contained 23.1 per cent of the Italian population; by 1981 this had fallen to 13.6 per cent. The plains have increased their share over the same period from just over one-third to nearly one-half. The intermediate hill districts have retained a more-or-less constant proportion, with slight tendency to decrease, at least until 1971.

Yet another basic geographic contrast is between the coast and the interior. This is manifested in different ways in the different macroregions of North, Centre and South. In the North the concentration of urban and economic activity has tended to be internal, in the Po Plain. Although there are some coastal cities, notably Genoa, Venice and Trieste, their growth as ports has tended to depend on economic progress in the interior hinterlands. Central Italy has few coastal settlements of any size and only mediocre ports. Some like Pisa and the Roman port of Ostia have declined because of silting. The major settlements tend to be inland, in basins (e.g.

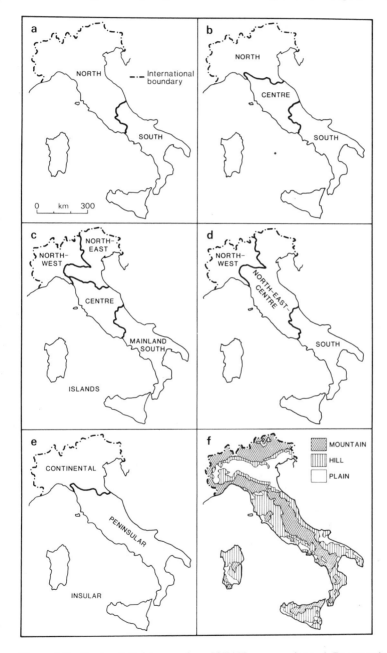

Figure 6.1 Regional divisions. a, b, c, ISTAT macroregions. d, Bagnasco's 'three Italies'. e, f, Physical divisions.

Table 6.1   Changing distribution of population by physical region, 1871–1981

| | % of population living in: | | |
	Plains	Hills	Mountains
1871	34.4	42.5	23.1
1951	41.9	40.6	17.5
1961	44.2	39.7	16.1
1971	47.1	38.6	14.3
1981	47.7	38.7	13.6

Source: ISTAT: *Censimento Generale della Popolazione, 1871, 1951, 1961, 1971, 1981.*

Florence) or on hills either high (e.g. Siena) or low (e.g. Rome). However, while the Tyrrhenian coast of central Italy is relatively deserted, the Adriatic coast is more densely settled, the population of Marche draining down to the Ancona region and its attendant beach resorts. It is in the South that the spatial contrast between coast and interior becomes most marked. Its colonial legacy has seen the development of outward-looking coastal cities and the exploitation and stagnation of the interior where, still today, no cities of major importance are found.

6.2.1 Administrative geography

Italy's administrative structure also contributes to an understanding of the country's geographical contrasts. The basic unit of local government is the commune, of which there are 8086. Historically the notion of the commune originated in the North and Centre as a new way of organizing society in contrast to the traditional feudal system. Typically, a commune consists of a town or village and its surrounding area. Some communes, especially in the South, consist of a single nucleated settlement — the typical southern agro-town — with no ancillary settlements; elsewhere a commune might consist of a major settlement plus one or more minor villages or hamlets, and dispersed farms and other residences. The commune is also the basic unit for local planning, the municipal master plan providing the framework for land use and settlement development within the communal territory.

The next level in the territorial and administrative hierarchy is the province, of which there are now 95 (compared to 59 at unification). These tend to be more significant as geographical areas than as units of local government, although they do have some important functions with regard to education and training, hospital and health services, public works and trade organizations. Although many provinces are of considerable antiquity, corresponding for instance to a major town and its surrounding constellation of minor towns and villages, others, more recently created, are artificial constructions without traditions or distinctive economic or social conditions to justify their separate existence. To the casual visitor to Italy perhaps the most visible manifestation of the existence of the provinces is their use on vehicle number plates; typically the number is prefixed by the first two letters of the province in which the vehicle is registered.

The third and, since the establishment of the regional governments in 1970, the most important level in the hierarchy is the region, of which there are now 20. As an inheritance from the past, regional feelings have always been strong in Italy, for many of the present regions had been independent states before they became part of united Italy. However, from unification until the Republican Constitution of 1948, regions were officially considered solely as statistical divisions which grouped together a given number of provinces. The state was keen to maintain a highly centralized structure in order to stifle any separatist movements which might undermine its territorial integrity; hence the regions had no legal or administrative functions. At the end of the Second World War, however, the pent-up sense of regional pride, combined with the demand for greater participation in self-government at the grass-roots, had the effect of generating pressure for devolution. The Constitution of 1948 provided for 5 'special' regions (see Chapter 1) and 14 'ordinary' regions (subsequently increased to 15 when Molise separated from Abruzzo in 1963). Confirmation of the 15 ordinary regions took 22 years of polemic and parliamentary debate, due largely to the procrastination of the DC. Several reasons account for this delay. First, doubts were expressed about the wisdom of creating yet another level of bureaucracy in addition to the national, provincial and commune levels. Second, there was the likelihood that certain regions would fall into the hands of Communist administrations. Third, the chequered experience of the Sicilian 'special statute' region showed that local elites could produce illogical, corrupt and factious administrations which were not only inept but frequently at loggerheads with central government.

Given this powerful opposition, how can the eventual decision to create the regions be explained? First, the Constitution provided for them, and failure to honour this threatened the legitimacy of the regime. Second, by the early 1960s the DC needed Socialist help in order to maintain a stable cabinet, and the price set by the Socialists for their collaboration included the establishment of the ordinary regions. Finally, regionalism tended to dovetail with another important reform movement — economic planning. The obvious inadequacy of local provincial and communal economic planning and the growing awareness of the need for a firmer and wider spatial base for regional planning favoured the establishment of the regional councils in 1970.

6.2.2 The regions: an opportunity missed?

The regional administrations were established amid great optimism. Protagonists of the regions thought that regional autonomy would be instrumental in destroying clientelism which, they believed, flourished mainly in a centralized political system. They argued that regional devolution would promote a high level of political participation because it would enable people to become more directly involved in dealing with their own problems. They also claimed that the weakening of the centralized power structure of the Italian state was a prerequisite for overcoming regional inequalities (Allum, 1973a).

Fifteen years after the first regional elections were held, few of these hopes appear to have materialized. This failure has not altogether been the fault of the regions themselves, but rather reflects the hostility of central government, and its agents in the courts and the civil service, to the whole idea of regional autonomy. The relationship between central and regional government has been characterized by tension: the central government trying to dominate the regions, the latter trying to maintain and extend their independence. Constitutional ambiguity as to the precise division of powers and responsibilities has fuelled mistrust on both sides.

The first wave of legislation setting up the regional governments in 1970 gave them only limited powers. More extensive devolution was granted in 1977. The regions now have power to legislate and plan — always within the guidelines laid down by central government — in four main spheres: administrative organization, social and cultural services, economic development and physical planning. To date, agriculture, most craft industries and tourism are the economic activities whose planning has been most tightly controlled by the regional authorities.

The regions vary greatly in size and population; reference back to Figure 1.3 (p. 26) and Table 2.3 (p. 59) will provide more precise details. Lombardy, with a population of 8.9 million in 1981, can therefore hardly be compared to Val d'Aosta with 109 000 or Molise with 325 000. The larger and more urbanized regions — Piedmont, Lombardy, Veneto, Emilia–Romagna, etc. — are the ones which have taken the lead in regional planning. Here opportunities are being used to develop planning tools specifically oriented to local issues. Subregions or *comprensori* have been drawn up as territories intermediate between the regions and the communes for the establishment and carrying through of strategic plans for population, employment, social, agricultural and environmental policies.

Elsewhere, however, the regions have made little progress. The most revealing indication of this is the accumulation of vast unspent reserves of regional funds. On average the regions have failed to spend 40 per cent of their total budgets; if one were to subtract routine and unavoidable expenditure such as rents and salaries, the proportion would rise to 70 per cent. Some unspent allocations are the result of construction delays or of decisions taken to invest in long-term projects rather than disburse short-term subsidies. But many of the delays arise from the obstructionist stance of central government in giving the necessary approval for spending by regional authorities, and from the bureaucratic inefficiency which has been reproduced in the ranks of the regional administrations themselves. A simple explanation lies behind this last fact: the vast majority of the staff taken on by the regions were simply civil servants transferred from central government ministries and field offices and from other semi-public agencies. Such personnel had little attachment to the regions to which they were transferred and, with their background of central administration, little sympathy for the regional ideal. Their inherited civil service ethos of elitism, pernickety legalism and an undemocratic outlook made them fundamentally ill-equipped to deal with the practical and technical problems facing the regional governments (Freddi, 1980).

Any hope that regional devolution would play a role in reducing regional inequality has been misplaced. Although allocation of funds to the regions favoured the poorer regions somewhat over the richer ones, the pattern of wealth remains stubbornly skewed in favour of the North. Table 6.2 shows that the index of gross output per inhabitant is considerably higher in the North, especially in the Northwest, than it is in the South. Moreover the increase in this index during 1971–81 has been greater in the North–Centre (29.1 per cent) than it has in the Mezzogiorno (23.5 per cent). With the exception of Abruzzo and Sardinia, no southern region exceeds 60 per cent of the national average figure of gross output per capita.

Table 6.2 enables us to reopen the discussion on Italian regional formations introduced at the beginning of this chapter. The 20 regions fall fairly neatly into the three macroregions identified by Bagnasco (1981) as constituting the three main models of postwar Italian development. The Northwest comprises regions which all have their per capita output figures well above the national norm yet which also have, with the exception of tiny Val d'Aosta, recent growth figures below the national average. The Northeast and Centre regions merge into one regional formation characterized by average or slightly below-average output figures, but with distinctly higher than average rates of increase of output per capita during 1971–81 (Latium is the notable exception here). Finally the South has well below-average output indices combined with low rates of increase south of Abruzzo–Molise.

Table 6.2   Output per capita by region, 1981

Region	Output per capita 1981 ('000 lire)	Italy = 100	Real increase in output per capita 1971–81 (%)
Northwest			
Piedmont	8718	105.1	27.5
Val d' Aosta	11 042	133.1	38.1
Lombardy	9331	112.5	27.6
Liguria	9245	111.5	21.5
Northeast			
Trentino–Alto Adige	8145	98.2	41.4
Veneto	7351	88.6	33.4
Friuli–Venezia Giulia	8446	101.8	36.0
Emilia–Romagna	8780	105.8	42.4
Centre			
Tuscany	7844	94.6	30.0
Umbria	6814	82.1	46.0
Marche	7073	85.3	40.4
Latium	7156	86.5	19.5
South			
Abruzzo	5680	68.5	36.5
Molise	4950	59.7	42.4
Campania	4818	58.1	23.4
Apulia	4916	59.3	26.3
Basilicata	4808	58.0	31.7
Calabria	4261	51.4	24.7
Sicily	4916	59.3	22.8
Sardinia	5214	62.9	13.1
Italy	8295	100.0	27.3

Source: ISTAT: *Annuario di Contabilità Nazionale, 1983.*

6.3 The South: stifled development

The problem of the backwardness of the South has been the foremost issue of national concern throughout the period since unification. No Italian topic has attracted so much polemic and scholarly debate both within the country and without (King, 1971). Although the historical origins of the North–South dichotomy are obscure, the consensus view places the beginnings of the problem at around the eleventh century with the advent of the Norman monarchy, the introduction of feudalism and the decline of the southern cities, at a time when communal civilization was beginning to flourish in the North–Centre. By 1861, in the opinion of Eckaus (1961), average per capita income in the South was about 20 per cent below that in the rest of the country.

This differential certainly widened during the ensuing 90 years. The cumulative effect of the growth process polarized both economic and social development in the North, and especially in the Northwest. Northern industrial growth was invigorated by closeness to other countries which had already started industrialization, and facilitated by financial organizations, external economies, hydroelectric power and a more favourable geographical setting. Relative to the North, the South suffered from poor soils, a plethora of steep and eroded uplands, a more adverse climate for farming, shortage of water and lack of mineral resources. In the social field, a more modernistic outlook in the North was backed up by wider opportunities for education and training, and a generally higher standard and quality of life. In short, the polarization process between 1861 and 1951 concentrated economic growth in the North, leaving demographic growth weighted in the South. By 1951 the South, with 40 per cent of the country's area and 37 per cent of its population, generated 32.8 per cent of national agricultural wealth, 18.2 per cent of industrial income and only 13.3 per cent of tertiary sector income. Yet the region was responsible for 50 per cent of the births and 75 per cent of the natural increase of Italy as a whole (Dickinson, 1955b). Basic to the problem of the South was the fact that agricultural production had failed to match the growth of a population which had doubled in the previous 70 years. Modern industrial development was virtually non-existent before 1960. It was also significant that the situation in the South was worsening: real per capita income actually fell by 7 per cent over the period 1938–51, whereas in the North it increased by 8 per cent (Tagliacarne, 1955). Bad housing, inadequate schools, poor health facilities, high infant mortality — all indicators of socioeconomic wellbeing — gave the same picture of southern backwardness as compared to the North.

6.3.1 The Cassa per il Mezzogiorno: 35 years of funding the South

The first really positive action to aid the development of the South took place in 1950, the year in with the Italian government passed the land reform laws (considered in detail in Chapter 5) and set up the Cassa per il Mezzogiorno or 'Fund for the South'. In its early years the Cassa did much good work in support of the land reform, reclaiming land, building irrigation ditches and providing roads, electricity and water for remote farming areas. These, however, were essentially rural policies which did little to stimulate the region's overall growth and certainly did nothing to attract industry to the South. Indeed, it was northern industry which benefited most from early Cassa policy, as northern firms were the suppliers of heavy machinery and of agricultural inputs like fertilizers (Allum, 1972).

Later in the 1950s the Cassa began to switch the thrust of its investment in the South away from agriculture and rural infrastructure to industry. Industrial credit was channelled to the South via three regional credit agencies — ISVEIMER for the mainland, SOFIS for Sicily and CIS for Sardinia. These agencies were to play an important, if largely unsung, role in financing southern industrial growth in ensuing decades.

The key intervention in promulgating a policy to industrialize the South was the Industrial Areas Law of 1957 which authorized the Cassa to offer generous inducements to industry, Italian or foreign, locating or expanding in the Mezzogiorno. The 1957 industrial policy for the South had three major facets: inducement by financial incentives, stimulation by direct state involvement, and spatial concentration via growth poles. The incentive package in turn had three main ingredients: capital grants, soft loans and tax concessions. Social security concessions were added in 1968. But the element of the 1957 law which was to have most effect in bringing industry to the South was the clause which compelled nationalized and state holding industries to locate at least 60 per cent of their new investment south of the Cassa boundary, even though location factors were more attractive in the North. Thus Italsider modernized the steelworks at Bagnoli near Naples and built the new plant at Taranto during the early 1960s. IRI also became active in the South in many other fields, including shipbuilding and repairing, port improvement and motorway construction.

The third aspect of the Cassa's industrial policy was its spatial articulation in the growth pole concept. Two types of pole were established: *industrial areas*, which were usually attached to the leading southern cities where major industrial expansion was predicted; and *industrial nuclei*, usually small towns of below 75 000 people, where the scale of industrial development was to be more modest, including a concentration on small rather than big industries.

Within a few years 42 localities had been designated as growth poles, and the number subsequently crept up to 48. Their locations are given in Figure 6.2. The question immediately arises as to whether this proliferation is such as to negate the very concept of spatial concentration of effort inherent in the growth pole concept (King, 1981). The large number of poles resulted largely from the desire of the government to maximize the political pay-offs of the policy; for the Cassa to have refused development pole status to any aspiring town would have lost votes in that area for the government. The political role of the Cassa thus has to be distinguished from its official function as a regional economic planning agency.

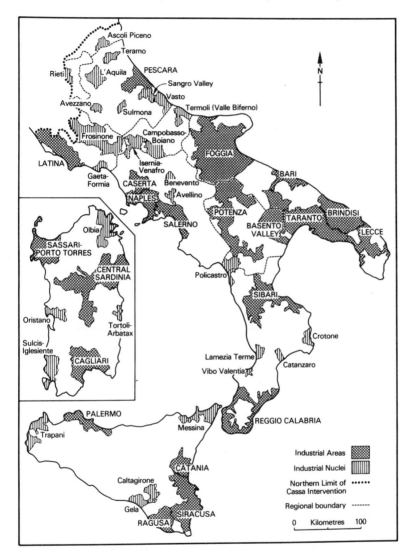

Figure 6.2 Areas and nuclei of industrialization in the Mezzogiorno.

More industrial development initiatives were taken by the Cassa and by central government in the 1960s and 1970s. In 1961 a new law created IASM, the Institute for the Assistance to Development in the Mezzogiorno.

Sponsored by the Cassa and the three credit agencies noted earlier, its remit was to promote the development and modernization of southern industry by the preparation of technical and feasibility studies. In 1963 a new public shareholding company, IN–SUD, was created, with Cassa capital, to enable the state to participate more directly in financing southern industrial development. Other institutional initiatives at this time included FOR-MEZ, a training and study centre set up in 1961 and revamped in 1965, and CIAPI, a centre for industrial training for southern workers.

Reforms introduced in the 1965 southern law, which extended the Cassa's life until 1980, attempted to deal with the problems of coordination between the Cassa initiatives and the operations of the rest of 'normal' government. Two main problems had arisen. The first concerned the lack of integration between Cassa activities and those of bodies like the Ministry of Agriculture or the Department of Public Works. The second concerned the lessening of commitment to the South on the part of the normal ministries produced by the very existence of the Cassa. The 1965 law streamlined the Cassa, aimed at greater coordination of intervention in the South at the various levels — national, regional, sectoral — and set up a new interministerial planning committee, CIPE, responsible for sanctioning all large-scale industrial development wherever it might be located. By its ability to approve or refuse permission for industrial expansion, CIPE was able to direct further industrial development towards the southern growth poles, particularly towards those half-dozen or so major poles which were emerging as successful regional nodes (Naples, Pescara, Bari–Brindisi–Taranto, Siracusa, Cagliari and Latina–Frosinone). This phase of southern policy was, however, rather hard on those 2 million southerners who lived in remote upland districts outside any kind of designated area.

The most recent phase of southern intervention started with the law of 1971, reinforced by supplementary legislation in 1976. Fresh initiatives were deemed necessary because of the disappointing results of the 1950s and 1960s. True, income per head had increased sharply since the commencement of the southern policy in the early 1950s, but the gap between the South and the rest of the country had scarcely been reduced. During the 1960s net imports into the region were equal to a massive 70 per cent of gross investment in the South, revealing the region's continuing dependence on outside support and its failure to initiate a process of self-sustaining development. Moreover the increases in employment created by the infrastructural and industrial projects had nowhere near matched the outflow from agriculture, or even equalled the natural increase in the labour force, so that total employment had declined and emigration accelerated. While the Cassa claimed (probably exaggeratedly) to have created 1.2 million new jobs (in all sectors of the economy) during 1961–71, 1.9 million people migrated from the South over the same decade — a silent protest against the continuing lack of economic opportunities in the Mezzogiorno.

The main features of the 1970s legislation were as follows. Additional funds were allocated to the Cassa, and the emphasis on industrial development was increased. A new system of grant and loan incentives which favoured smaller and labour-intensive activities over large, capital-intensive initiatives was put into operation, while the state holding firms were required to locate 80 per cent, not 60 per cent as before, of their new investments in the South. Strong support for basic infrastructure like roads, drainage and irrigation continued. Even more than the 1965 law, the 1971 law treated the South as the central problem of national economic planning, and the coordination between southern and national economic planning was improved, at least in theory. The role of CIPE was strengthened by the addition of a committee of regional chairpersons, since it became necessary after the early 1970s to integrate the role of the newly formed regional administrations into southern development planning. The function of the Cassa thus changed: it became less of an overall regional development agency and more of an advisory body concentrating on key projects, particularly those affecting more than one region or dealing with special problems such as the expansion of metropolitan areas or the conservation of natural resources. The so-called 'special projects' assumed increasing importance in the 1970s, accounting for one-tenth of Cassa assistance to the South during 1971–75 and one-fifth during 1976–80 (Ronzani, 1980; Spooner, 1984). Among the special projects so far initiated are the following: completion of interregional water supply schemes such as that to the driest region of Apulia; the provision of infrastructure in the two 'crisis cities' of Naples and Palermo; construction of the big new canal-port at Cagliari in Sardinia; development of key agricultural sectors like citrus fruits, intensive meat production and marketing; and the decontamination of the badly polluted Bay of Naples, accorded top priority after the 1973 Naples cholera epidemic was traced to contaminated fish. Finally, the spatial strategy of southern industrial development also changed in 1971. Extra help was given to the nuclei and areas which had failed to attract much industry and there was an attempt to diffuse industrial development along 'axes of penetration' into the backward interior — a marked reversal of the concentrated growth pole planning of the 1960s.

Since its long-term funding ran out in 1981 the position of the Cassa has been increasingly uncertain. A pattern of annual finance made any long-term planning impossible, and the Cassa finally went into liquidation in 1984 when not enough members of parliament turned up to vote for its continuation. Although a majority of government opinion probably believes that some kind of 'fund for the South' is still needed, there is as yet no clear indication of what form the Cassa's successor body will take.

6.3.2 Southern industrial development: an assessment

There is no doubt that the various incentives offered by the government via the Cassa to industries locating in the South have had a significant impact. The volume of industrial investment in the South increased by seven times over the period 1951–75, compared to a twofold increase in the North–Centre (Podbielski, 1978). Part of the discrepancy, however, is explained by the much lower base levels in the South, so that dramatic percentage increases are somewhat misleading. Moreover, the investment increase was not matched by a concomitant growth in industrial employees, whose increase during 1951–71 was only 33 per cent in the South, compared with 58 per cent in the North–Centre (*see* Table 3.1, p. 83). Since 1971, however, the South has increased its industrial workforce more rapidly than the North–Centre, by 22 per cent as against 7.5 per cent for the decade 1971–81.

More spatially precise data issued by IASM on the industrial impact of the Cassa show that by 1980 2427 new factories employing a total of 305 000 workers had settled in the 48 areas and nuclei of industrialization. If factories in the course of construction and at the planning stage are included, the IASM figures rise to 4050 factories and 390 000 workers. Some of the major establishments which have located in the South include the Italsider steelworks at Taranto, the Montedison petrochemical plants at Brindisi and at Priolo in eastern Sicily, the Alfa Sud car plant at Pomigliano d'Arco, Olivetti's factory at Pozzuoli and SIR's plastics and chemicals plant at Porto Torres in Sardinia.

The new industrial development attracted by the Cassa is highly concentrated sectorally (King, 1985). Nearly three-quarters of the jobs are in three branches of industry — metallurgy, mechanical industries and chemicals. In metallurgy and chemicals each new job has represented an expenditure of more than £100 000 — a very expensive way of solving the South's unemployment problem. There has been only limited development of small and medium-sized firms producing traditional goods like foodstuffs, clothing and furniture, although there have been some encouraging signs of industrial diversification in Abruzzo and Apulia in the past 10 years.

Spatially there has been marked concentration of industrial growth since 1957 in four major areas. These are Latina–Frosinone (39 000 new industrial jobs), Naples–Caserta–Salerno (65 000), Bari-Brindisi–Taranto (51 000) and Catania–Augusta–Siracusa (22 000). Together these four nodes account for 58 per cent of the 305 000 Cassa-induced industrial jobs created by 1980. Moderate increases in industrial employment have been recorded in Pescara (9000 new jobs), Vasto (8000), Lecce (10 000), the Basento Valley (6000), Palermo (6000), Gela (6000), Cagliari (8000) and Sassari–Porto Torres (7000). On the other hand some designated industrial growth areas have actually experienced a decline in industrial employment since 1957; this is the case with Isernia, Campobasso and Benevento, all in the southern Apennines, together with Reggio Calabria and Catanzaro in Calabria, and Caltagirone and Trapani in Sicily. Overall Rodgers (1979) found that between 1951 and 1971 the industrial areas and nuclei had experienced an 81.4 per cent increase in manufacturing employment, whereas outside the designated areas the manufacturing workforce decreased by 16.1 per cent.

Industrial development has undoubtedly led to sharper regional differentiation within the South. At a regional level Abruzzo, Apulia and Sardinia have advanced to a position whereby their per capita incomes are only about 20 per cent below the national average, although partly this is a false prosperity produced by large-scale emigration and a fall in the working population. At the other end of the South's prosperity spectrum, Calabria, Basilicata and Molise remain deeply rural regions with average incomes still around half the national level. On the northern fringes of the Mezzogiorno the encroachment of the Cassa boundary into southern Latium has led to the establishment of industrial plants in an area which is not really depressed and has at times even experienced a labour shortage. Around Latina many firms, including American companies such as Proctor and Gamble, Palmolive and Pfizer, have set up factories under the dual attraction of Cassa aid and proximity to the lucrative Rome market. In the adjacent Frosinone industrial area 250 new industries employing 14 000 workers have sprung up around motorway exit points on the Autostrada del Sole, Fiat's Cassino plant being the most important of these factories (Pacione, 1982). Such dynamic industrial development in the north of the Mezzogiorno has led to suggestions that the Cassa should shift its boundary southwards or that there should be a system of graduated incentives to encourage more industry to settle south of Naples where the highest unemployment and worst poverty are to be found.

Latina and Frosinone apart, the greatest disappointment of southern industrialization has been the lack of diversification away from the 'base' industries of metallurgy and petrochemicals. The demonstration and multiplier effects of the state industries have been particularly limited, leaving the vast, expensive complexes as white elephants or 'cathedrals in the desert'. The state holding sector has never been successful at developing and managing small firms. This is an important deficiency given the public commitment since 1976 to develop smaller concerns as the main thrust of current southern industrialization policy. Although there are the beginnings of secondary industrial development in Abruzzo and Apulia and in some of the major port cities like Naples, Palermo and Cagliari, modern, diversified and competitive industry has yet to emerge on a broad front (Giannola, 1982).

The industrialization model relied on for stimulating growth in the South in the 1960s and early 1970s is now in crisis. It was based on the hypothesis that the Italian South, the white manpower reserve of the EC, was a suitable area for transferring European manufactures with easily acquired technology. But now these industries are moving beyond the Mediterranean, towards countries with lower labour costs. The South has lost its attraction now that wage differentials have been virtually eliminated. It has also been adversely affected by the problems afflicting the state holding sector. During the recessions of the 1970s and early 1980s the public sector was increasingly called on to perform massive salvaging operations of enterprises which found themselves in difficulty, thereby diverting state funds from the task of developing the South to rescue operations in other parts of the country. The state sector thus failed to match the requirement of locating 80 per cent of its new industrial development in the South, as stipulated by the 1971 legislation. There was, in addition, a marked deterioration in the quality of state holding sector management, which during the 1970s became more conditioned by political interests.

Perhaps the saddest example of government mishandling of southern industrial development is the case of the Gioia Tauro steelworks. In the early 1970s, when the expansion of the big Italsider plant at Taranto was thought still to leave some spare demand for steel, it was decided to build a fifth integrated steel complex at Gioia Tauro on the Calabrian coast north of Reggio di Calabria. This site was chosen for political reasons, to create employment (7500 jobs were promised) and assuage the discontent which had erupted in the Reggio riots of 1970. A site in Reggio Province was obligatory since, of the other two Calabrian provinces, Catanzaro had been made regional capital and Cosenza had been given the new University of Calabria. The post-1973 economic crisis confirmed what many had feared all along — that the plant could never be viable. The proposals were also blocked by the EC. Plans for the project were first scaled down and then cancelled entirely, even though work had already started on the port and a large area of rich agricultural land, including mature citrus and olive groves, had been cleared. The South's final, and probably most bizarre, cathedral in the desert was thus never built.

6.3.3 Is the South catching up with the North?

This is a question which is frequently asked at the end of discussions which attempt to evaluate the success of the Cassa per il Mezzogiorno. Yet few commentators bother to stop and ponder whether the question is fair. In retrospect it hardly seems realistic to have expected the South to 'catch up' with the North, given the fact that the latter region had one of the fastest growth rates in Europe during the period 1950–73. Instead, the fact that the southern growth rate kept pace with that of the North–Centre should perhaps be cause for satisfaction. On the other hand a large proportion of southern growth has been the result of outside help with net imports averaging 27 per cent of southern income and half of all industrial investment made since 1959 coming from state firms which have had no option but to shift to the South (Rodgers, 1984).

Statistics on the growth of output per head between 1951 and 1983 show that the South has barely encroached on the North–Centre. The South increased its output per capita by 2.02 times at current prices compared to the North–Centre's 1.93 times. Whereas output per head in the South was equivalent to only 53.2 per cent of the average of the rest of the country in 1951, by 1983 this proportion had risen to 61.7 per cent. But the gap is still obviously very wide and, at the above rates of progress, would take several decades to eradicate. Indeed the rate of closure has markedly slowed down since 1974; between 1974 and 1983 there was only a 0.4 per cent narrowing (Buxton, 1985). The recessions of the past 10 years or so have thus blocked the recovery of the Mezzogiorno.

Since the bulk of the South's socioeconomic improvement vis-à-vis the North took place before 1973, Table 6.3 details some of the characteristics of this improvement between the two census years of 1951 and 1971. It can be seen that the South's performance was generally rather better on social indicators (diet, housing, hospital bed provision, etc.) than it was on economic indicators such as income, industrial employment or electricity consumption. Tagliacarne's synthesis of 21 socioeconomic indices (the 10 in Table 6.3 plus 11 others) showed that over the period 1951–71 the six regions which improved the most were all southern — in order of improvement Apulia, Sardinia, Basilicata, Abruzzo–Molise, Calabria, Sicily — whereas the four slowest improving regions were all northern — Piedmont the slowest, followed by Liguria, Lombardy and Trentino–Alto Adige (Tagliacarne, 1973). Recent data for 1981 show that while the social indicators in Table 6.3 have continued to improve (number of telephones per 100 population rising to 60.4 per cent of the North–Centre figure, number of radio/TV licences to 67.4 per cent, number of motor cars to 60.3 per cent, number of rooms to 78.9 per cent, number of hospital beds to 77.1 per cent), the economic indices have tended to stagnate, with the South's per capita income, as a percentage of that of the North, dropping by nearly 2 percentage points between 1973 and 1980 (Amatucci, 1984).

Table 6.3 Regional socioeconomic indices, 1951–71

	North–Centre		South		1951–71 change (%)		South as % of North–Centre	
	1951	1971	1951	1971	North–Centre	South	1951	1971
Industrial workforce (000s)	3508	5540	734	984	57.9	34.1	38.8*	33.1*
Income per capita ('000 lire at current prices)	193	1267	104	684	555.8	558.8	53.8	54.0
Consumption of electricity for lighting (kWh/cap/year)	69	219	30	133	217.4	343.3	43.5	60.7
Meat consumption (kg/cap/year)	18	35	10	29	94.4	190.0	55.6	82.9
Tobacco consumption (kg/cap/year)	0.75	1.40	0.49	1.15	86.7	134.7	65.3	82.1
No. telephones/100 inhabitants	4.2	21.1	0.8	10.3	402.4	1187.5	19.0	48.8
No. radio/TV licences/100 inhabitants	9.9	24.8	4.3	16.5	150.5	283.7	43.4	66.5
No. motor cars/100 inhabitants	1.9	24.2	0.7	13.9	1173.7	1885.7	36.8	57.4
No. of rooms/100 inhabitants	90.0	127.4	59.3	97.3	41.6	64.6	65.9	76.4
Hospital beds/1000 inhabitants	9.2	11.9	4.3	8.0	29.3	86.0	46.7	67.2

Source: Tagliacarne (1973).
* Standardized by population (65 per cent in North–Centre; 35 per cent in South).

6.3.4 Dependent development

Quantitative indications of the status of the South compared to the rest of Italy are only part of the story. Of possibly greater importance are the terms of the evolving relationship between the Mezzogiorno and the Italian economy. Graziani (1978) has stated that the mechanism of southern development has transformed the Mezzogiorno from a poor, self-sufficient region to one which is less poor but more strictly dependent on the rest of the country. The nature of this dependency involves not so much a simple reliance on outside aid as a control over how the resources of the South are utilized. The same author has destroyed the myth of the Mezzogiorno as a huge millstone suspended round the neck of the national economy, entirely dependent on subsidies from the North–Centre, by pointing out that social security expenditure per capita is 40 per cent higher in the North than in the South (Graziani, 1983). The core of the dependency relationship is contained in the style of industrial development and in the ownership of capital. Control of the 'technostructures' of southern industry — managerial functions, origin of capital, destination of profits, marketing, research and development — remains rooted firmly in the North. Hence the factories in the southern industrial poles can be regarded as outposts of the northern economy. The southern development programme has thus been functional to the overall development of the Italian industrial economy. Wade (1979) has argued that the concentration of heavy industry in the South came about because Italian industrialists producing goods for export wanted an enlarged modern heavy industry sector to provide them with cheap basic inputs, and such expansion was cheaper in the South because of lower land prices, more abundant labour, easy access to sea transport, less opposition to industrial pollution and an unsaturated infrastructure (especially housing for workers). The reliance on capital-intensive industry preserved an army of reserve labour for the North, while migrant workers' remittance transfers boosted the size of the market for northern consumer products. This interpretation sees what took place in the South as a 'reflexive' type of dependent development, reflecting the interests of owners of industry and capital in the North (Wade, 1980).

Modernization and growth have taken place in the South, but not true development. There has been a rise in personal incomes, the agricultural population has declined sharply, public works have mushroomed, consumer products are more widespread, and access to education, information and political party membership are all now virtually on a par with those of the North. All of this is a consequence of closer contact with industrial regions in the North and with the seat of government in Rome, rather than a result of significant expansion of productive capacity *in situ*. The capital invested in and applied to the South — loans, grants, subsidies, pensions, unemployment benefits, etc. — is fundamentally welfaristic in nature and, moreover, has spawned an expansion of bureaucratic agencies ostensibly responsible for administering such policies but which have also functioned to distribute civil service sinecures to the local bourgeoisie who might otherwise have been unemployed. Here, too, is a powerful mechanism of political control, for the recruitment of such administrative personnel is closely related to networks of personal clientelism and political patronage. This has been well illustrated by studies of Sardinian rural society in the 'post-peasant' era which show the involutionary character of tertiary sector development, both in the private sector with the multiplication of bars, shops, service garages, etc., and in the state bureaucracy with the proliferation of local-level officials and technicians (Weingrod, 1979).

Polarized industrial development, bureaucratic welfarism and varying incidences of emigration have been key factors contributing to the economic differentiation of zones within the South, making it increasingly difficult to generalize about the evolution of the region as a whole. Drawing on data which refer to the mid-1970s, Graziani (1983) has produced a most interesting map (Figure 6.3) which posits the existence of three main styles of 'development' (or lack of it) in the South. First, there is the *productive Mezzogiorno*, where a process of autonomous local development has emerged, based either on the results of the massive investments of the Cassa in industrial estates and irrigation, or on the development of small firms (either legitimate or as part of the 'underground economy'). In these 'autonomous development areas' at least 90 per cent of income is locally generated. The productive Mezzogiorno is to be found mainly around the South's provincial capitals and along certain of its coasts which have become popular as centres of residential growth and tourism (Pescara, Neopolitan Riviera, Sardinian Costa Smeralda, etc.). Second, there is the *emigrant Mezzogiorno* whose income is sustained to a significant extent (at least 5 per cent of local income) by payments sent by emigrants abroad. These are mainly interior and mountain areas where emigration has been a long-established tradition, especially Molise, the high Apennines between Avellino and Potenza, parts of Calabria, and central Sicily. Remittance areas hardly exist in Apulia and Sardinia partly because these two regions have weaker, and more recently developed, emigration traditions, with a greater proportion of the outmovement directed to northern Italy (no data are available on remittances from internal migrants). The third area is the *subsidized Mezzogiorno*. This is an extensive area of rural territory, comprising mainly hill and mountain country but also including some economically weak lowlands such as the Salentine Peninsula south of Lecce and the Sardinian Campidano which stretches between Cagliari and Oristano. In

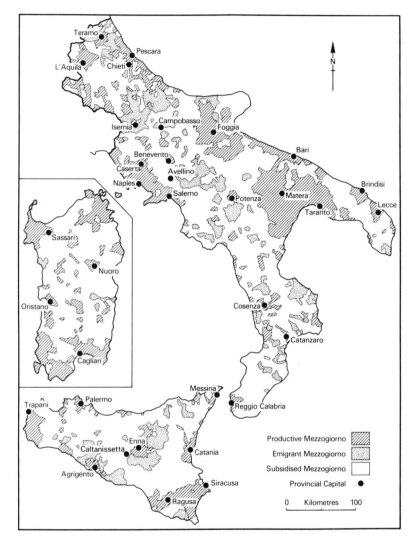

Figure 6.3 The Mezzogiorno: productive, emigration and subsidized areas.

these areas remittances are not significant and autonomous growth has not occurred. Instead the once self-sufficient rural economy has effectively collapsed and explicit subsidies such as unemployment benefits and pensions of various kinds have to be provided to sustain the population.

With the South's new demographic dynamism, resulting from the fall-off of outmigration since the early 1970s and a birth rate which is still significantly higher than that of the North and Centre, the Mezzogiorno is becoming once again a region of chronic labour surplus. Between 1981 and 1991 ISTAT estimates that Italy will experience an increase in population of around 1.9 million, 1.4 million of which will occur in the South. Merely to keep unemployment at its present (high) level means the creation of at least 500 000 jobs over the next few years; to significantly reverse the trend of continuing high unemployment would require at least 1 million new jobs; and it is inconceivable that an outmigration of the scale that took place in the 1950s and 1960s could rescue the situation. Furthermore, the nature of the new 'labour reserve' is different than formerly. Whereas the southern unemployed of the 1950s constituted a mass of semi-literate and untrained peasants, the unemployed of today have respectable educational qualifications; two-thirds possess a high-school diploma and many are graduates. How to provide satisfying and remunerative work for this new generation of educated southerners is the great challenge of the late 1980s.

6.4 The Northwest: deindustrialization in the core of Italy

Although Rome is the capital of Italy, and has been for 115 of the Italian state's 125 years of existence, few would deny that the economic core of the country lies in the North, and especially in the two big powerful regions of Piedmont and Lombardy. The North's economic prominence is traceable at least to the Middle Ages when many powerful commercial cities developed in the region. After unification all the geographical factors pointed to the Po Plain as the best location for industry. The Northwest was the new seat of government, at Turin; it was nearest to the more advanced regions of Europe; it had greater supplies of labour and credit, and better communications; it had rich agriculture and sources of power; and further investment in social overhead capital soon resulted from the initial industrial growth. By about 1910 most of the giants of Italian industry had been founded, and they all started in the Northwest, mainly in Turin or Milan. The first 65 years of the present century did little to disturb this trend of progressive spatial polarization.

The link between economic growth and political development can hardly be overstressed. The events of the nineteenth century which produced the modern Italian state centred around Piedmont, Turin and Count Camillo Cavour. An avowed nationalist, a brilliant statesman and an astute politician, Cavour identified the policies of his Piedmontese kingdom with the creation of an Italian national state. He made Turin, the Piedmontese capital, a haven for nationalist exiles from other Italian states, and used

Piedmontese foreign policy to gain friends and allies for the cause of unification. Historically, therefore, the evidence for the western Po Plain as Italy's core area is incontrovertible (McManis, 1967).

By proximity, treaties and even occupation, French influence has lent a common external tone to Piedmont. The Alpine watershed was not the historical boundary of northwest Italy, for the Duchy of Savoy straddled the mountains to hold both Turin and Chambery under unified rule. In subsequent years French power and influence extended down the eastern mountain slopes to form a ring around the plain. Nowadays the French ethos of centralization and efficiency is still more characteristic of Piedmont than is the 'Italian style' of bureaucratic inertia. Compared to the troubled and corrupted South, efficiency reigns in Piedmont and scandals are rare. Development plans for Turin and its region are among the most detailed to be found in Italy; indeed regional planning in Italy was pioneered in this region (Arcangeli, 1982).

In further contrast to the South, very little Piedmontese industry is under state control. Fiat, symbol of Italian private industrial enterprise, dominates the economy of the region, accounting for two-thirds of the employment in Turin, one-third directly and one-third indirectly in Fiat's supply companies. A further reflection of Turin's private enterprise character is its possession of Italy's only university-level business school, founded in 1957.

Yet Turin is not without its problems. A city which is overdependent not only on one industry but on one firm has a dangerously narrow economic base, and the slump in the international automobile industry, which brought 23 000 Fiat redundancies in 1980, has had its effect on the Piedmontese capital. By 1983 Turin had 92 000 unemployed, half of whom were young people searching for their first job. The city's social problems have been compounded by the rootlessness of a workforce, 86 per cent of whom were not born in the city. Especially between 1969 and 1976 the city was greatly afflicted by urban unrest. Although action was directed at specific problems — lack of services, shortage of housing, excessive fares — it also reflected a wider political opposition to Turin's development as a city of monopolistic capitalism.

Milan and Lombardy, with a more broadly based economic structure than Turin and Piedmont, have weathered the economic crises of the past dozen years rather better. Milan is unquestionably the economic capital of Italy. The iron crown of Lombardy, which may be seen in the cathedral at Monza, now a suburb of Milan, is a symbol of north Italian industry. Milan hosts most of the headquarters of the major Italian firms, as well as the country's stock exchange and principal trade fair. Unlike Turin, which is surrounded by a rural region dotted with villages and small country towns, Milan meshes with a huge industrial conurbation which stretches for 70 km between the Ticino and the Adda rivers. Seveso, site of the 1976 dioxin disaster, lies almost exactly at its centroid. Altogether this is an area of 3500 sq km with a population of 5.7 million and an average density of 1600 per sq km, the nearest thing to an Italian megalopolis.

Milan Province, one of seven in Lombardy, generates nearly 12 per cent of national income, 40 per cent of industrial exports and 35 per cent of the Treasury's tax revenue from business transactions; yet it contains only 7 per cent of the national population. Despite these figures, industry in the Milan region is characterized by a predominance of medium-sized rather than large firms. Even the biggest enterprises — Alfa Romeo, Autobianchi, Innocenti, Pirelli, Falck, Franco Tosi, Breda and Magnetti–Marelli — are modest in comparison to Fiat's dominance over Turin. Walker (1967) makes the comparison between Milan and Birmingham as great broad-based engineering centres. In contrast to the South where the industrial structure takes the form of a number of artificially stimulated and spatially isolated nodes with weak linkages to the surrounding regional economies, industry in the Lombardy belt consists of functionally linked assemblages of enterprises deriving considerable external economies and based on a network of interlacing capital which also extends to other parts of the Po Plain as well as north to Switzerland and south to Genoa (Mikus, 1982).

Genoa is the weakest node of the Northwest's industrial triangle, although Liguria's income figures do not reveal this since industrial decline is financially offset by an influx of rich pensioners who settle along the mild and pretty Riviera coast. Genoa's urban areas now extend along the littoral for more than 25 km, west to Voltri and east to Nervi. The main industrial concentrations are at Cornigliano (steel) and Sestri (shipbuilding and oil terminals). Encroaching relief confines the width of the Genoan conurbation to less than 2 or 3 km, except for tongues extending up the valleys inland, the main one being the Pontedecimo which carries main road, railway and now motorway routes across the Giovi Pass to the inland plains. For at least 50 years, Genoa's economy has been too dependent on the declining heavy industries of the IRI state holding group (Rodgers, 1957); here there is a much weaker tradition of local economic dynamism than in Milan. Lack of level land is a major factor curtailing industrial expansion, while the port has a reputation for high fees, bureaucratic red tape and militant dockers and is losing trade to other ports like Savona, Leghorn and even Marseille.

The end of the long boom in 1963 and the shift in the balance of relations between capital and labour brought about by the 'hot autumn' were the key acts which terminated the process of progressive polarization of large-scale industry and wealth in the Northwest. The number of manufacturing workers in the region fell by 4.7 per cent during 1971–81, although nationally there was a 9.6 per cent increase. In 1961 the Northwest accounted for 51.4 per cent of the Italian manufacturing employment; by 1981 this proportion had fallen to 43.2 per cent, reflecting the contraction of many key industries — metallurgy, engineering, textiles, shoes, oil products — in the industrial heartland. Traditional manufactures like clothing and footwear declined particularly rapidly in the industrial core (but not elsewhere in Italy), as increasing labour costs could not be matched by higher productivity in these technologically backward industries. Meanwhile firms operating in sectors which were more advanced technologically, such as cars, mechanical trades, chemicals, etc., resorted to the reduction of working hours and to the use of the government redundancy fund (*Cassa Integrazione*) to reduce output and allow temporary lay-offs of surplus labour. In sectors employing backward and intermediate technology, firms adopted where possible a strategy of decentralizing parts of the productive process to small subcontracting firms, located both within and outside the Northwest, and even, again where feasible (as with footwear), of using the putting-out system to exploit cheap home-workers. The aims were twofold: to reduce the cost of labour by employing non-unionized workers; and to regain the flexibility not available to monolithic enterprises to respond to short-term fluctuations in the market.

6.5 The Northeast and Centre: a new model for Italian economic and social life?

With the South's economic take-off sabotaged by the recession and with the Northwest showing signs of deindustrialization and a less-than-convincing transition to a post-industrial state, Italian economic dynamism is confined to the third regional formation of the Centre and Northeast. Although traditionally split by the ISTAT macrodivisions of North and Centre, this belt contains seven regions — Tuscany, Umbria, Marche, Emilia–Romagna, Veneto, Trentino–Alto Adige and Friuli–Venezia Giulia — which generally exhibit similar economic and demographic behaviour, as reference to Tables 2.2, 2.3 and 6.2 will show. Although part of the Centre macroregion, Latium is the exception; this region's character is distorted by the presence of Rome, and is generally more 'southern' anyway.

The seven regions of 'middle Italy' increased their share of national value-added in manufacturing from 28 to 32 per cent during the period 1968–80 (cf. a fall in the Northwest's share from 55 to 49 per cent over the same period). A similar contrast in trends in industrial employment exists, the Northeast and Centre macroregions increasing their industrial workforces during 1971–81 by 17.7 and 17.9 per cent respectively, compared to the Northwest's already noted fall of 4.7 per cent. 'Peripheral development' in the Northeast and Centre has thus been the major force for the spatial reshaping of the Italian economy over the past 15–20 years (Arcangeli *et al.*, 1980).

What, then, is so special about this belt of 'middle Italy' that stretches between Rome and Trieste (or, perhaps more accurately, between Grosseto and Gorizia)? Why is industrial development taking place here but no longer elsewhere in Italy? Two main processes seem to be at work.

The first we have already mentioned: this is the process of productive decentralization whereby after the 1960s it became easier to expand in 'intermediate' areas than in the Piedmont–Lombardy core or in the heavily subsidized but still unattractive South. The brief 1963–64 depression and the 'hot autumn' were the turning points after which the regions of the Centre and Northeast stopped declining and began to redevelop traditional industries, especially in the fields of textiles, clothing, footwear, furniture and some mechanical trades such as vehicle and motorcycle parts, often through subcontracting from 'core' firms. In contrast to the Northwest, the Northeast and Centre had no shortage of industrial sites, for their open urban framework of small and medium-sized towns had yet to develop congested metropolitan structures. Above all labour was cheaper, more flexible, less unionized and less militant. This decentralized industrial development tended not to transfer to the South where, quite apart from locational peripherality, industrial growth was guided by official policy and by big state concerns operating large, basic industry under regulated wage levels and newly organized unions.

Generally the stages of production which have been decentralized are labour intensive and low skilled. Productive decentralization obviously implies the feasibility of vertically fragmenting the stages of production without loss of efficiency or of economies of scale. With certain technologies and productive processes, there is no advantage in manufacturing all the components of a product under a single roof; whether they produce similar or different pieces, 20 lathes or 20 knitting machines have substantially the same productivity if they are gathered together or dispersed in separate locations. Likewise the assembly of motorcycles or tractors can take place irrespective of the location of manufacture of the various components. Productive decentralization also takes place when demand is diversified and varies over time, as with fashion clothing and footwear, or with customized mechanical products; the small firm has the flexibility to respond to such short-term or small-scale demand fluctuation. This leads on to the second process underpinning central and northeastern industrial growth: the emergence of thousands of new, small firms which do not merely cater for the subcontracted low-skill stages of big firms' production cycles, but which are independent, innovative enterprises in their own right. Such firms often exhibit marked spatial specialization — some examples are Carpi and Modena for knitwear, Bologna for bicycles, Ascoli Piceno for shoes, Poggibonsi for furniture, Reggio Emilia for ceramics and agricultural machinery.

6.5.1 The Emilian model of microcapitalism

Brusco (1982) has labelled this style of development the 'Emilian model', after one of the regions where the process has been most notable. The term encapsulates three interconnected features held to underlie the region's remarkable recent economic growth: decentralized production in small and medium-sized rural towns; geographical specialization in the kind of product made; and a high degree of mainly female sweated labour in small factories, craft workshops and homes. Curiously the 'Emilian model' is a close parallel to the kind of production being carried out in the early textile towns in the years *leading up* to the English industrial revolution! A further interesting feature is the fact that this fiercely independent 'microcapitalism' has as its regional setting the greatest Communist stronghold of the Western world, for the PCI has controlled the regional government of Emilia–Romagna since the advent of regional autonomy in 1970, and it has ruled Bologna city council since the end of the Second World War. This feature is not, in fact, an anomaly since the PCI has always been strongly male protectionist, especially of men working in skilled employment in medium-sized firms.

With the exception of Ferrara and Ravenna, most of Emilia–Romagna's principal settlements and industrial activities are aligned along its central transport axis, from the Romans' crossing of the Po at Piacenza (now very much under the influence of Milan) to Rimini where the Emilian Way bends a little, realigning itself for the journey down the Adriatic coast to Brindisi. This linear urban system is underlain by a rich agriculture based on owner-cultivation of small but intensively worked farms supported by a strong cooperative tradition and the highest consumption of fertilizers and degree of mechanization in Italy. Along with Verona in Veneto, Bologna Province has the highest agricultural income in the country. Fruits are the main revenue earner, with dairying well developed in parts. Vines, cereals and beef cattle complete the rural economy. Not surprisingly, with such agricultural wealth and diversity, the food industries are more highly developed in Emilia than anywhere else in Italy. Spaghetti bolognese, Parma ham, parmesan cheese, Bologna salamis and Lambrusco wine are examples of food specialities that appear on menus and in delicatessens the world over. Further out in the plain, Ferrara and Ravenna have large sugar refineries. The food industry provides a platform of labour-intensive activity on which many other industrial lines have been built: agricultural machinery, machine tools, clothing, furniture, electric motors, household appliances, construction materials and many more. Many of these activities are in the hands of medium-sized firms which have recently expanded on the outskirts of towns and along the motorways. Helped by their modest size, these new firms have blended well with the existing population and settlement structure, requiring no new massive investment in housing or infrastructure. With the exception of the petrochemicals plants at Ferrara and Ravenna, both of which are the result of non-local investment (Montedison and ANIC respectively), no industrial plant in Emilia–Romagna employs more than a few hundred workers. The characteristics of independent enterprise, product distinctiveness and hard work come from a well-established tradition of solid peasant farming and the craft skills of generations of artisans. The region hardly felt the effects of the recessions of the past dozen years, for Emilia's small firms are resilient, adaptable to market changes and adept at taking advantage of export openings. The region boosted its share of national export earnings from 6 per cent in 1963 to 9.4 per cent in 1980. By 1983 Modena had overtaken Milan as the richest province in Italy, a remarkable advance for a province that was 17th in the league table as recently as 1970.

6.5.2 An economic revolution in the making?

Is the 'Emilian model' a new path to economic growth? Fuà (1983) insists that the twin processes of productive decentralization and independent dispersed industrialization constitute a model of development which holds great promise for the future. Certainly the happy blend of prosperous farming, rural social stability, widely scattered industries, noble towns, fine architecture, picturesque landscapes and varied tourist and tertiary activities offers a vision which is immensely more palatable than the urban congestion, working-class alienation, industrial decline and environmental pollution of the Northwest, or the triple evils of rural degradation, industrial bankruptcy and political corruption prevalent in the South. The Emilian model has shown that it is possible to pass from one economic structure to another — from an agrarian society to a more economically balanced system — in a relatively short time without sacrificing the heritage of culture, organization and buildings amassed over the centuries, and without the concentration of population in large cities or of workers in big factories and office blocks. The Italy of this regional formation now extends over nearly 30 per cent of the total national population and area. Emilia–Romagna, Veneto and Tuscany — three large regions which are geographically and culturally closest to the Northwest — are the regions which have been affected most strongly. Based around the three marvellous cities of Florence, Bologna and Venice, these regions have succeeded in marrying balanced development with the preservation of all that is finest in Italian urban and rural landscapes. Umbria and Marche are also strongly affected; here agriculture is less wealthy but these two regions are full of historic urban centres with long traditions of efficient and democratic civic government and of commercial and craft skills. By contrast Trentino–Alto Adige and Friuli–Venezia Giulia are less strongly involved and Latium, although conventionally included as part of the Centre, not at all.

The question may be asked as to why this model of 'peripheral development' has not taken root in the South. Industrial growth in the Northeast and Centre has been based mainly on local private enterprise, supported only recently by government incentives favouring small firms; it has been built up on firm foundations of rural independence and craft skills which are part of the fabric of society in middle Italy but which are generally absent in the South, with its social polarization between landed gentry and a disinherited landless proletariat. There is, however, some evidence that the 'Emilian model' is extending down the Adriatic flank from Marche into Abruzzo and Apulia, where there has been a considerable recent development of small firms around towns such as Pescara, Chieti, Bari and Lecce. Similar industrial developments have been noted in and around the Naples conurbation (Giannola, 1982). A revealing indicator of this southern small factory development has been the increasing consumption of electricity monitored by statistics on industrial power consumption, both by quantities consumed and by number of users (Lizzeri, 1979). The 1981 Industrial Census also revealed clear evidence of small-firm growth in the localities mentioned in sectors such as footwear, clothing, gloves and handbags. However, the mechanical and engineering branches common in Emilia–Romagna, Veneto and Friuli are absent. The southern firms are thus technologically backward and are probably based more overtly on the exploitation of cheap, marginalized labour in the slum districts of Naples and in overcrowded rural areas such as southern Apulia where outwork is well developed.

There are, nevertheless, weaknesses in the peripheral small-firm model. These have become apparent since the late 1970s, but as yet are not so severe as to portend the system's imminent collapse. The following main weaknesses may be mentioned (Arcangeli *et al.*, 1980). First, it is becoming more and more difficult to increase and even maintain the level of exports. Since Italy joined the European Monetary System the strategy of devaluation is less readily available for counteracting increasing labour costs; meanwhile stronger competition is being felt from products made in developing countries with even lower labour costs. Second, there are the economic problems of some of the medium-firm sectors such as textiles, white goods and some branches of engineering which are now facing saturated markets, both at home and abroad. Third, it is becoming increasingly difficult for diffuse industrialization to continue to expand because of competition from other sectors — agriculture, tourism, the construction industry — for land and labour. The most obvious manifestation of this is the increasing price of land for industrial sites. Fourth, in response to the above three problems, it is difficult to obtain public sector aid for industrial growth and infra-structural improvement (the latter is still needed in the hilly areas of Marche and Umbria for instance) because of the continuing priority of public policy towards the Mezzogiorno. Finally, and perhaps most decisively, there are signs that the reserves of marginal labour are diminishing. In particular young people appear to be refusing to work for a pittance in low-status, insecure and non-unionized jobs. This entails a progressive reliance on older elements of the labour market and naturally implies a less certain future in the long term. In any case, basing an 'economic revolution' — if such it is — on sweated labour and tax evasion is hardly to be praised. Yet this is Italy's natural reaction to the recession. The strength of the country's underground economy has grown to such an extent that it now accounts for an estimated one-fifth of the workforce. To tamper with it would, in the short term at least, adversely affect the lives of millions of people and destroy the most dynamic sections of the economy. Survival, Italian style, means eschewing such suicidal strategies, however morally just they might be.

BIBLIOGRAPHY

Acquaviva, S.S. and Santuccio, M. (1976) *Social Structure in Italy*. London: Martin Robertson.

Alberoni, F. (1970) 'Aspects of internal migration related to other types of Italian migration'. In Jansen, C. J. (ed.) *Readings in the Sociology of Migration*. Oxford: Pergamon, pp. 285–316.

Allen, K. J. and Stevenson, A. A. (1974) *An Introduction to the Italian Economy*. London: Martin Robertson.

Allum, P. (1972) 'The South and national politics, 1945–50'. In Woolf, S. J. (ed.) *The Rebirth of Italy 1943–50*. London: Longman, pp. 95–120.

Allum, P. (1973a) *Italy — Republic without Government?* London: Weidenfeld and Nicolson.

Allum, P. (1973b) *Politics and Society in Postwar Naples*. Cambridge: Cambridge University Press.

Allum, P. (1980) 'Some reflections on the "historic compromise" '. *Peuples Méditerranéens*, 12, 75–90.

Allum, P. (1981) 'A social earthquake in Naples'. *New Society*, 966, 308–310.

Amatucci, A. (1984) 'Social aspects of policies for the South of Italy'. *Mezzogiorno d'Europa*, 4, 473–487.

Amin, A. (1982) 'State intervention in southern Italy: the case of Alfa Sud'. *Mezzogiorno d'Europa*, 2, 75–105.

Amin, A. (1985) 'Restructuring in Fiat and the decentralisation of production into southern Italy'. In Hudson, R. and Lewis, J. (eds) *Uneven Development in Southern Europe*. London: Methuen, pp. 155–191.

Angotti, T. (1977) *Housing in Italy: Urban Development and Political Change*. New York: Praeger.

Apicella, V. (1978) 'The evolution of the Italian motorway system'. *Banco di Roma Review of Economic Conditions in Italy*, 32, 331–346.

Arcangeli, F. (1982) 'Regional and subregional planning in Italy: an evaluation of current practice and some proposals for the future'. In Hudson, R. and Lewis, J. (eds) *Regional Planning in Europe*. London: Pion, pp. 57–84.

Arcangeli, F., Borzaga, C. and Goglio, S. (1980) 'Patterns of peripheral development in Italian regions, 1964–77'. *Papers of the Regional Science Association*, 44, 19–34.

Archibugi, F. (1965) 'The growth of cities in Italy'. *Banco di Roma Review of Economic Conditions in Italy*, 19, 42–58.

Arlacchi, P. (1983) *Mafia, Peasants and Great Estates: Society in Traditional Calabria*. Cambridge: Cambridge University Press.

Astengo, G. (1952) 'Towns and regional planning in Italy'. *Town Planning Review*, 23, 166–181.

Bagnasco, A. (1981) 'Labour market, class structure and regional formations in Italy'. *International Journal of Urban and Regional Research*, 5, 40–44.

Balbo, L. and May, M. P. (1975) 'Women's condition: the case of postwar Italy'. *International Journal of Sociology*, 5, 79–102.

Banfield, E. C. (1958) *The Moral Basis of a Backward Society*. Glencoe: The Free Press.

Barberis, C. (1968) 'The agricultural exodus in Italy'. *Sociologia Ruralis*, 8, 179–188.

Barberis, C. (1971) 'Men, farms and product in Italian agriculture'. *Banco di Roma Review of Economic Conditions in Italy*, 25, 398–412.

Barbero, G. (1972) 'Agricultural mechanisation and employment in southern Italy'. *International Labour Review*, 106, 415–444.

Bardazzi, S. (1984) 'Italy'. In Williams, R. H. (ed.) *Planning in Europe*. London: Allen and Unwin, pp. 26–36.

Barzini, L. (1964) *The Italians*. London: Hamish Hamilton.

Bethemont, J. and Pelletier, J. (1983) *Italy: A Geographical Introduction*. London: Longman.

Bielli, C. (1973) 'Aspects of the social integration of immigrants in Milan'. *Genus*, 29, 183–192.

Blinkhorn, M. (1984) *Mussolini and Fascist Italy*. London: Methuen Lancaster Pamphlets.

Blok, A. (1966) 'Land reform in a west Sicilian latifondo village: the persistence of a feudal structure'. *Anthropological Quarterly*, 39, 1–16.

Blok, A. (1969) 'South Italian agro-towns'. *Comparative Studies in Society and History*, 11, 121–135.

Blok, A. (1974) *The Mafia of a Sicilian Village 1860–1960*. Oxford: Blackwell.

Botto, G. (1975) 'Situation and prospects of the Italian wool industry'. *Banco di Roma Review of Economic Conditions in Italy*, 29, 293–302.

Bracco, F. (1976) 'The Italian chemical industry: prospects and problems'. *Banco di Roma Review of Economic Conditions in Italy*, 30, 109–118.

Brusco, S. (1982) 'The Emilian model: productive decentralisation and social integration'. *Cambridge Journal of Economics*, 6, 167–184.

Buxton, J. (1985) 'Economic breakthrough still awaited'. *Financial Times Survey of Southern Italy*, 24 January 1985, p. 12.

Cafagna, L. (1971) *The Industrial Revolution in Italy, 1830–1914*. London: Fontana.

Cafiero, S. and Busca, A. (1970) 'Metropolitan development in the Seventies'. *Banco di Roma Review of Economic Conditions in Italy*, 24, 391–409.

Calabi, D. (1980) 'The genesis and special characteristics of town planning instruments in Italy, 1880–1914'. In Sutcliffe, A. (ed.) *The Rise of Modern Urban Planning 1800–1914*. London: Mansell, pp. 55–69.

Calabi, D. (1984) 'Italy'. In Wynn, M. (ed.) *Planning and Urban Growth in Southern Europe*. London: Mansell, pp. 37–70.

Calavita, N. (1983) 'Urban planning, the state and political regimes: the Italian case'. *Society and Space*, 1, 377–396.

Caroli, B. B. (1970) *Italian Repatriation from the United States, 1900–1914.* New York: Center for Migration Studies.

Cavallari, C. and Faustini, G. (1978) 'Labour costs and employment in Italy and the EEC'. *Banca Nazionale del Lavoro Quarterly Review*, 126, 251–270.

Cavazzani, A. (1976) 'Social determinants of part-time farming in a marginal region of Italy'. In Fuller, A. M. and Mage, J. M. (eds) *Part-Time Farming: Problem or Resource in Rural Development.* Norwich: Geo Abstracts, pp. 100–113.

Cesare, M. B. (1982) 'The women in the Italian family in the light of socio-cultural conditions'. *International Review of Sociology*, 18, 376–382.

Cesaretti, P., De Benedictis, M., De Filippis, F., Giannola, A. and Perone-Pacifico, C. (1980) *Regional Impact of the Common Agricultural Policy: Italian Report.* Naples: Centro di Specializzazione e Ricerche Economico-Agrarie per il Mezzogiorno.

Clapperton, C. (1972) 'Patterns of physical and human activity on Mount Etna'. *Scottish Geographical Magazine*, 88, 160–167.

Clark, M. (1984) *Modern Italy 1871–1982.* London: Longman.

Clough, S. B. (1964) *The Economic History of Modern Italy.* New York: Columbia University Press.

Clough, S. B. and Livi, C. (1956) 'Economic growth in Italy: an analysis of the uneven development of North and South'. *Journal of Economic History*, 16, 334–349.

Clough, S. B. and Saladino, S. (1968) *A History of Modern Italy.* New York: Columbia University Press.

Cole, J. P. (1968) *Italy.* London: Chatto and Windus.

Colombino, U. (1984) 'An economic investigation into the condition of children in Italy'. *World Development*, 12, 365–380.

Colombo, U. (1980) 'The role of nuclear power in the energy prospects of Italy'. *Isveimer Bulletin*, 29/30, 11–39.

Corna Pellegrini, G. and Zerbi, M. C. (1983) 'Urban geography and urban problems in Italy'. *Progress in Human Geography*, 7, 357–369.

Cosgrove, D. (1982) 'The myth and the stones of Venice: an historical geography of a symbolic landscape'. *Journal of Historical Geography*, 8, 145–169.

Dandri, G. (1978) 'The evolution of the Italian housing situation from 1951 to 1978'. *Banco di Roma Review of Economic Conditions in Italy*, 32, 137–152.

Dean, G. and De Benedictis, M. (1964) 'A model of development for peasant farms in southern Italy'. *Journal of Farm Economics*, 46, 295–312.

De Benedictis, M. (1981) 'Agricultural development in Italy: national problems in a Community perspective'. *Journal of Agricultural Economics*, 32, 275–286.

Delano Smith, C. (1979) *Western Mediterranean Europe: A Historical Geography of Italy, Spain and Southern France since the Neolithic.* London: Academic Press.

Della Seta, P. (1978) 'Notes on urban struggles in Italy'. *International Journal of Urban and Regional Research*, 2, 303–329.

Del Panta, L. (1979) 'Italy'. In Lee, W. R. (ed.) *European Demography and Economic Growth.* London: Croom Helm, pp. 196–235.

de Wolfe, I. (1963) *The Italian Townscape.* London: Architectural Press.

Dickinson, R. E. (1955a) 'Geographic aspects of unemployment in Italian agriculture'. *Tijdschrift voor Economische en Sociale Geografie*, 46, 86–97.

Dickinson, R. E. (1955b) *The Population Problem of Southern Italy: An Essay in Social Geography*. Syracuse: Syracuse University Press.

Di Comite, L. (1980) 'The demographic transition process in Italy'. *Economic Notes by Monte dei Paschi di Siena*, 9, 174–196.

Di Comite, L. and Imbriani, C. (1982) 'Age structure of the population and the labour market in Italy's Mezzogiorno'. *Mezzogiorno d'Europa*, 2, 495–502.

Douglass, W. A. (1983) 'Migration in Italy'. In Kenny, M. and Kerzer, D. I. (eds.) *Urban Life in Mediterranean Europe*. Urbana: University of Illinois Press, pp. 162–202.

Drake, R. (1984) 'The Red Brigades and the Italian political tradition'. In Alexander, Y. and Myers, K. A. (eds) *Terrorism in Europe*. London: Croom Helm, pp. 102–140.

Eckaus, R. S. (1961) 'The North–South differential in Italian economic development'. *Journal of Economic History*, 21, 285–317.

Eisenhammer, J. (1985) 'The politics of the state steel industry in Italy: the art of muddling through'. In Quartermaine, L. and Pollard, J. (eds) *Italy Today: Patterns of Life and Politics*. Exeter: Exeter University Press, pp. 35–58.

Ellwood, D. W. (1985) *Italy 1943–1945*. Leicester: Leicester University Press.

Evans, R. H. (1979) 'Regionalism and the Italian city'. In Romanos, M. C. (ed.) *Western European Cities in Crisis*. Lexington: D. C. Heath, pp. 215–231.

Fazio, A. (1981) 'Inflation and wage indexation in Italy'. *Banca Nazionale del Lavoro Quarterly Review*, 137, 147–170.

Flower, R. (1978) *Chianti: The Land, the Wine, the People*. London: Croom Helm.

Fofi, G. (1970) 'Immigrants in Turin'. In Jansen, C. J. (ed.) *Readings in The Sociology of Migration*. Oxford: Pergamon, pp. 269–284.

Fogagnolo, G. (1975) 'Contribution of the Italian nuclear industry to the solutions of the energy crisis'. *Banco di Roma Review of Economic Conditions in Italy*, 29, 205–223.

Franklin, S. H. (1961) 'Social structure and land reform in southern Italy'. *Sociological Review*, 9, 323–349.

Fraser, J. (1981) *Italy: Society in Crisis, Society in Transformation*. London: Routledge and Kegan Paul.

Freddi, G. (1980) 'Regional devolution, administrative decentralisation and bureaucratic performance in Italy'. *Policy and Politics*, 8, 383–398.

Fried, R. C. (1967) 'Urbanization and Italian politics'. *Journal of Politics*, 29, 505–534.

Fried, R. C. (1971) 'Communism, urban budgets and the two Italies'. *Journal of Politics*, 33, 1008–1051.

Fuà, G. (1977) 'Employment and productive capacity in Italy'. *Banca Nazionale del Lavoro Quarterly Review*, 122, 215–244.

Fuà, G. (1978) 'Lagged development and economic dualism'. *Banca Nazionale del Lavoro Quarterly Review*, 125, 123–134.

Fuà, G. (1983) 'Rural industrialisation in later developed countries: the case of Northeast and Central Italy'. *Banca Nazionale del Lavoro Quarterly Review*, 147, 351–378.

Furlong, P. (1985) 'The changing role of the Vatican in Italian politics'. In Quartermaine, L. and Pollard, J. (eds) *Italy Today: Patterns of Life and Politics*. Exeter: Exeter University Press, pp. 59–76.

Gentilcore, R. L. (1970) 'Reclamation in the Agro Pontino, Italy'. *Geographical Review*, 60, 301–327.

Gentileschi, M. L. (1976) 'Immigration flows to the regional capitals of Italy'. In Pecora, A. and Pracchi, R. (eds) *Italian Contributions to the 23rd International Geographical Congress 1976*. Rome: Consiglio Nazionale delle Ricerche, pp. 73–80.

Gerschenkron, A. (1955) 'Notes on the rate of industrial growth in Italy, 1881–1913'. *Journal of Economic History*, 15, 360–375.

Giannola, A. (1982) 'The industrialisation, dualism and economic dependence of the Mezzogiorno in the 1970s'. *Banco di Roma Review of Economic Conditions in Italy*, 36, 67–92.

Ginatempo, N. (1979) 'The structural contradictions of the Italian building industry'. *International Journal of Urban and Regional Research*, 3, 465–491.

Ginatempo, N. and Cammarota, A. (1977) 'Law and social conflict in the cities of southern Italy: an analysis of the housing question in Messina'. In Harloe, M. (ed.) *Captive Cities*. Chichester: Wiley, pp. 111–122.

Giugni, G. (1971) 'Recent trends in collective bargaining in Italy'. *International Labour Review*, 104, 307–328.

Giugni, G. (1984) 'Recent trends in collective bargaining in Italy'. *International Labour Review*, 123, 599–614.

Glass, D. V. (1967) *Population Policies and Movements in Europe*. London: Cass.

Golini, A. (1983) 'Present relationships between migration and urbanisation: the Italian case'. In Morrison, P. A. (ed.) *Population Movements: their Form and Function in Urbanisation and Development*. Liège: Ordina, pp. 187–209.

Graziani, A. (1978) 'The Mezzogiorno in the Italian economy'. *Cambridge Journal of Economics*, 2, 355–372.

Graziani, A. (1983) 'The subsidized South'. *Mezzogiorno d'Europa*, 3, 79–85.

Grindrod, M. (1968) *Italy*. London: Ernest Benn.

Gutkind, E. A. (1969) *Urban Development in Southern Europe*. New York: Free Press.

Hildebrand, G. H. (1965) *Growth and Structure in the Economy of Modern Italy*. Cambridge, Mass.: Harvard University Press.

Houston, J. M. (1964) *The Western Mediterranean World: An Introduction to its Regional Landscapes*. London: Longman.

Keyser, W. and Windle, R. (1978) *Public Enterprise in the EEC: Italy*. Alphen aan den Rijn: Sijthoff and Noordhoff.

King, R. L. (1971) *The Questione Meridionale in Southern Italy*. Durham: University of Durham Department of Geography, Research Paper 11.

King, R. L. (1973a) 'Poverty and banditry: pastoral anarchy in Sardinia'. *Geographical Magazine*, 46, 127–132.

King, R. L. (1973b) *Land Reform: The Italian Experience*. London: Butterworth.

King, R. L. (1976) 'Long-range migration patterns in the EEC: an Italian case study'. In Lee, R. and Ogden, P. E. (eds) *Economy and Society in the EEC*. Westmead: Saxon House, pp. 108–125.

King, R. L. (1981) 'Italy'. In Clout, H. D. (ed.) *Regional Development in Western Europe*. Chichester: Wiley, pp. 119–149.

King, R. L. (1985) *The Industrial Geography of Italy*. Beckenham: Croom Helm.

King, R. L. and Strachan, A. J. (1978) 'Sicilian agro-towns'. *Erdkunde*, 32, 110–123.

King, R. L. and Strachan, A. J. (1980) 'Spatial variations in Sicilian migration: a stepwise multiple regression analysis'. *Mediterranean Studies*, 2, 62–87.

King, R. L. and Took, L. J. (1983) 'Land tenure and rural social change: the Italian case'. *Erdkunde*, 37, 186–198.

Kogan, N. (1981) *A Political History of Postwar Italy*. New York: Praeger.

Lacci, L. (1973) 'Agriculture's contribution to Gross National Product in Italy'. *Banco di Roma Review of Economic Conditions in Italy*, 27, 236–250.

Lane, D. (1980) 'Mini-farming in the Italian South'. *Geographical Magazine*, 53, 177–179.

Leonardi, R. (1984) 'The Italian parliamentary elections of 1983: the making and unmaking of myths'. *West European Politics*, 7, 188–191.

Levi, C. (1948) *Christ Stopped at Eboli*. London: Cassell.

Lizzeri, G. (1979) 'Power consumption and industrial development in southern Italy'. *Isveimer Bulletin*, 17/18, 15–37.

Lopreato, J. (1967) *Peasants No More*. San Francisco: Chandler.

Low-Beer, J. R. (1978) *Protest and Participation: The New Working-Class in Italy*. Cambridge: Cambridge University Press.

Lutz, V. (1962) *Italy: A Study in Economic Development*. London: Oxford University Press.

Mack Smith, D. (1959) *Italy: A Modern History*. Ann Arbor: University of Michigan Press.

Mannucci, C. (1970) 'Emigrants in the Upper Milanese area'. In Jansen, C. J. (ed.) *Readings in the Sociology of Migration*. Oxford: Pergamon, pp. 257–267.

Manuelli, E. (1958) 'Situation and prospects of the Italian steel industry'. *Banco di Roma Review of Economic Conditions in Italy*, 12, 567–579.

Marcelloni, M. (1979) 'Urban movements and political struggles in Italy'. *International Journal of Urban and Regional Research*, 3, 251–268.

Martinelli, A. (1979) 'Organised business and Italian politics: Confindustria and the Christian Democrats in the postwar period'. *West European Politics*, 2, 67–87.

Masera, F. (1967) 'Italy in ten years of the Common Market'. *Banco di Roma Review of Economic Conditions in Italy*, 21, 363–388.

Maxwell, G. (1957) *God Protect Me From My Friends*. London: Longman Green.

Maxwell, G. (1959) *The Ten Pains of Death*. London: Longman Green.

Mazzaoui, M. F. (1972) 'The cotton industry of Northern Italy in the Late Middle Ages'. *Journal of Economic History*, 32, 262–286.

McManis, D. (1967) 'The core of Italy: the case for Lombardy-Piedmont'. *Professional Geographer*, 19, 251–257.

Medici, G. (1952) *Land Property and Land Tenure in Italy*. Bologna: Agricole.

Mikus, W. (1982) 'Types of spatial interactions in industry with examples from Northern Italy'. In *Scritti in Onore di Aldo Sestini*. Florence: Società di Studi Geografici, pp. 727–736.

Milone, F. (1957) 'Land transformation in southern Italy'. *Banco di Roma Review of Economic Conditions in Italy*, 11, 395–415.

Montini, L. (1955) 'The Parliamentary Inquiry into Destitution in Italy'. *International Labour Review*, 71, 60–78.

Moss, L. W. and Cappannari, S. C. (1962) 'Estate and class in a south Italian hill village'. *American Anthropologist*, 64, 287–300.

Mottura, G. (1980) 'Notes for a study of work organization in Italian agriculture'. *International Journal of Urban and Regional Research*, 4, 388–404.

Mottura, G. and Pugliese, E. (1980) 'Capitalism in agriculture and capitalist agriculture: the Italian case'. In Buttel, F. H. and Newby, H. (eds) *The Rural Sociology of Advanced Societies*. London: Croom Helm, pp. 171–199.

Neri, F. (1982) 'The supply of foreign labour in Italy: the case of Friuli Venezia Giulia'. *Banco di Roma Review of Economic Conditions in Italy*, 36, 445–459.

Neufeld, M. F. (1960) 'The inevitability of political unionism in underdeveloped countries: Italy, the exemplar'. *Industrial and Labour Relations Review*, 13, 363–386.

O'Riordan, N. J. (1975) 'The Venetian ideal'. *Geographical Magazine*, 47, 418–426.

Pacione, M. (1974a) 'Italian motorways'. *Geography*, 59, 35–41.

Pacione, M. (1974b) 'The Venetian problem: an overview'. *Geography*, 59, 339–343.

Pacione, M. (1976) 'Italy and the energy crisis'. *Geography*, 61, 99–102.

Pacione, M. (1979) 'Natural gas in Italy'. *Geography*, 64, 211–215.

Pacione, M. (1982) 'Economic development in the Mezzogiorno'. *Geography*, 67, 340–343.

Padovani, L. (1984) 'Italy'. In Wynn, M. (ed.) *Housing in Europe*. London: Croom Helm, 247–280.

Pantaleone, M. (1966) *The Mafia and Politics*. London: Chatto and Windus.

Panunzio, V. (1978) 'The Italian ports and their problems'. *Banco di Roma Review of Economic Conditions in Italy*, 32, 27–40.

Pasquino, G. and Pecchini, U. (1975) 'Italy'. In Hayward, J. and Watson, M. (eds) *Planning, Politics and Public Policy*. Cambridge: Cambridge University Press, pp. 70–92.

Patella, L. V. (1978) 'Changes in transhumance in the central Apennines'. *Geographia Polonica*, 38, 215–222.

Peruzzi, D. (1965) 'The mezzadria: a decaying system of land tenure and management in Italy'. In Simpson, E. S. (ed.) *Agricultural Geography: IGU Symposium*. Liverpool: University of Liverpool Department of Geography Research Paper 3, pp. 49–54.

Pettenati, P. (1982) 'The labour market and inflation in transitional growth: lessons from the Italian experience'. *Banca Nazionale del Lavoro Quarterly Review*, 35, 165–180.

Picarelli, A. (1977) 'The Italian textile industry: problems and prospects'. *Banco di Roma Review of Economic Conditions in Italy*, 31, 43–68.

Pieroni, O. (1982) 'Positive aspects of part-time farming in the development of a professional agriculture: remarks on the Italian situation'. *GeoJournal*, 6, 331–336.

Podbielski, G. (1974) *Italy: Development and Crisis in the Postwar Economy*. Oxford: Clarendon Press.

Podbielski, G. (1978) *Twenty-Five Years of Special Action for the Development of Southern Italy*. Rome: SVIMEZ.

Podbielski, G. (1981) 'The Common Agricultural Policy and the Mezzogiorno'. *Journal of Common Market Studies*, 19, 333–350.

Predetti, A. (1982) 'Some aspects of the labour market in Italy'. *Banco di Roma Review of the Economic Conditions in Italy*, 36, 405–426.

Procacci, G. (1970) *History of the Italian People*. London: Weidenfeld and Nicolson.

Quartermaine, L. (1985) 'Speaking with one voice: society and mass media in postwar Italy'. In Quartermaine, L. and Pollard, J. (eds) *Italy Today: Patterns of Life and Politics*. Exeter: Exeter University Press, pp. 1–16.

Rey, G. M. (1982) 'Italy'. In Boltho, A. (ed.) *The European Economy: Growth and Crisis*. Oxford: Oxford University Press, pp. 502–527.

Reyneri, E. (1980) 'Emigration and sending area as a subsidized system in Sicily'. *Mediterranean Studies*, 2, 88–113.

Rodgers, A. (1957) 'The role of the state in the industrial development of the port of Genova'. *Papers and Proceedings of the Regional Science Association*, 3, 290–300.

Rodgers, A. (1958) 'The port of Genova: external and internal relations'. *Annals of the Association of American Geographers*, 48, 319–351.

Rodgers, A. (1978) 'Mediterranean Europe'. In Trewartha, G. T. (ed.) *The More Developed Realm: A Geography of its Population*. Oxford: Pergamon, pp. 79–97.

Rodgers, A. (1979) *Economic Development in Retrospect: The Italian Model and its Significance for Regional Planning in Market Oriented Economies*. New York: Wiley.

Rodgers, A. (1984) 'Recent developments and proposed changes in Italian regional policy: their impact and political implications'. In Demko, G. (ed.) *Regional Development: Problems and Policies in Eastern and Western Europe*. London: Croom Helm, pp. 174–199.

Ronchey, A. (1979) 'Guns and grey matter: terrorism in Italy'. *Foreign Affairs*, 57, 921–940.

Ronzani, S. (1980) 'Regional incentives in Italy'. In Yuill, D., Allen, K. and Hull, C. (eds) *Regional Policy in the European Community*. London: Croom Helm, pp. 134–156.

Rossi-Doria, M. (1958) 'The land tenure system and class in southern Italy'. *American Historical Review*, 64, 45–53.

Saraceno, E. (1986) 'The occupational resettlement of returning migrants and regional development: the case of Friuli–Venezia Giulia'. In King, R. L. (ed.) *Return Migration and Regional Economic Problems*. London: Croom Helm, pp. 69–78.

Sarti, R. (1971) *Fascism and the Industrial Leadership in Italy, 1919–1940*. Berkeley: University of California Press.

Saunders, G. R. (1980) 'Peasant life in Piedmont'. *Current Anthropology*, 21, 827–828.

Saville, L. (1968) *Regional Development in Italy*. Edinburgh: Edinburgh University Press.

Sicca, L. (1978) 'The food industry and its growth prospects in Italy'. *Banco di Roma Review of Economic Conditions in Italy*, 32, 121–136.

Signorelli, A. (1980) 'Regional policies in Italy for migrant workers returning home'. In Grillo, R. D. (ed.) *'Nation' and 'State' in Europe*. London: Academic Press, pp. 89–103.

Silverman, S. (1970) 'Exploitation in rural central Italy: structure and ideology in stratification study'. *Comparative Studies in Society and History*, 12, 327–339.

Slater, M. (1984) 'Italy: surviving into the eighties'. In Williams, A. M. (ed.) *Southern Europe Transformed*. London: Harper and Row, pp. 61–83.

Slater, M. (1985) 'Italy's changing political economy'. In Quartermaine, L. and Pollard, J. (eds) *Italy Today: Patterns of Life and Politics*. Exeter: Exeter University Press, pp. 17–34.

Solinas, G. (1982) 'Labour market segmentation and workers' careers: the case of the Italian knitwear industry'. *Cambridge Journal of Economics*, 6, 331–352.

Spooner, D. J. (1984) 'The Southern Problem, the Neopolitan Problem and Italian regional policy'. *Geographical Journal*, 150, 11–26.

Strachan, A. J. and King, R. L. (1982) *Emigration and Return Migration in Southern Italy: A Multivariate, Cluster and Map Analysis*. Leicester: Leicester University Geography Department Occasional Paper 9.

Tagliacarne, G. (1955) 'Italy's net product by regions'. *Banca Nazionale del Lavoro Quarterly Review*, 35, 215–231.

Tagliacarne, G. (1973) 'The regions twenty years later: socio-economic dynamics of the regions between 1951 and 1971'. *Banco di Roma Review of Economic Conditions in Italy*, 27, 127–161.

Tagliacarne, G. (1974) 'The state of housing in Italy'. *Banco di Roma Review of Economic Conditions in Italy*, 28, 524–536.

Tarrow, S. (1979) 'Italy: crisis, crises or transition?' *West European Politics*, 2, 166–186.

Toniolo, A. R. (1937) 'Studies of depopulation in the mountains of Italy'. *Geographical Review*, 27, 473–477.

Treves, A. (1980) 'The anti-urban policy of fascism and a century of resistance to industrial urbanization in Italy'. *International Journal of Urban and Regional Research*, 4, 470–484.

Venino, C. (1976) 'Italian livestock farming with reference to the EEC and the rest of the world'. *Banco di Roma Review of Economic Conditions in Italy*, 30, 209–224.

Vercellone, P. (1972) 'The Italian Constitution of 1947–48'. In Woolf, S. J. (ed.) *The Rebirth of Italy 1943–50*. London: Longman, pp. 121–134.

Vigorelli, P. (1969) 'Returning migrants re-employed in Italian industry'. *Migration News*, 18, 3–13.

Wade, R. (1979) 'Fast growth and slow development in southern Italy'. In Seers, D., Schaffer, B. and Kiljunen, M. L. (eds) *Underdeveloped Europe: Studies in Core-Periphery Relations*. Hassocks: Harvester Press, pp. 197–221.

Wade, R. (1980) 'The Italian state and the underdevelopment of southern Italy'. In Grillo, R. D. (ed.) *'Nation' and 'State' in Europe*. London: Academic Press, pp. 151–171.

Waley, D. (1978) *The Italian City-Republics*. London: Longman.

Walker, D. (1967) *A Geography of Italy*. London: Methuen.

Webster, R.A. (1975) *Industrial Imperialism in Italy 1908—1915*. Berkeley: University of California Press.

212   *Italy*

Weingrod, A. (1979) 'Industrial involution in Sardinia'. *Sociologia Ruralis*, 19, 246–265.

Weingrod, A. and Morin, E. (1971) 'Post-peasants: the character of contemporary Sardinian society'. *Comparative Studies in Society and History*, 13, 301–324.

Wertman, D. (1982) 'The Catholic Church and Italian politics: the impact of secularisation'. *West European Politics*, 5, 87–107.

White, P. E. (1985) 'Modelling rural population change in the Cilento region of southern Italy'. *Environment and Planning*, 17, 1401–1413.

Wiskemann, E. (1971) *Italy since 1945*. London: Macmillan.

Zanetti, G. (1983) 'The industrial structure and efficiency of the Italian economy: trends and planning aspects'. *Banco di Roma Review of Economic Conditions in Italy*, 37, 249–300.

Zariski, R. (1972) *Italy: the Politics of Uneven Development*. Hinsdale: Dryden Press.

PLACE INDEX

SUBJECT INDEX